MW00560368

EARLY CHILDHOOD EDUCA

Sharon Ryan, *Editor*

To look for other titles in this series, visit www.tcpress.com

(continued)

Thinking Critically About Environments for Young Children

Bridging Theory and Practice

Edited by

Lisa P. Kuh

Teachers College, Columbia University
New York and London

Published by Teachers College Press, 1234 Amsterdam Avenue, New York, NY 10027

Library of Congress Cataloging-in-Publication Data

Thinking critically about environments for young children : bridging theory and practice / edited by Lisa Kuh.
    pages cm. -- (Early childhood education series)
Includes bibliographical references and index.
ISBN 978-0-8077-5545-7 (pbk. : alk. paper)
ISBN 978-0-8077-7308-6 (ebook : alk. paper)
    1. Classroom environment. 2. Outdoor recreation for children. 3. Virtual reality in early childhood education. 4. Early childhood education--Environmental aspects. I. Kuh, Lisa Porter.
LB3325.C5T49 2014
372.21—dc23   2014002133

ISBN 978-0-8077-5545-7 (paper)
ISBN 978-0-8077-7308-6 (ebook)

Printed on acid-free paper
Manufactured in the United States of America

21 20 19 18 17 16 15 14   8 7 6 5 4 3 2 1

Contents

Acknowledgments

Lisa P. Kuh

This book is dedicated to those early childhood educators who came before us, as well as those today who strive for beauty and creativity in their work. Thanks to my family, Ed, Evan, and Josh, whose love and support made this project possible.

Megina Baker and Judith Ross-Bernstein

We acknowledge the young children and their teachers from Denmark, Norway, and Sweden who inspired us to see beyond our own culture.

Laura Beals

I would like to thank my family for their support, especially my husband, Aaron, and my two lovelies, Adelaide and Charlotte. I would also like to extend my thanks to my colleagues at the Developmental Technologies Research Lab (especially C.C. and K.S.), and in particular Marina Bers, the lab director and my mentor throughout my (many) years at Tufts.

Clement Chau and Iris Chin Ponte

Many thanks to the teachers, children, and faculty at the Eliot-Pearson Children's School, especially Debbie LeeKeenan, George Scarlett, Nathan Render, Hadeel Alessa, Heather DiGiovanni, and Kate Schellie.

Angela Eckhoff

Thank you to all the museum staff from the various institutions mentioned in this chapter. Your time and dedication to parents, teachers, and children served to build the foundation for the ideas presented here.

Carley Fisher-Maltese

To my husband and sons for their boundless love and support—you are the center of my world and I could not have done this without you.

Anna Housley Juster

With gratitude to Lisa Kuh for her hard work in developing this important book and to my husband, Ken, and parents everywhere who find ways to support play in the midst of it all—thank you.

Tiffany R. Lee and Leah A. Bricker

We extend deep gratitude to the children, youth, families, and teachers who participated in the studies we reference in this chapter, as well as our LIFE Center colleagues for their intellectual influence and collaboration. We also wish to thank the National Science Foundation for the opportunity to pursue these lines of research (Awards SBE-0354453 and SBE-0835854), although any opinions expressed in this chapter are solely our own.

Morgan Leichter-Saxby

With thanks to Anna, for her skills and patience during the writing process; the great thinkers, writers, educators, and players who have gone before us; and the children, always running on ahead.

Melissa Rivard

I am grateful to the Reggio Emilia educators who, for fifty years, have relentlessly pursued educational experiences that are at once joyful and of the highest quality for children, families, and teachers. You are my inspiration.

Patricia Tarr

I would like to thank Susan Fraser for her memories and comments on this chapter.

Introduction

Thinking Critically About Environments

Lisa P. Kuh

The shelves above the cubbies are piled high with bright blue plastic rest mats. The carpeted meeting space is home to an area rug depicting a busy street scene bordered by the alphabet and the numbers 1–10 in primary and secondary colors. Wall spaces have plastic pocket calendars, bulletin board decorations with scalloped edges in various designs, and posters depicting names of shapes, colors, and feelings—all from catalogs. Some children's work is also displayed—one piece of artwork from each child, each barely discernible from the other. Shelves are stacked with materials: a pegboard atop a floor puzzle atop a tub of pattern blocks. Outdoors a large plastic and metal climbing structure dominates a flat landscape, surrounded by wood chips.

I visit many environments, both formal and informal, indoors and out of doors, every year, and I find myself asking, "Why is that object there? What is its purpose? What is the teacher's (or community's, parent's, museum director's) goal in offering this object, this arrangement, and this space to children?" These are questions that practitioners, policymakers, and designers must ask themselves regularly. Unfortunately, the answers are not usually related to creating meaningful spaces that promote play, exploration, and rich learning experiences. The early childhood classroom described above, which was assembled quite intentionally, represents what is widely accepted as high-quality school design for young children. On the surface, things may look quite cheerful, but the ever-present primary colors and catalog items also symbolize tensions related to environments for young children.

This book considers the ways in which environments for children promote and hinder experiences in them, how social constructs about what is good for children influence environmental design, and what practitioners can do to develop effective learning environments for young children, be they in schools, playgrounds, museums, or virtual worlds. The classroom described at the opening of this chapter reflects a typical early childhood classroom and can serve as a starting point for rethinking and expanding the notion of environments. There are many books about setting up classrooms, but few of them ask educators to respond critically to the messages sent to children as a result of the choices adults make in establishing learning environments. This book seeks to combine the philosophical and practical aspects of environments for young children so that readers can both understand and articulate how and why thinking carefully about young children's spaces is crucial to their growth and development.

DEFINING ENVIRONMENTS

Before we consider the colorful catalog classroom described above and examine what makes it problematic, let us stop and consider some definitions of the word *environment* as applied to spaces for young children. The word *environment* is carefully chosen and has roots in education, environmental psychology, cultural geography, and architecture. Montessori used the term *prepared environment*, specifying characteristics such as materials and furniture in proportion to the child and his or her needs; beauty, order, and harmony in design; the cleanliness of the environment; and an arrangement that facilitates movement and activity (Standing, 1957). Important in this notion of environment is that the child has access to spaces where he or she can choose materials and develop independence. Environmental design scholars also note the importance of choice in environments and view them as places that support development by affording opportunities to try out predefined roles in conventional settings. This involves promoting children's exploration of unprogrammed and undefined spaces where preschoolers can manipulate the environment and engage in pretend play, and practice independence (Heft & Chawla, 2006).

Interestingly, progressive classrooms in the early 1900s share some important similarities with classrooms of today. Over time there were shifts in what "counted" as a high-quality early childhood environment, and certain trends garnered favor according to the social and political climates of the day. Classroom practices related to block play, nature exploration, loose parts, high-quality wooden furniture, real objects such as glass and china, didactic materials, and their uses were part of past early childhood curricula inspired by educational theories and philosophies such as those of Froebel, Montessori, Dewey, and the Bank Street College of Education. Although vestiges of these early environmental developments still appear in today's classrooms in the form of child-sized furniture and materials designed specifically for children, Progressive Era innovations are disappearing, as evidenced by classrooms without blocks, the prevalence of primary-colored plastic furniture and materials, and the elimination of outdoor play in some settings.

The Reggio Emilia approach takes a strong stance regarding environments in schools and in broader communities, and characterizes the classroom environment as a "third teacher" (after parents and educators) (Gandini, 1998). From this perspective, children have the right to be educated in thoughtfully designed spaces that support their development (Stremmel, 2012). Architect Mark Dudek (2005) uses the word *environment* in connection with designed spaces for young children to describe a "landscape" for exploration and play within and beyond the classroom. All of these conceptions of spaces for young children, which we call environments, denote formal, informal, and virtual areas where children have the opportunity to express themselves and make choices as they encounter what the environment has to offer. In this conceptualization, *environment* is an aggregate term referring not only to the actual spaces and the objects within them, but also to the social and cultural forces that shape them—and are in turn shaped by those who use them.

PROBLEMATIZING ENVIRONMENTS FOR LEARNING: RETURNING LANDSCAPES TO THE CHILDREN

Let's return to the classroom description that began this chapter. Is it really so bad? Consider the primary-colored and letter-and-number-adorned meeting area rug. On the surface, it serves a very functional purpose. It provides a soft space in the classroom and a place for children to gather or spread out materials. But it is not a neutral rug. What messages do the primary-colored images and the letters and numbers on it send? That primary colors are the most important colors? That you must drive your train only on the prescribed "road" on the rug? What if children want to build with blocks on it—does the rug now dictate what they should build? Such highly commercialized materials send strong messages to children about what is important and how they should play. In addition, for young children who are sorting out the sensory stimuli in their environments, building with multicolored blocks on a visually busy rug might be an overwhelming experience, especially for those grappling with visual stimuli or sensory issues. I have seen children sitting in rows on these rugs, with piles of Cuisenaire rods, small chalkboards and handwriting books, or beginning readers, in close proximity to one another, being asked to read, write, sort, and respond—an enormous task that is made more challenging by the environmental constraints of the classroom.

The messages children absorb from their environment are especially important, considering the amount of time children spend in controlled, structured, scheduled, directed activity. Play experiences indoors and outside may be few and far between as recess time in schools diminishes and structured, scheduled activity takes the place of outdoor play after school hours (Rivkin, 1995). Dudek (2005) and others lament that "landscapes" for children are no longer freely available to children and that our role as parents, teachers, designers, and policymakers is to return these landscapes to the children.

The loss of play space and time is also related to policy regarding children's learning. The emphasis on standards and learning outcomes has in many ways superseded teacher thinking about the fuller range of experiences that children might have in a given environment (Heft & Chawla, 2006). In this light, the colorful rug is a misappropriation of curricular intention. More and more, it seems that every object must now overtly teach something very specific to a child who comes into contact with it. This phenomenon is seen in the tic-tac-toe boards on playground equipment where design communicates a mode of play that is directed at the child, as opposed to inviting children to extend ownership and creativity to their play narrative. In our efforts to have our environments be as educationally instructive as possible, we actually limit what children can or will do in these environments. If there is little for children to "take up" in their classrooms, if classrooms are specifically designed to minimize responses and interactions with the space in ways that don't follow prescribed curricular goals, then children must rely on the adult to manage their responses and guide their interactions.

This can be especially problematic in light of research on children living in poverty. Annette Lareau (2003) asserts that poor children are repeatedly instructed to defer to adults in institutional settings and are not often exposed to the idea of choice. Louise Derman-Sparks and Patty Ramsey (2011) add another layer of complexity, noting that there are ranges of antibias categories with which children might identify related to race, class, sexual orientation, ability, and ethnicity and that some children enter into learning environments not having any of their personal characteristics addressed or reflected in the space. What has to change in our thinking about environments that impacts the kind of programming we provide for young children, especially those living in poverty, coming from marginalized groups, or those looking to see themselves in their learning spaces? Robert C. Pianta, in the introduction to the *Handbook of Early Childhood Education*, poses this question another way, wondering: How can restructuring environments for young children increase the quality of care for young children, especially our most vulnerable (Pianta, Barnett, Justice, & Sheridan, 2012)? Although the colorful rug with the letters on it may look innocuous, it comes with an inventory of meaning about learning that may exclude entire groups of children from being able to fully engage in their own learning.

HEALTHY RISK-TAKING: DEVELOPMENTALLY APPROPRIATE PRACTICE AND SAFETY FIRST

Responses to diversity in our student population often result in tightening the technical aspects of our work, of which furnishing a classroom is one. The standardization of what counts as a classroom, schoolyard, or learning environment regardless of children's context is an unsurprising response to the growing diversity and achievement gap in education. The cost, however, is that the specifics of what to include, and who gets to decide what to include, are limited to a prescribed menu of items. Flexibility in design considerations and openness to out-of-school learning venues are largely missing from conversations about classroom quality, especially in environments that serve poor children.

Complicating this issue is that developmentally appropriate practice (DAP) has become synonymous with safety and not with the kinds of healthy risks that we hope teachers and children will take in their interactions with one another and in their environments. Although licensing and accrediting organizations perform important functions in establishing and maintaining high standards for quality in early childhood settings, they also limit children's exposure to the real world and perpetuate a materials industry that is out of touch with what children need to learn. Creating environments that trust children and encourage competency is especially important for all children whose experiences may be limited due to lack of access to high-quality environments, loss of play spaces, and overly structured experiences that hinder child-centered explorations.

Safety standards in early childhood are designed to keep children from harm, yet the definitions of what is harmful and what might be an interesting provocation for learning are confusing. Genuine logs brought from a neighbor's yard after a tree fell in a storm could result in a splinter. If notions of safety are our primary concern, then clearly a prefabricated composite material "log" is a better choice. As a classroom teacher, I stored my colored pencils in a variety of glasses from a secondhand shop. The children loved choosing which glass to take to a table and had classified the glasses according to attributes (the "bumpy" glass, the "bubble" glass). On the rare occasion that a glass was dropped, we carefully swept it up. In my 25 years of teaching, perhaps four glasses have been broken, and I have never had a child cut by broken glass. However, during a licensing visit at one school, we removed all glass and china from the classroom before the inspection so as not to draw attention to items that could be deemed "dangerous." More and more, furniture is required to be bolted down, making flexible rearrangement of classrooms more difficult. Although no one wants a child to be injured, children (and teachers) can be trusted to use materials safely if they are shown how to handle them carefully. Furnishings can be selected that are low to the ground and accessible to children, as opposed to tall, heavy, adult-height shelving piled high with materials.

Both being careful and taking risks are important work in the life of a child. It takes self-control to carry a tray of fragile items from one side of the classroom to another; it takes physical control, stamina, and perhaps teamwork to carry a large log across the playground. Children, deprived of these experiences, are also deprived of the chances to practice "taking care" and reaping the joy and self-awareness that comes with this. Teachers need practice, too. They must learn to form partnerships with licensors and regulators and to articulate an environmental philosophy that applies to indoor settings, outdoor spaces, and virtual learning contexts.

The school equipment and materials industry sends a strong message about what a high-quality classroom should have in it and what it should look like. This message is so pervasive that some "teachers who take a different approach may even feel pressure from other teachers or parents to decorate so that their room looks like a classroom should look" (Tarr, 2004, p. 1). However, the current early childhood field has not specifically addressed how or which components of environments are important for promoting high-quality interactions with environments and child-centered learning experiences. Rating scales and curriculum checklists itemize materials and characteristics that should be present indoors and out, but what they are to look like and how they are to be arranged is unclear. Although this vagueness promotes flexibility and interpretation, it also allows commercial institutional uniformity to define what is "good" for children (Beatty, 1995). Yet the early childhood community and the culture at large do not often question the value of particular design norms and the educational stance they represent.

Although DAP guidelines do address the trend toward the "narrowing of the curriculum scope" and the constraints of teaching to ever-increasing academic standards, they stop short of proposing or advocating for possible environmental counterbalances to these restrictions (Copple & Bredekamp, 2009). The reality is that the environments we provide for children are within our control, while some policy constraints such as adhering to standards or a specific curriculum are not. Notwithstanding these policies, teachers can develop a strong philosophical stance toward environmental design for young children that accommodates policy constraints while at the same time providing a space for learning that inspires. Given that the environment is to serve as a "teacher" and that children will learn from the spaces in which they spend time (for better or for worse), then thinking carefully about the current state of prepared and spontaneous environments is an important endeavor (Gandini, 1998). If, as some espouse, childhood is the time when individuals begin to see and use the environment imaginatively, environments should inspire children to do just that.

NEW NOTIONS OF ENVIRONMENTS FOR YOUNG CHILDREN

The notion of environments for young children is broadened to include multiple contexts for learning and growth. As such this book is organized into three parts that address a span of conceptualizations of environments for young children. Part I (Chapters 1–3) provides historical background and addresses aesthetics, politics, and space configurations in school environments for young children. Chapters 4–6 in Part II take up outdoor play spaces, beginning again with a historical overview moving to intentionally designed outdoor playscapes, children's gardens, and improvisational play venues. Part III (Chapters 7–9) considers the role of environments outside school, including informal learning environments that promote science knowledge, museum spaces, and virtual environments.

Those contributing to this book have noted ways in which children respond to the environments around them, and the contributors share a common critical stance related to the impact of spaces for children. The authors in this book also share a practice-based focus as well as a researcher lens. They substantiate their writing with examples from practice, lessons learned, and illustrations and photographs of key aspects of the environments they discuss. They bridge the practitioner–researcher divide and draw upon their diverse backgrounds in and out of the "schoolhouse." Many of the authors have grounded their work in a particular theoretical perspective. The purpose here is not to project one theory, but to put theories to work as guides for practice or the practice of others. Each chapter includes implications for practice and discussion questions related to the topic to assist readers in adopting an active stance toward building a new notion of environments for young children.

In my Conclusion, I ask readers to think about the environments in which they do their best learning. This question is for teachers and administrators looking to make changes in their schools, students who may be using this book in a class, or professors assigning chapters as part of a class. In higher academia, we do not often follow environmental guidelines for maximizing learning with our own students, nor do schools take these into consideration when designing professional development for teachers. Tools for educators are presented so that those using this book have some ways to shape the learning environments they establish for their own students. Drawing from the work of the School Reform Initiative, I provide protocols for looking at text, structuring meaningful conversation, and engaging in environmental learning walks. We hope these chapters inspire shifts in thinking about environments for young children and support new approaches and practices for those who design, teach about, and live or work in the many spaces in which our children dwell.

REFERENCES

Beatty, B. (1995). *Preschool education in America: The culture of young children from the colonial era to the present.* New Haven, CT: Yale University Press.

Copple, C., & Bredekamp, S. (Eds.) (2009). *Developmentally appropriate practice in early childhood programs serving children from birth through age 8* (3rd ed.). Washington, DC: NAEYC.

Derman-Sparks, L., & Ramsey, P. G. (2011). *What if all the kids are white? Anti-bias multicultural education with young children and families.* New York, NY: Teachers College Press

Dudek, M. (2005). *Children's spaces.* Oxford, UK: Architectural Press.

Gandini, L. (1998). Educational and caring spaces. In C. Edwards, L. Gandini, & G. Forman (Eds.), *The hundred languages of children: The Reggio Emilia approach—Advanced reflections* (2nd ed., pp. 161–178). Greenwich, CT: Ablex.

Heft, H., & Chawla, L. (2006). Children as agents in sustainable development: The ecology of competence. In C. Spencer & M. Blades (Eds.), *Children and their environments: Learning, using, and designing spaces.* Cambridge, UK: Cambridge University Press.

Lareau, A. (2003). *Unequal childhoods: Race, class, and family life.* Berkeley, CA: University of California Press.

Pianta, R. C., Barnett, W. S., Justice, L. M., & Sheridan, S. M. (Eds.). (2012). *The handbook of early childhood education.* New York, NY: Guilford Press.

Rivkin, M. (1995). *The great outdoors: Restoring children's rights to play outside.* Washington, DC: National Association for the Education of Young Children.

Standing, E. M. (1957). *Maria Montessori, her life and work.* London, UK: Hollis & Carter.

Stremmel, A. (2012). A situated framework: The Reggio experience. In N. File, J. J. Mueller, & D. B. Wisneski, (Eds.) *Curriculum in early childhood: Re-examined, rediscovered, renewed.* New York, NY: Routledge.

Tarr, P. (2004). Consider the walls. *Young Children 59*(3), 88–92.

PART I

SCHOOL AND INDOOR ENVIRONMENTS

This section encourages readers to consider their own classroom environments and make informed choices about the spaces they create, what they put into these spaces, and why. In Chapter 1, Lisa P. Kuh and Melissa Rivard explore the notion of an early childhood aesthetic, define some important characteristics of Montessori and Reggio environments, as well as that advocated by Dewey, and juxtapose them with current early childhood environments. Early childhood classrooms in the United States (and internationally) have begun to look surprisingly similar as catalog materials and notions of what elements make up a "high-quality" environment influence the design and content of spaces for young children, which may not be meeting the learning needs of young children or teachers. The authors advocate for teacher agency and urge teachers to determine just what they have control over in their classrooms.

In Chapter 2, Patricia Tarr begins with a description of her own classroom, circa 1971, and moves through the classroom of the 1980s and early 2000s, and encourages readers to think about values and evolving aesthetics of classrooms today. Tarr then focuses on some of the specifics of Reggio-inspired classrooms that have begun to influence classroom design in both early childhood and some elementary contexts. She revisits the spaces she describes early in her chapter, explicitly naming the micro-elements of an early childhood aesthetic and how teacher choices represent teacher images of children. Readers are invited to reflect on their own spaces and what is revealed about their image of the child.

Chapter 3 looks cross-culturally to places where there is an articulated and culturally rooted philosophy of what constitutes the "good childhood." Specifically, Megina Baker and Judith Ross-Bernstein take a close look at schools and public spaces in the Nordic countries to understand the intentions and values communicated through the design of both indoor and outdoor spaces. Referencing examples from Sweden, Norway, and Denmark, the authors examine the relationship between a unified ideological stance and the environmental and aesthetic aspects of education and care. The chapter concludes with possibilities for what can be learned about the development of childhood resilience and applied to early childhood education in the United States.

CHAPTER 1

The Prepared Environment

Aesthetic Legacies of Dewey, Montessori, and Reggio Emilia

Lisa P. Kuh
Melissa Rivard

Where do you do your best work? What environmental qualities enable you to think, play, rest, concentrate, or collaborate? How do you want your environment to look, sound, feel? Between the two authors of this chapter, we visited more than 30 classrooms over the course of a year in the United States and internationally in some cases—all of which look surprisingly similar. Clearly, there are certain design norms afoot as catalog materials and notions of what elements make up a "high-quality" environment influence the design and content of spaces for young children. Your environment—be it a home, a workplace, a classroom or school building, or a place for leisure activity—impacts the way you feel, the way you think, and how you learn (Lillard, 2005; Spencer & Blades, 2006; Weinstein & David, 1987). In schools, the "look" of environments and the items in them make up a particular aesthetic code that may not be meeting the needs of young children (Tarr, 2004).

Aesthetics refers to the visual qualities of objects and environments, as well as the deep feelings associated with physical spaces that objects can engender (Flannery, 1977). Aesthetics also refers to the branch of philosophy that deals with the nature of beauty. Early childhood educators Carter and Curtis (2008) note that for young children (and adults, for that matter), cultivating an aesthetic sense promotes the ability to experience, appreciate, and produce beauty. This chapter examines design norms that persist in schooling and looks back at some of the important aesthetic legacies that influenced classroom design—some of which have persisted, and others of which have been left behind and replaced by commercial and consumer-driven design norms that dominate classroom décor, arrangement, and curriculum. We first briefly examine the general look and feel of early childhood classrooms and what researchers say about an early childhood aesthetic.

Then we will turn to the legacies of John Dewey, Maria Montessori, and early childhood educators in Reggio Emilia and their influences on classrooms today. Dewey's philosophy, which has guided much of educational philosophy since the 20th century, helps ground our reasoning as to why particular aesthetic aspects of the Montessori and Reggio Emilia approaches might serve children well. In particular, we consider how environmental design/aesthetic choices impact teaching and learning through children's access to and ownership of curriculum, and their relationships—with teachers, with one another, with families, and with the community. We examine the relationship between commercialism and aesthetics, turning a critical eye on the mass-produced materials and furnishings that permeate our schools yet do not reflect the philosophies and aesthetics that Dewey, Montessori, and Reggio educators espouse, nor do they promote the optimal atmosphere for children's learning and well-being. We end with a consideration of what we as early childhood educators have "taken up" and what we have left behind from our philosophical ancestors and how teachers might examine their own schools and classrooms and make intentional aesthetic choices that support teaching and learning.

WHAT DO ENVIRONMENTS FOR YOUNG CHILDREN LOOK LIKE TODAY?

As pointed out in the Introduction, the elements in an early childhood classrooms today typically include rugs with primary colors and letters, pictures of cartoon frogs holding shapes or colors, words placed out of sight between wall and ceiling, materials stacked in brightly colored bins but not accessible to children, and "anchor charts" that stay up all year to become "visual noise." Such spaces suggest that little thought was given to who the children are and what they might need in an environment where they spend 8 or more hours a day. Yet when teachers make choices about what to put in their classrooms, their selections represent more than just the objects themselves—they tell a story of what is important to teachers about learning and their beliefs about children.

The field of environmental psychology has identified ways in which environment impacts how we think, feel, and behave in a particular space. Studies show that children are more cooperative and have more positive interactions in spaces where there is aesthetic attention to wall color, to placement of objects, and to wall decorations (Maslow & Mintz, 1956; Murray-Teige, 2012). Research examining the use of posters and wall charts finds that they do not play a significant role in the instructional process and that there are few instructional opportunities that support self-directed learning related to such charts (Huben-thal, 2009). In addition, art educators and early childhood educators have documented children's ability to appreciate aesthetics and participate in the development of an aesthetically pleasing experience. Even very young children can talk about and appreciate nuances of art, color, light, and line (Booyeun, 2004; Dhanko-Mcgee, 2006; Johnson, 2007).

Books about curriculum are largely devoid of directives about what makes "good" classroom décor. If décor is mentioned, it is not correlated with peda-gogical notions of choice, accessibility, independence, or collaboration among children. Although aspects such as light, color, and "areas" devoted to particular activities are sometimes referenced, what goes on the walls and the design and presentation of furnishings and materials often default to a particular aesthetic code taken up by early childhood environments in the United States today. Ac-cording to this code, brighter, busier, and more bountiful are apparently better.

Before examining the Montessori and Reggio approaches to aesthetics, we first turn briefly to Dewey, who, like scholars in fields such as environmental psychology, architecture, and design and philosophy, posited that there is a connection between aesthetics and personal experience.

PROGRESSIVE ERA NOTIONS OF ENVIRONMENTS FOR YOUNG CHILDREN

Dewey believed it is the responsibility of the educator to "select those things within the range of existing experience that have the promise and potentiality of presenting new problems" (Dewey, 1938, p. 26). Dewey goes on to say that a teacher must see what is in the environment not as a "fixed possession," but as an "instrument of agency" that capitalizes on the child's powers of obser-vation and intelligence. When children and teachers are part of a classroom where they are collaborative creators of the space, the environment becomes both a process and product of the learning experience. As one early child-hood educator expressed to us, "I felt like such steward and guide in my own classroom full of materials I made myself. . . . I felt at home there. There is a kind of authoritarianism to the (catalog) materials—the rug, the calendar, the curriculum kits—[I used to feel,] how could a little person like me challenge that or make anything better?"

We argue that, when the spaces and objects children encounter in school, such as commercial rugs, posters, and spatial arrangements, become and re-main "fixed possessions" and are used in "predetermined ways," no intelli-gence or agency is required or activated on the part of the child or the teacher. How many students, Dewey wonders, have lost the impetus to learn because of the way they experienced learning? Like Vygotsky (1978), Dewey (1938) acknowledges the importance of context:

The primary responsibility of educators is that they not only be aware of the general principle of the shaping of actual experience by environing conditions, but that they also recognize what surroundings are conducive to . . . experiences that lead to growth. Above all they should know how to utilize surroundings, physical and social, that exist so as to extract from them all that they have to contribute to building up experiences that are worthwhile. (p. 40)

Dewey argues, and this is our concern as well, that traditional education can actually dodge this responsibility, and does so systematically by the very organizational structures on which it relies. He notes that "desks in rows, black-boards, and small uninteresting school yards" were not designed to connect with a community or to invite children into an environment for learning that is based on children's experiences (Dewey, 1938, p. 40).

Dewey, however, stops short of issuing a clear directive on what classrooms should look like and what materials teachers might choose. Maria Montessori (who developed her method in Italy around the same time that Dewey was theorizing in the United States) and Loris Malaguzzi (who, along with other progressive educators, artists, and parents, developed what is now known as the "Reggio Emilia approach" in northern Italy after World War II) were clearer in their delineation of methods, aesthetic choices, and teacher training. Therefore, they had a more direct impact on the environment, materials, and curricula developed by educators who sought to follow their examples. Although we can trace this legacy back to Pestalozzi, Rousseau, Froebel, and Dewey, we have chosen to focus on the Montessori and Reggio Emilia approaches because they have most directly manifested themselves in organized schooling. Programs bear their names, and they have become synonymous with curricula, materials, professional development, and specific and explicit aesthetic codes.

However, the early childhood educational community in the United States and globally made choices, both explicit and implicit, over time about what they took up and what they would continue to employ from these approaches. We turn now to an examination of the aesthetic norms and forms behind the Montessori and Reggio Emilia pedagogies—developed decades apart—and consider which aspects of these legacies continue to impact early childhood classrooms.

MONTESSORI'S PREPARED ENVIRONMENT: MEETING CHILDREN'S NEEDS IN THE "CHILDREN'S HOUSE"

Montessori's first school, founded in 1907 in one of the poorest neighbor-hoods in Rome, was called the *Casa de Bambini*, or the Children's House, as many Montessori schools around the world are known. The word *house* was chosen very intentionally. The furnishings and materials reflected a home-like environment, but were proportioned for a child and allowed the school to be a place of order and calm that might not have existed in some children's lives. The children in these first schools came from impoverished neighborhoods, and Montessori, the first woman physician in Italy, known for her work with children with developmental delays, was asked by the mayor of Rome to use her methods with children who were on the boundaries of the school and social systems. Montessori felt that the atmosphere in the classroom should be conducive to reflection and concentration (Lillard, 1997). She saw the environment as existing in relationship to the teacher and the child, with no one element at the center (see Figure 1.1).

Montessori developed her approach by observing children, paying attention to what she perceived as a natural sense of order in children's movements, choices of activity, and social-emotional lives (Lillard, 1997). Certainly influenced by Froebel's materials connected with the kindergarten movement of the mid-1800s and the turn of the 20th century, she noticed that children had a preference for certain objects and tended to create order out of these materials (Montessori, 1966). Montessori designed a series of didactic materials for math, language, senses (color, shape, weight, texture, smell, and taste), science, culture, and practical life (materials that support care of self and the environment, food preparation, and fine-motor work). In this section, we first examine Montessori philosophy related to minimalism, beauty, and order as attributes of the prepared environment. Then we discuss accessibility, choice, and independence as both environmental characteristics and goals for learning.

Minimalism, Beauty, and Order

Montessori saw order in the environment as a basic human need that could combat children's stress and instill a sense of calm. In fact, she found that children returned to materials that were simple and clean, and could be accessed again and again. She referred to classrooms as the "prepared environment" to denote the intentional choosing of materials and furnishings, and their arrangement in a space (Montessori, 1976).

One of Montessori's hallmarks is the advent of child-sized furniture. The "charm of a house is its cleanliness and order, with everything in its place, dusted, bright and cheerful" (Montessori, 1967a, pp. 277–278). She used words like *tidy, calm,* and *dignified* to describe the classroom and felt that these aspects were needed so that the child could engage in intellectual work (Martin, 1992). Figure 1.2 shows a Montessori classroom that reflects the aesthetic of the Montessori philosophy. Desks and tables are not the focal point, but rather shelving with carefully arranged materials and open floor space to work with them are central to the design. Montessori called for the abolition of desks and furniture bolted to the floor. Furnishings, especially tables, should be "firm but light" and easy for children to carry and move so that children can work either together or alone, depending on their needs (Montessori, 1967b).

Figure 1.1: Relationship Among the Environment, Teacher, and Child

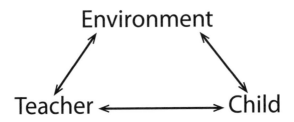

Figure 1.2: A Typical Montessori Classroom

This classroom includes natural light, plants, low and open shelving, open spaces for work on tables or the floor, and artifacts that represent the population of children who attend the school.

Low cupboards, open shelving, movable furniture, and mats that children can spread on the floor to work on were intended to help the children make themselves comfortable and find their own place in the classroom.

Montessori displayed materials in a color-coordinated manner with trays matching bowls, matching other materials, allowing children to easily see what is before them and to see the patterns and categories of materials in the room. This also helped children identify what they wanted to work with and where things belonged in the classroom. Each set of materials is arranged in its own area of the room, each in a specific place, so children know exactly where to find and return them.

Part of the Montessori aesthetic also included plants, lots of light, and un-cluttered spaces (refer to Figure 1.2). She went so far as to say that the room should be adorned with "pleasing artistic pictures" (Montessori, 1914/1965, p. 40), that children's environments be "decorated" or adorned with artwork that might stimulate children's thinking, reflect their environment, or simply pro-vide something interesting to look at. This denoted the perspective that chil-dren could be influenced by their surroundings, and that they appreciate and thrive in an environment that evokes beauty, order, and interesting content.

Accessibility, Choice, and Independence

Despite current interpretations of the Montessori method as cultivating only individual pursuits by children, Montessori actually advocated for chil-dren being free to collaborate and develop a sense of community. Classrooms were comprised of mixed ages so children could teach one another. This was part of Montessori's reaction to the individualistic norms of participation in Italian schools, where children were isolated at their desks and were not free to move about the room (Lillard, 1997).

Montessori felt that the environment should inspire choice-making on the part of the child, and in her prolific writing, the word *environment* is rarely mentioned without the word *choice*. She believed that children should be able to choose to work together or independently and that the structure of the class-room and its furnishings and materials should allow for both (Montessori, 1976). However, choice in the Montessori philosophy means something very different from what is found in contemporary early childhood classrooms. Typical early childhood classrooms have children working at "centers" set up by teachers for specific activities, or children can choose from limited areas or materials—for example, an art project, dramatic play, block area, light table, writing center, and perhaps a manipulative set up on a rug. A Montessori classroom does not limit children to these centers; rather, children can choose from dozens of activi-ties within each area of the room. The materials are available for children to choose from shelves during long periods of uninterrupted time, often up to 2 or even 3 hours. In addition, opportunities to be outside in nature were considered very important. Whenever possible, Children's Houses allowed children to move freely between the indoor and outdoor spaces during the work period.

But what did Montessori mean by "pleasing pictures" or an environment that was "bright and cheerful"? Aren't these subjective ideals? The activity rug in most early childhood classrooms might be characterized as "cheerful" by some. Like Dewey, Montessori wanted the objects in the classroom to be taken up by children for their needs, not to remain as a "fixed possession" outside a child's agenda. Subtle, neutral tones and objects were preferred. The environment was to be arranged carefully so that children could func-tion in it as independently of the teacher as possible. Montessori felt, as did

Dewey, that the environment should reflect children's experiences. Although the didactic materials she developed have remained consistent in design for over 100 years, their aesthetic is neutral enough to blend in with a classroom whose décor reflects a given population or location. She went so far as to say that pictures of "children, families, landscapes, flowers, historical incidents" must be included, that the environment should represent the children in it—a perspective directly related to current diversity ideals in many environmental inventories such as NAEYC (National Association for the Education of Young Children) accreditation and ECERS-R (Early Childhood Environment Rating Scale) (Lillard, 1997). Her work in Italy and India (where she was exiled post–World War II), and subsequently the United States, honored the routines and values of the schools that adopted her approach.

Montessori left us with child-sized furnishings, didactic materials (many of whose designs have been taken up by educational materials manufacturers and are widely distributed), areas of the environment, and a minimalist aesthetic that evokes calm, clean lines, and an uncluttered space. Let us now turn to Reggio Emilia and see what aesthetic legacies might have their origins in this approach.

THE REGGIO EMILIA AESTHETIC

It is nearly impossible to fully understand Reggio Emilia's aesthetic without first considering its historical, cultural, and political origins because it remains so deeply grounded in them. Construction of the first "Reggio school" began 6 days after the end of World War II, using bricks salvaged from ruined buildings and proceeds from the sale of a tank and several horses left behind by the German troops. Loris Malaguzzi, founder of the Reggio Emilia philosophy of education, told Reggio Children liaison Lella Gandini in an interview that when he heard that a school for young children was being built on donated farmland by a group of parents, he was so amazed that he biked out to see it. The school was to be the first of a collective of cooperative, parent-run schools dedicated to "breaking from the past"—an oppressive Fascist regime and authoritarian approach to education—and toward building a more tolerant, equitable, and humane society. Malaguzzi's meeting with these parents represented the beginning of a long relationship that ultimately culminated in the creation of Reggio Emilia's 34 municipal infant-toddler centers and preschools, the first of which opened in 1963 (Malaguzzi, 1998).

The "origin story" of the Reggio schools reveals that they came into existence through the direct participation of parents and the community, and that they reflect a vision of schools as a central force in rebuilding society in ways that align with the socially progressive values of the Emilia Romagna region

(Gandini, 1998). Reggio educators speak of the environment as "the third teacher" (Gandini, 1998; Strong-Wilson & Ellis, 2007), which, along with the teacher and parents, transmits its own messages and has a powerful impact on how children come to think, feel, and behave. Every aspect of the environment is thoughtfully designed both to create "an amiable environment, where children, families, and teachers feel at ease" (Malaguzzi, 1998, p. 63) and to support a pedagogy that nurtures relationships, democracy, and an aesthetic sensibility. Reggio's pedagogical philosophies and the environment align via a number of design concepts, qualities, and characteristics that have become closely associated with "the Reggio aesthetic." In the next sections we will talk about the pedagogy of relationships, democracy, and aesthetics and how each is reflected in the physical environment.

Designing for a Pedagogy of Relationships

The physical layout and arrangement of space in Reggio schools are designed to maximize interaction among children and adults inside the school, while also allowing for solitary work when desired (Malaguzzi, 1998). Every school has a central piazza or "town square" where people "can encounter, socialize with and exchange ideas with others in the school community," with smaller spaces opening off the piazza that allow for small group and individual work (Malaguzzi, 1998, p. 64) and provide a sense of "connected play" (Alexander, Ishikawa, & Silverstein, 1977, p. 342). The inclusion of all of these spatial elements is necessary to support different kinds of learning and is in keeping with universal principles of design. In the seminal work *A Pattern Language: Towns, Buildings, Construction*, architect and design theorist Christopher Alexander and his colleagues identify hundreds of "timeless" design elements with deep biological roots—ways for built spaces to meet the functional and affective needs of their inhabitants. "Common land" (such as the piazza) is considered key to fighting a sense of social isolation and creating a sense of connection to a larger social system (p. 337). This deep need is often ignored in typical schools, where most classrooms open onto hallways. More like roads or sidewalks than a common or square, they serve the primary purpose of orderly "distribution" (Ceppi & Zini, 1998, p. 38), and along with many of the adults in the school, send the message to "keep moving." Communication and interaction in these spaces are tacitly, and often explicitly, discouraged.

The use of *transparency* in the physical space creates "the possibility of looking through from one space to another" (Ceppi & Zini, 1998, p. 42), thereby creating relationships, connections, and a sense of continuity within and between spaces. Interior windows, clear walls, and partial divisions provide a sense of separate, yet not isolated, space (as well as some sound barrier) necessary for focusing on solitary or small-group activities while helping children feel connected and safe (Alexander et al., 1977; Ceppi & Zini, 1998). One might think of transparency as a mechanism for sending visual "invitations" to the inhabitants of a space to remain aware of and perhaps choose to participate in nearby activities.

Exterior windows *bring the outside in* (Ceppi & Zini, 1998; Gandini, 1998), enable inhabitants to "sense" the space outside the school, and form a continuous relationship with the surrounding community and environment, both considered important contexts for learning (Malaguzzi, 1998). They allow children and teachers to observe daily life and natural phenomena—unexpected events that can be woven into learning experiences and become part of the emergent curriculum of Reggio schools. Windows and other openings allow for an abundance of light (Gandini, 1998) that greatly enhances our perception of space and objects, how we feel, and, therefore, how we relate to others and our environment. Plants, textured fabric and paper, children's work on transparent materials, and other objects placed near the windows filter and texturize the light (Gandini, 1998; Ceppi & Zini, 1998), creating patterns and shadows that become material to be explored.

Walls and other spaces are considered in terms of their *communicative possibilities*—an essential aspect of strengthening the relationships among and between children, teachers, families, and others. For instance, special care is given to what is placed in the entrance hall (Gandini, 1998), where teachers display children's work with the intention of not merely informing families and others of what is happening in the school, but of shaping their beliefs about the capability of children (Malaguzzi, 1998). In the classrooms, consideration is given to the height at which documentation (visual artifacts of children's and adult's learning processes) is placed—higher for an adult audience and lower for the children—so it can serve as a reference point for learning.

Designing for a Pedagogy of Democracy

Like Montessori, Malaguzzi (1998) believed that each environment should reflect the identity and culture of its inhabitants. This means that all members of the community need opportunities to contribute to the creation of that culture and that each individual is reflected in the space—important tenets of a democratic society. Children are considered citizens from the moment of birth and should be allowed to participate in every aspect of life and of the communities of which they are part (Rinaldi, 2006). Families participate in setting up the space, building furniture, and providing toys and materials. Making the children, the teachers, their activities, and their learning visible to one another and to parents and other visitors is held at a premium in Reggio and reinforces a sense of identity and belonging (Gandini, 1998).

From a Reggio perspective, space should not limit or dictate what can happen but should be open to modification that both reflects and supports the children's and teacher's practices. Educators in Reggio Emilia design for *transformability* so spaces can be used in a multitude of ways and "manipulated by the children and adults" according to their needs (Ceppi & Zini, 1998, p. 38). Open-ended materials and objects that can be repurposed, used, and formed in a multitude of ways not only sustain children's interest but are believed to encourage creative and flexible ways of thinking. When children literally *see* an object transform from one thing into another—either in their own or another person's hands—they can make important mental shifts that allow them to hold first impressions less rigidly.

Many design elements work in concert to focus attention on, rather than compete with, the unique contributions of the children, teachers, and families. There is a marked difference in the quantity and quality of what gets put on the walls in Reggio schools compared with typical schools, which can be full of "visual noise." Reggio schools, like their Montessori predecessor, take a more minimal approach, aiming for an environment that is "slightly bare, so that the best balance is reached when the space is inhabited" (Ceppi & Zini, 1998, p. 61). Neutral and low-saturation colors are used on the walls and furniture and serve as a background for the elements they want to highlight. Tiziana Filippini, a pedagogical leader in Reggio, says, "The role of the teacher is to differentiate" (T. Filippini, personal communication, December 11, 2007). By being selective about what they put up, including their own interpretations and making conscious graphic design choices, teachers become "curators" of children's learning and help shape a classroom's and school's identity.

Designing for an Aesthetic Sensibility

Reggio educators are deeply committed to "bringing the arts out of the margins" (Malaguzzi, 1998, p. 74), both because of the role the arts play in developing critical dispositions—such as the ability to recognize and consider multiple perspectives—and for the communicative possibilities that the symbolic languages afford to young children (Vecchi, 1998). This value is reflected in the existence and prominence in each school of the *atelier* (a studio or laboratory-like space where children are able to manipulate, explore, and build with a wide range of materials) and the *atelierista* (a teacher trained in the visual and expressive arts). Unlike in typical schools, where children are sent to a specialist to "do art" that is disconnected from other learning and is valued for the time it gives the "real teachers" to plan, in Reggio schools, work with visual and symbolic languages is an integral part of the curriculum and the overall school environment. Along with documentation, the artwork that children create becomes the "second skin" of the school (Ceppi & Zini, 1998, p. 55).

In her keynote address to the International Atelierista Study Group, Vea Vecchi (2006), an *atelierista* who began working alongside Malaguzzi in 1970, declared, "An aesthetic sensibility is the greatest protection we can raise against

violence and indifference [personal, cultural, and environmental] . . . and must
be sustained and nourished at all costs." Aesthetics and beauty are considered
an essential part of the human experience and key in the development of empathy for other beings, places, and things (Vecchi, 2006). Aesthetics include,
yet go beyond, an appreciation for beauty and are considered an "attitude" or
sensibility that, like other languages, needs to be nurtured from a young age
and must permeate the environment. *Niete senza gioia* (to do nothing without
joy)—words that greet visitors at the entrance of some Reggio schools—is a
central precept (Gandini, NAREA website). Great care is taken with every
aspect of the environment—the visual as well as multisensorial dimensions—to
achieve an overall sense of harmony. Color and light play important roles here.
Nothing should be "aggressive or even violent" to the senses, so primary colors
and "overly bright institutional lighting" (both abundantly present in typical
U.S. schools) are avoided (Ceppi & Zini, 1998, p. 68). Space should be neither
visually nor acoustically "loud."

No possibility for appealing to the senses (and to cognition) is overlooked.
Visitors to Reggio schools frequently comment on the bathrooms, which stand
in stark contrast to those in their own schools. One might find mirrors of
different shapes hung at the children's height in passageways to inspire children to play with their reflections, and clear bottles filled with colored water
are placed on shelves in overlapping patterns—encouraging discoveries about
color mixing as children move their position in relation to them.

The choice of materials, and the appealing and "provocative" ways in
which teachers make them available to the children, is inspired by the ubiquitous market stalls in the city where children have gone with their families
to browse and make selections. (Like the re-creation of the piazza in schools,
the market is another cultural object borrowed by the schools to "bring the
outside in.") When displaying materials this way, teachers send children "invitations to explore" and make discoveries about the world (Gandini, 1998).
Many of the materials are brought from home or gathered outdoors—lending
a sense of appeal because of their authenticity and connection to the "real
world," unlike most materials found in schools worldwide that are manufactured specifically for school and appear nowhere else in children's lives.

MAKING INTENTIONAL AND INFORMED CHOICES ABOUT CLASSROOM ENVIRONMENTS

Although there are elements of classrooms that are fixed and may fall outside
a teacher's immediate control (placement of windows, plumbing, room shape
and size), teachers must give themselves permission to go beyond the assump-
tion that the environments they offer must look like the environments in the
catalogs or the room next door. Those who work with young children can

begin to reconsider the environment from the standpoint of what they want to teach, how they hope children will feel, and what and how the environment ultimately encourages and enables children to do and to learn. Dewey called the environment an "instrument of agency," and we posit that, for many teachers, seeing it through this lens involves challenging well-established aesthetic norms and a willingness to venture into new territory, such as learning about principles of design and involving children in decisions about what is made visible inside and outside of the classroom and how the space is arranged. Such changes may be met with resistance from other stakeholders (e.g., administrators, colleagues, parents) who are operating under different assumptions about what early childhood environments should look like and who has a say in the design, materials, and set up of spaces for learning.

Agency describes the ability to organize and direct behavior to "create new ways of being" (Holland, Lachicotte, Skinner, & Cain, 1998; Wandrei, 2001). Wandrei (2001) describes agency as having three components, summarized below:

1. The capacity for self-controlled action that plays an organizing role in how people regulate emotion and thought
2. A sense of "alternativism" and "oppositionality" that actually frees the individual from being defined by status quo patterns, and in turn contributes to creativity
3. The adoption of new language and symbolic systems that make one able to form new connections and new ways of thinking

Dewey (1938) posits that we cannot change who children are at any given time, but that teachers do have control over what he calls the "objective conditions" (p. 45). "Objective conditions" cover a wide range—including not only what an educator does and how but also the equipment, books, apparatus, toys, games played, and the "total set-up of the situations in which a person engages" (p. 45). There are a number of lessons we can take from Montessori and Reggio that point to "objective conditions" that teachers (and by extension, students) have control over. We focus on three considerations here: (1) What do early childhood educators make available to children in school settings, and how do they make those choices? (2) What do educators put on their walls in classrooms, and schools, and why? and (3) Who participates in the appearance and care of the environment?

What Do Early Childhood Educators Make Available to Children?

As we see in both the Montessori and Reggio examples, there are some positive aspects to having some standards with respect to aesthetics in the environment, as long as what is considered standard intentionally reflects and supports cultural values and pedagogical beliefs. But, just as with curricula and assessments, there are perils as well as promise associated with any move toward standardization. One peril is to allow industry, rather than the members of the school community themselves, to drive what schools and classrooms look like.

As the primary consumers of mass-produced classroom materials, teachers have more control over what goes into classrooms and schools than they might think. There is evidence that school movements can change classroom design trends. For example, as progressive education spread to public elementary via the post-kindergarten movement era, the primary grades did come to resemble kindergarten. Bolted-down desks were replaced by small movable desks or even tables. Teachers began using group games and more hands-on activities. Similarly, Froebel's "gifts or occupations"—the small architectural blocks for construction, counting, and parquetry; lacing, sewing, and cutting activities; paper folding; and clay—spread internationally and, through the urging of leaders in the kindergarten movement, Milton Bradley began manufacturing them in the United States (Brosterman, 1997). This paved the way for the mass production of educational materials for young children in the United States.

As consumers, early childhood educators have more agency over what goes into classroom spaces than they might think. The idea of the market driving industry is not new. Educators send a strong message through what they purchase, and the educational materials industry will respond to demand from its customers. Relatedly, a colleague noticed something interesting in the exhibit hall at a recent NAEYC conference. A display of classroom furniture showed chairs—some of primary-colored plastic and some of blond wood—sitting side by side. Seeing this made her think that the company knew there was a market for different aesthetics and that they needed to produce for both.

Teacher agency involves thinking about what makes each classroom unique and clarifying your intentions as you prepare environments for young children. It means thinking differently about the choices you make when you set up your classroom. How might involving children in the creation of materials, signs, and other components of the classroom environment allow children to have a sense of agency and representation, while offering opportunities to learn and work on skills as well? (See Figures 1.3 and 1.4.) Might a commercial poster of the four seasons be replaced with children's observational drawings or photographs of what the seasons look like where they live, perhaps juxtaposed with images from other parts of the world at the same time of year? Not only would such a change better correspond with the children's own experience of the world, it offers opportunities for learning about geography and diverse climates. Could an alphabet rug be replaced by one donated by (or purchased from) a family or local business or artisan? Then children could learn the alphabet in more meaningful ways, perhaps by searching out and photographing objects in their local environment that have the shape of each letter and posting these images in the room. And perhaps the standard, mass-produced materials made available to children—materials often characterized by their hardness (for durability), impermeability (for cleanliness), and smoothness (for safety)—could be augmented with tools and objects from home and recycled and natural objects collected by the children and their families. These would offer a sense of authenticity and a greater range of tactile qualities to children (Ceppi & Zini, 1998).

What Do Teachers Put on Their Walls, and Why?

A prevalent and decidedly "non-Montessori" and "non-Reggio" aesthetic that exists as an accepted early childhood convention is the idea of early childhood classrooms as loud, messy, and cluttered—a "more is better" approach. Stemming from Dewey's notions of an experiential approach and well-intentioned and important free-play movements of the 1960s and 1970s, the idea was developed by some educators who rightly promoted childhood "messing about" as a natural and necessary part of young children's experience. This has since been translated as "more mess + more noise = more fun!" and, in some contexts, teachers, parents, and children have been conditioned to see early childhood classrooms as inevitably loud and chaotic. But such an environmental aesthetic can be counterproductive for many children who benefit from time to focus and concentrate in a quiet and orderly space, a space in which one can also "mess about."

The teachers and *atelieristas* of Reggio Emilia seek ways to build children's capacity to sustain a deep relationship with the environment, which, they believe, is best supported in a space that has been intentionally designed, not filled haphazardly with visual "noise." For Reggio Emilia, the development of an aesthetic sensibility (and the empathy that engenders for both the animate and inanimate aspects of the environment) is a political act. The notion of a teacher as a "curator" of a classroom may help instill the agency and stewardship that educators need to be selective and make careful choices about what goes up on the walls.

This is about more than just beautiful classrooms and walls painted in soft tones. Lillard (2005) cites studies in which children's autonomy, choice, and sense of control in the classroom were linked to more adaptive risk-taking, higher levels of performance on Thematic Apperception Test, and overall well-being. The juxtaposition of furnishings, arrangement of materials, and the specific provocations they offer are all potential entry points for children's

Figure 1.3: Signs Collaboratively Created by a Teacher and Students in a Boston Public Preschool Classroom Using the Drawings of the Children

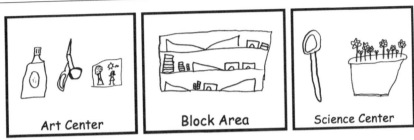

Art Center   Block Area   Science Center

Figure 1.4: Handmade Sign Situated in the Classroom Context

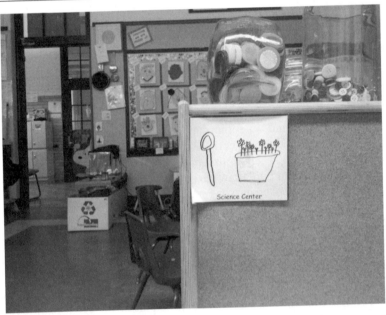

learning. How will these characteristics direct the eye and the body or affect thinking and emotions? We posit that these behaviors are directly linked to the ways in which the environment promotes them, and the arrangement of the space, its aesthetic, and the choices teachers and schools make about what goes into classrooms can impact the experiences children have. For example, teachers might consider, rather than displaying *all* children's artwork connected to a specific activity, allowing children choose a piece of artwork for a gallery space in the classroom. Or group projects such as murals or sculptures can be thought of as a historical record of a classroom's body of work, and remain on display year after year to inspire and tell the story of what children can do. We encourage teachers to think beyond the color palette of primary and secondary colors. A kindergarten teacher we know recently covered her bulletin boards with a creamy cotton fabric, adding soft texture and light to the room. Upon consideration, she realized that—with purple walls, green cupboards, and checkerboard linoleum floor—the butcher paper and patterned borders she typically used for her bulletin boards were difficult on the eyes and she decided to change them. A group of toddler teachers we work with recently did a "primary color inventory" in their classroom in order to remove overly stimulating visuals from the room, creating a more neutral learning aesthetic.

Who Participates in the Appearance of and Care for the Environment?

Both the Montessori and Reggio Emilia approaches encourage the development of empathy and care for the environment. There is a false dichotomy that children will either be learning a skill *or* stewardship. One can learn stewardship *via* skills and vice versa. In both Montessori and Reggio schools, it is important for children to know that things have a purpose and that there are rituals that accompany their life in school, such as how they prepare for learning, how they take meals, and how they clean up. Montessori believed engaging children in the care of the environment would develop their sense of autonomy and ownership. Skills such as caring for plants, sweeping, washing tables, dusting, and tasks often designated for the home such as polishing silver were seen as entry points for this connection with the environment and with society, and they remain a vital part of the Montessori curriculum today. Montessori classrooms always have large floor mats for children to work on, keeping materials clean, protecting them from being stepped on, and guiding children where to walk in the space. There are also small mats for tables that help children define their workspace and organize themselves for learning.

In both Montessori and Reggio schools, the rituals connected to routines involve children in preparing the environment for one another—setting tables with real china and silverware and placemats, cleanup and preparation of the space for the next day or next activity. In Reggio Emilia, lunch is a formal affair. The cook is an important and visible member of the school community, tables are set with real china and silverware, and children take on the coveted role of waiter. The visual essay "Conta" highlights the degree to which children value participating in this way. In it, Reggio educators tell the story of children in one classroom coming to suspect that their method of selecting the day's waiter—Conta (or "Eeny Meeny Miny Moe")—was unfair and that some children were getting to perform this cherished role more than others. This launched a lengthy investigation during which children analyzed data, represented their findings graphically, and developed a new system that distributed the role of waiter more fairly (Krechevsky et al., 2012).

In Montessori classrooms even lunch brought from home is served on a placemat, and snack often involves a self-service where children set the table, use real glasses and dishes, and wash their plates and area afterward. This stands in contrast to snack and lunch rituals in many schools today where crackers are unceremoniously set (or even spilled) onto a bare tabletop; beverages are drunk out of cartons, bottles, or cans; and when children are finished (usually in 20 minutes or less), everything goes in the trash and an adult quickly sanitizes the surface with a chemical wipe while the children line up for the next activity.

OUR LEGACIES: EMPOWERING TEACHERS TO MAKE AESTHETIC CHOICES

We concur with Dewey, Montessori, and Reggio educators who all agree that certain aesthetic codes are beneficial (not to mention make the job of setting up the environment easier in some respects), but, when overutilized, they can overwhelm the space and disconnect children and adults from the educational experience. Certain aesthetic codes have persisted because they are easy to implement, require little thinking about individual children and their needs, and need not be connected to ongoing and ever-changing curriculum. Many environments, Montessori- and Reggio-inspired classrooms included, reflect only what the catalogs tell teachers to include (Hainstock, 1986/1997). However, classrooms *should* look different from one another. The spirit of the Montessori and Reggio philosophies is meant to empower teachers to make aesthetic choices that reflect the children they teach and to prepare an environment where the organization of materials and furnishings promotes simplicity, beauty, access to a range of materials, and a sense of connection and belonging to a larger community for children and for teachers.

We return to our original questions posed at the beginning of this chapter and encourage educators to think about these as they evaluate their own settings. Consider the design of your schools and classrooms for children (and for yourselves if you are in an adult learning setting). What kind of environment inspires you to learn or creates a climate for learning? What do you need from your surroundings to do your best learning? Teachers need to consider that their classroom and school environments might be communicating that school is *not* part of the "real world," but is instead an artificial environment intended for only specific kinds of learning. We believe that relying on prefabricated, standardized objects, such as commercial posters and primary-colored alphabet rugs, sends implicit (and often cumulative) messages that school, and what is experienced there, is separate and disconnected from the other parts of life. Our aesthetic legacies hold promise for bridging the gaps between the environments that teachers create for children and what teachers want the children to learn and become.

Discussion Questions

- How does a particular aesthetic inspire ritual and structure, as well as children's participation in these structures?
- What is the relationship between aesthetics and children's choice-making ability?
- In what ways do you see the current aesthetic of your classroom contributing to or inhibiting children's sense of well-being, their ability to participate in and make choices about their environment, and their desire to learn?
- In what ways does your space (or this space, if you are observing) exhibit the values of relationship, democracy, and beauty?
- What message or directive does Montessori's idea of the "prepared environment" send to you?
- What aesthetic constraints do you work under and what is within your power to change, modify, embellish?

REFERENCES

Alexander, C., Ishikawa, S., & Silverstein, M. (1977). *A pattern language: Towns, buildings, construction.* New York, NY: Oxford University Press.

Booyeun, L. (2004). Aesthetic discourses in early childhood settings: Dewey, Steiner, and Vygotsky. *Early Child Development and Care, 174*(5), 473–486.

Brosterman, N. (1997). *Inventing kindergarten.* New York, NY: Harry N. Abrams.

Carter, M., & Curtis, D. (2008). *Learning together with young children: A curriculum framework for reflective teachers.* St. Paul, MN: Red Leaf Press.

Ceppi, G., & Zini, M. (Eds.). (1998). *Children, spaces, relations: Metaproject for an environment for young children.* Reggio Emilia, Italy: Reggio Children.

Dewey, J. (1938). *Experience and education.* New York, NY: Kappa Delta Pi.

Dhanko-Mcgee, K. (2006). Nurturing aesthetic awareness in young children: Developmentally appropriate art viewing experiences. *Art Education 59*(3), 33–35.

Flannery, M. (1977). The aesthetic behavior of children. *Art Education, 30*(1), 18–23.

Gandini, L. (1998). Educational and caring spaces. In C. Edwards, L. Gandini, & G. Forman (Eds.), *The hundred languages of children: The Reggio Emilia approach—Advanced reflections* (2nd ed., pp. 161–178). Westport, CT: Ablex Publishing.

Gandini, L. (2013). A history of the experience of the Reggio Emilia municipal infant-toddler centers and preschools. Available at www.reggioalliance.org/reggio_emilia_italy/history.php

Hainstock, E. G. (1986/1997). *The essential Montessori: An introduction to the woman, the writings, the method, and the movement.* New York, NY: Plume.

Holland, D., Lachicotte, W., Skinner, D., & Cain, C. (1998). *Identity and agency in cultural worlds.* Cambridge, MA: Harvard University Press.

Hubenthal, M. (2009). Wallpaper or instructional aids: A preliminary case study of science teachers' perceptions and use of wall posters in the classroom. Presented at the meeting of the National Association of Research in Science Teaching Annual International Conference, Garden Grove, CA.

Johnson, H. L. (2007). Aesthetic experience and early language and literacy development. *Early Childhood Development and Care 177*(3), 311–320.

Krechevsky, M., Mardell, B., Filippini, T., & Gardner, H. (2012). Creating powerful learning experiences in early childhood: Lessons from good teaching. *Defending Childhood: Keeping the Promise of Early Education, 192.*

Lillard, A. S. (2005). *Montessori: The science behind the genius.* New York, NY: Oxford University Press.

Lillard, P. P. (1997). *The Montessori classroom: A teacher's account of how children really learn.* New York, NY: Schocken Books.

Malaguzzi, L. (1998). History, ideas, and basic philosophy: An interview with Lella Gandini. In C. Edwards, L. Gandini, & G. Forman (Eds.), *The hundred languages of children: The Reggio Emilia approach—Advanced reflections* (2nd ed., pp. 49–97). Westport, CT: Ablex Publishing.

Martin, J. R. (1992). *The schoolhome: Rethinking schools for changing families.* Cambridge, MA: Harvard University Press.

Maslow, A., & Mintz, N. (1956). Effects of esthetic surroundings 1: Initial short-term effects of three esthetic conditions upon perceiving energy and well-being in faces. *Journal of Psychology, 41,* 247–254.

Montessori, M. (1914/1965). *Dr. Montessori's own handbook.* New York, NY: Schocken Books.

Montessori, M. (1966). *The secret of childhood.* New York, NY: Ballantine.

Montessori, M. (1967a). *The absorbent mind.* New York, NY: Henry Holt.

Montessori, M. (1967b). *The discovery of the child.* New York, NY: Ballantine.

Montessori, M. M. (1976). *Education for human development: Understanding Montessori.* New York, NY: Schocken Books.

Murray-Teige, D. (2012). *A review of the research literature on classroom spaces.* Paper presented at the meeting of the National Art Education Association, New York, NY.

North American Reggio Emilia Alliance. (NAREA). http://www.reggioalliance.org/index.php

Rinaldi, C. (2006). *In dialogue with Reggio Emilia: Listening, researching and learning.* New York, NY: Routledge

Spencer, C., & Blades, M. (Eds.). (2006). *Children and their environments: Learning, using, and designing spaces.* Cambridge, UK: Cambridge University Press.

Strong-Wilson, T., & Ellis, J. (2007, Winter). Children and place: Reggio Emilia's environment as third teacher. *Theory Into Practice, 46*(1), 40–47.

Tarr, P. (2004). Consider the walls. *Young Children, 59*(3), 88–92.

Vecchi, V. (1998). The role of the atelierista: An interview with Lella Gandini. In C. Edwards, L. Gandini, & G. Forman (Eds.), *The hundred languages of children: The Reggio Emilia approach—Advanced reflections* (2nd ed., pp. 161–178). Westport, CT: Ablex Publishing.

Vecchi, V. (2006, February 2). The role of the atelierista. Reggio Children, First International Atelierista Study Tour. Reggio Emilia, Italy.

Vygotskty, L. S. (1978). *Mind in society: The development of higher psychological processes.* Cambridge, MA: Harvard University Press.

Wandrei, M. L. (2001, August). *Agency, constructivism, and social constructionism.* Paper presented at the Annual Meeting of the American Psychological Association, San Francisco, California.

Weinstein, C. S., & David T. G. (Eds.). (1987). *Spaces for children: The built environment and child development.* New York, NY: Plenum Press.

CHAPTER 2

If the Environment Is the Third Teacher, What Is It Teaching Us?

Patricia Tarr

Those of us inspired by the Reggio philosophy have come to look at what it means to create intentional learning environments that reflect an image of the child and of ourselves as educators in new and different ways, yet ways that are rooted in the history of early childhood education in North America. The phrase "the environment as the third teacher," as I will use it in this chapter, comes from Lella Gandini's definition in *The Hundred Languages of Children*, "The environment is seen here as educating the child; in fact, it is considered 'the third educator' along with the team of two teachers" (Gandini, 1993, p. 148; Gandini, 2012, p. 339). In the pages that follow, I will pick up on some of the themes that Kuh and Rivard introduced in Chapter 1 and explore what these mean for educators in the North American context. I present this chapter as a challenge to reexamine our assumptions and values as we create educational spaces.

Educational spaces have a profound long-term effect on us. Christopher Day (2004) has written, "Our environment is part of our biography. It is part of the stream of events and surroundings that help make us what we are" (pp. 26–28). Anita Rui Olds (2001) has concurred, writing, "Our attitudes and beliefs are the legacy we leave our children. Our thoughts, as reflected in our designs, in turn shape children's beliefs about themselves and life" (pp. 12–13). The ideas in these quotations may seem obvious—of course our environment influences us—and I think it is easy to dismiss this as "common sense." Yet if we reflect on these ideas and bring them into our consciousness in our role as educators, they highlight the moral and ethical responsibility that we have to carefully and intentionally plan educational spaces for children. These statements can serve as a provocation for us to consider how spaces, surroundings, and events have shaped us as individuals and as educators.

To begin this discussion of educational environments, I want to take you on a walk through a series of early childhood classrooms over a span of 35 years. I invite you to reflect on the changes these environments have undergone, as well as what design norms have persisted. Later in the chapter we will revisit each space to examine the changes through the lens of Reggio principles. I will conclude with provocations in the form of questions that we must ask ourselves in order to challenge our assumptions and to provide equitable, intentional, and meaningful learning environments for children.

VISITING EARLY CHILDHOOD CLASSROOMS SPANNING 35 YEARS

We will begin our series of visits with the classroom where I taught 4-year-olds in a university lab preschool located in the Pacific Northwest in the 1970s and 1980s, interspersed with my kindergarten classroom in 1973. Next, I offer a composite description of classrooms I have visited in the early 2000s, followed by a profile of a North American Reggio-inspired classroom. These environments both reflect and shaped me as an educator.

An Early Childhood Center in 1971

We enter the small old wooden building that serves as the school office to be greeted by the secretary and center director. Leaving our lunch in the fridge in the kitchen, we head into the play yard that features a large tree with a bench around it in the middle. Large wooden boxes, with openings at each end and one side, planks, wooden stairs, wooden sawhorses—all painted in dark green, blue, red, and yellow—are scattered around the yard. There is an A-frame metal climber and horizontal ladders, swings, a slide, old tires, wagons, and tricycles that can be ridden along an asphalt path. A sandbox contains shovels and buckets, and nearby are the remnants of a vegetable garden. There are many movable parts here.

As we enter the first building, a postwar portable with a wide veranda that houses the class of 4-year-olds whom I teach, you can see furnishings of low medium-brown wood shelving arranged around the room, with some set at right angles to create particular areas: art center, housekeeping center, science center, puzzle table with an adjacent shelf holding wooden puzzles, some of Montessori's wooden cylinders and color tablets to sort, and other small construction sets. Many of the furnishings date from the opening of the center in 1961. To the left of the entry, there are counters over storage cupboards that line the lower part of the wall. A large hooked rug in front of these cabinets serves as the group meeting area. The wall at one end has a window looking into the second room. Under this window and next to the rug sits a freestanding bookshelf filled with picture books.

From where we stand you can see the art area with shelves for collage materials, mostly scrap construction paper and small pieces of fabric, felt pens, crayons, scissors, and glue; a housekeeping area with a wooden stove, fridge, small table and chairs, doll bed, and dress-up clothes. There is an area with wooden unit blocks made from maple for its weight, and a wooden train with interlocking track; a wood ferryboat; small cars and trucks of wood, metal, and plastic; and realistic plastic farm animals. You can see wooden trucks that are sturdy enough for children to ride on and a wooden rocking boat. In this room, windows line the opposite wall, providing natural light and a place to grow seeds or other plants. Nearby are a balance-beam scale and a three-legged stool with a magnifying glass in the center of the seat. Looking to your right, you can see the corridor lined with built-in cubbies, with one-piece rain suits for playing outside in the frequently rainy weather, but minus the backpacks you might see today.

As we look through into the second room, you can see a full-size kitchen counter, sink, stove, and fridge lining most of the wall. There are tables for cooking and snack. You notice a woodworking table covered with indoor/outdoor carpet to deaden the noise, with real, not plastic, tools: child-sized hammers, saw, drill and screwdrivers, screws, and nails. The easel is there, and a transparent plastic water table on legs. Children's paintings are tacked up on the wall, perhaps mounted on a larger sheet of poster board or colored construction paper.

If we stay to watch the 2½-hour program, you will observe a circle time where children choose their activities before they head off to play in one of the centers. There might be specific art materials set out on a table as an invitation, play dough at a small table, and maybe a cooking activity happening in the kitchen area. There will be a short "rest time" with children stretched out with blankets, doing their best to relax and rest, a circle time with songs and a story, snack, and at least 30 minutes or more of outdoor play, regardless of the weather.

We might visit on a day when there is a field trip to the fire station, a freighter in the harbor, the supermarket, or another venue considered appropriate for young children. These trips are used to create interest areas for children's play. You will hear us speak about educating the "whole child" and note us observing children to discover their interests in the materials we set out. We provide art materials but offer little instruction, beyond care of their use, based on the belief that we want to support children's natural creativity.

My memories are reinforced when I peruse educational texts published at this time (e.g., Kritchevsky & Prescott, 1969/1977; Read, 1976; Rudolph & Cohen, 1964). The photographs of children engaged in classroom activities and outdoors show the wooden shelves, tables, and rather plain, neutral walls and multipurpose outdoor equipment that I remember from this time.

Read (1976) describes Freud, Erickson, and Piaget as the key influences on early childhood educators' understanding of human behavior. In teacher training programs, behavioral objectives were beginning to take hold in lesson planning, but they had not yet impacted our planning in the preschool.

A Public School Kindergarten in 1973

Join me in my move into my own kindergarten classroom to teach a morning and afternoon class in a public school 2 years later. The furniture is very new, since kindergarten is a recently legislated requirement for each school district. The furnishings consist of blond movable storage units and shelving that can be arranged around the room, along with yellow laminate round tables for snack or art. The room is neutral in tones yet much brighter than the lab school, with light furniture and colorful laminate tables. The blocks and woodworking table are there, as well as an easel, materials for an art center, listening center, bookshelf, housekeeping center, sand or water play, and a construction set consisting of large plastic interlocking pieces that can be put together to create cubes large enough for children to climb on and enter. Linoleum covers about one-third of the floor space near the coat hooks and sink, creating a wet/messy area for sand, water, and art in the room. We still attempt to have a rest time on the carpet during our 2½-hour day. A typical day includes circle and story time, center time that includes free-choice snack, and some outdoor play.

A Classroom in the 1980s

Return with me to the lab preschool 12 years later, in the mid-1980s. Bright yellow and muted orange laminate tables, like those in my kindergarten class, have replaced some of the original tables, but essentially you will see that the mood and the overall aesthetic of the classroom has remained the same, with one difference: A new teacher has decorated the classroom with hanging mobiles of cartoon characters and some commercial educational posters. These foreshadow the growing trend to bring commercial materials into the classroom. It is now popular to hang signs above the centers identifying their purpose—the art center, science center, book center, and housekeeping center—as part of an increasing emphasis on literacy. The outdoor play yard remains essentially the same, with freshly painted wooden equipment scattered around. Playing outside remains an important part of the program.

The Commercial Classroom of 2005

Now let's jump forward to 2005. We enter a typical early childhood class located in an elementary school where the walls are covered with commercial alphabet letters, numbers, posters identifying colors, shapes, birthday charts, calendar and weather charts, and the phrases "Yesterday was___, today is___, tomorrow will be__," as part of the materials essential for the morning ritual. Neutral colors of the brown or blond wood have been replaced by primary colors in furniture, as well as storage shelves. The atmosphere is certainly bright and colorful, but it also appears crowded and cluttered. Children's work is on the walls, but it is almost invisible against bulletin boards with colorful backgrounds and scalloped borders. (See Tarr, 2004, for a detailed description.)

A Reggio-Inspired Classroom

Walk now into a North American classroom that has been inspired by the Reggio philosophy. If it is in an elementary school, you will probably find evidence of the history and evolution of the philosophies of a previous time. Although the furniture may include the yellow or orange tables of 1980s, the ubiquitous U-shaped "teaching" table, and storage shelves with colorful plastic bins, you will see changes. The room has an intentional clarity in the way it is organized. Gone is the flat light created by fluorescent fixtures, replaced by area lights that illuminate particular places. A light table and overhead projector with baskets of transparent recycled materials provide intentional opportunities to work with light and shadow. Mirrors backing shelves or placed under objects create reflective surfaces that provide multiple points of view of an object. Computer screens create additional sources of light. An interactive whiteboard and laptop cart take up a corner of the class, and these determine the meeting space for the group. Translucent fabric or wood lattice pieces hang by wires from the ceiling to define a particular area with filtered light and a lowered ceiling. Recycled and natural materials are organized in clear containers that make their qualities visible. There is a wide variety of drawing media accessible to the children: pencils in degrees of softness, fine-tipped black drawing pens, charcoal, ballpoint pens, sticks of graphite, oil pastels, chalk pastels, crayons, colored pencils, and felt pens organized by kind and color. Papers of assorted sizes, colors, and textures are arranged in attractive arrays. There is a container of wire of different colors and gauges along with wire cutters and needle-nose pliers. Near the window space are a variety of plants that relate to the trees outside. A prism hangs in the window, creating rainbows on the floor. The housekeeping area has a variety of real cooking and eating utensils, covered jars of beans, plastic foods, and articles of clothing that reflect the ethnic diversity of the children in the class. Close to the block area filled with wooden unit blocks are containers of small colorful tiles, transparent glass gems, cardboard and plastic cylinders, and plastic people and animals.

Fiction and nonfiction books are readily available on the bookshelves or placed around the room as relevant to particular areas of investigations. There is a table to create messages or books supplied with paper, writing implements, staples, punches, and glue sticks. An alphabet created from natural materials hangs at the children's eye level near this table. Another table provides an invitation to create patterns with stones, pinecones, shells, and sticks, part of mathematical understanding.

The space has a calm, inviting atmosphere. The rich and complex assortments of materials are organized as invitations for the children. The materials are cared for and not chaotic. What is quickly apparent is the visibility of the learning that happens here. The bulletin boards, painted in neutral colors, are covered with documentation panels: visual images, texts, and artifacts that bring to life children's voices and thinking. You can see traces of past projects, and evidence of current investigations.

CLASSROOMS IN CONTEXT

I have presented these classroom descriptions as an entry point into my discussion of "If the environment is the third teacher, what is it teaching us?" to illustrate an evolutionary approach to this question. Classrooms exist as part of particular places: whether they are located in a purposely built early childhood center, in a church or community building, or in part of an elementary school. These are all buildings that have a history. According to Burke and Grosvenor (2008), "The design of school buildings, both the exterior shell and the interior ordering of spaces and furnishings, is in a symbiotic relationship with ideas about childhood, education and community" (p. 12).

If we step out of the classroom momentarily to reflect on this history and the relationship between schools and society, we can see how the multistoried urban schools built early in the 20th century served the need of housing many student populations that resulted from laws enacted across Europe and North America making education compulsory for all children. Influenced by the Prussian model of education, students were divided by age into graded classrooms. Buildings were designed to hold large numbers of students, to make it easy to control their movements and for teachers to watch and control their charges. Burke and Grosvenor (2008) state:

> Many aspects of a society and its government were made clear to its citizens though the establishment of these specialized sites of instruction. Pupils learned their place in the world; they were graded and selected; they learned systems of

classification, and studied objects from the locality, the country and the world. It was at school that they were taught their responsibilities, their duty and their sense of place. (p. 17)

The single-story schools that emerged in the 1950s to house the postwar baby boom population in the suburbs reflect the availability of larger tracts of land for school sites and a modernist approach to architecture. Regardless, both structures maintained similar relationships of individual classroom spaces to the larger school, classrooms connected by long corridors designed to move children quickly and efficiently from outdoors to indoors. They were often designed to meet the economic needs of school districts, based on traditional assumptions about pedagogy. Teachers, families, or children were not consulted. In the 1960s, when North America was influenced by the British Infant School and open education, again, designs may have changed but largely without the input of those teaching in these spaces. This often meant that teachers in open-classroom spaces constructed walls and continued to teach in the way they were accustomed.

Although education for young children developed around ideas originating with Froebel (see Brosterman, 1997), Dewey, Montessori, the McMillan sisters, Patty Smith Hill, and others, once kindergarten became housed in elementary schools, it became subject to the tensions and pressures of pushed-down curriculum that live now in the standardization of goals and learning outcomes for young children, prior to 1st grade.

REVISITING THE CLASSROOMS

As we revisit the classrooms described previously, we will do so by keeping in mind the following quotations from Loris Malaguzzi and Lella Gandini:

- "The space has to be a sort of aquarium that mirrors the ideas, values, attitudes, and cultures of the people who live within it." (Malaguzzi in Gandini, 2012, p. 339)
- "A visitor to any institution for young children tends to size up the messages that the space gives about the quality of care and about the educational choices that form the basis for the program." (Gandini, 2012, p. 318)
- "There are hundreds of different images of the child. Each one of you has inside yourself an image of the child that directs you as you begin to relate to the child. This theory within you pushes you to behave in certain ways; it orients you as you talk to the child, listen to the child, observe the child. It is very difficult for you to act contrary to this internal image." (Malaguzzi, 1994, pp. 52)

It is with these words as a lens that I want to return to the schools described earlier, with the following questions in mind:

- What messages do we take from these classrooms?
- How did they reflect the values, ideas, and cultures of those who lived in this space?
- What is the image of the child conveyed?

Lab School in 1971

We enter the play yard. I begin here because outdoor play was an essential part of our program, and it conveys a great deal about our image of the child. In our play yard, although there is the typical fixed equipment in the form of swings and a slide, most of the equipment is flexible and movable by children with some assistance from adults as needed. The large wooden boxes, planks, and sawhorses are always in the process of becoming. They support values of creativity, imagination, collaboration, and group play. They provide physical challenges that are open-ended and changing, whether it is climbing, balancing, lifting, or pushing and pulling. The surface of the yard offers sand, mud, and grass as natural surfaces to explore. The flexible equipment reflects an image of an active and moving child, a social child, and a child capable of challenging his or her own physical skills. It reflects adults who trust children to know their bodies and abilities and a value of outdoor free play, relatively unstructured by adults who are available but not overly intrusive in children's play. Under a teacher's watchful care, children's safety is a concern, but it is not the key driving force for planning the space.

When we enter this 1970s preschool classroom, we are struck by the calm colors and creamy yellow-colored walls. The materials and spaces acknowledge elementary school subject areas of literacy, science, social studies, mathematics, and art, but there are none of the overt representations that indicate teaching specific concepts directly linked to learning outcomes. It is clear that the program places a value on children learning through play, exploration, and discovery.

From our Reggio perspective, we can see that although the room is comfortable and materials are accessible for children, suggesting a value for supporting children's independence and autonomy, it does not exemplify the care and attention to sensory and aesthetic qualities quickly apparent in the Reggio-inspired classroom. In 1971, we valued organization as a means of classroom and behavior management through the flow between spaces and the number of chairs placed in a particular area, indicating the number of children believed could work comfortably in the space. We can see connections to Dewey's learning from experience, Montessori's self-correcting materials, and the tall, thin, and short, wide, clear cylindrical containers in the water table that reflect our growing understanding of Piaget's research in children's thinking. In the art center, the materials and their organization reflect the value of free expression and creativity, and limited teacher intervention. We believed that children will progress through drawing and painting stages of development, if we offer them the materials and support, but without formal instruction. We might model a way to use a separate brush in each paint color, or roll a coil in clay, but this was done usually informally when we were sitting at a table where children were working. Finger painting was valued as an important sensory experience. We created murals with a group of children in a single session because we did not consider children capable of revising drawings and planning the mural over a period of time. Children's drawings and paintings on the walls of the class reflected our expectations for children's artistic expression based on our understanding of their developmental stages in art.

The space reflects, on one hand, a strong image of a child as capable of learning through play and social interaction. It is, as compared with our contemporary thinking, also a diminished image of the child. We believed that young children needed a rest break during a 2½-hour program, although in reality, this was an exercise in control of bodies. Influenced as we were by Piaget's stages of development and a notion of children's learning that progressed from the simple to complex, we offered a less complex environment than a Reggio-inspired class does today. We did not actively instruct children in literacy or mathematics, although we engaged in informal modeling of reading and writing, and picture books were an important part of the program. This is not to suggest that we stood back and let things unfold as they would. We did plan specific activities, generally open-ended ones, and changed the centers such as the housekeeping center to a restaurant, store, or hospital that might integrate writing and symbolic representation, depending on field trips or children's interests. We did not see children, as do the Reggio educators, as creators of culture (Rinaldi, 1998), but as living out a culture of childhood that we expected (Tarr, 2003).

Guided by developmental psychology and a scientific view of ourselves as objective observers of children, we watched children carefully and listened to their thinking so that we could determine if they were within expected norms of development, or to influence the planning of future activities. This is very different from Reggio-inspired documentation and a "pedagogy of listening" (Rinaldi, 2006, p. 65) that promotes dialogue with children so they see themselves as learners and contributors to the culture of the group.

Although I have not revisited the kindergarten classroom in detail, the values and assumptions remained essentially the same as for the preschool, even though it was operating within a public school setting. While the children did not spend as much time playing outside, neither was there the pressure to teach literacy skills and mathematics concepts as there is today.

The 1980s Classroom

Fast-forward to the classroom of the mid 1980s, and we can see a gradual shift in the environment as replacement furniture becomes more colorful and more plastic materials are introduced. We see the creeping commercialism with the addition of information posters and cartoon characters. We also begin to see a shift in programming. Five-year-olds go off to the museum with clipboards and pencils in hand to record what they see, something that we would have considered far too advanced for them in 1971. The signs labeling centers seem to provide evidence of a growing awareness of ways to teach literacy, but it is unclear to whom the signs are directed. If they are for the children, they are usually too high for children to read, even if they were capable of reading. If they are for the parents, do they indicate that we have provided the centers expected in a high-quality early childhood program? Do they serve another purpose: to suggest to teachers that specific kinds of learning happen in specific places? Are they preparation for elementary school, where such subjects are frequently taught separately? Do these signs shut down "border crossings" of materials and disciplines contrary to the holistic way that young children naturally explore the world?

As I reflect on the 1980s and the 1990s, I see a growing influence of Vygotsky's (1978) social constructivist thinking, first apparent in language education, and subsequently influencing education more broadly. It provided the teacher with a role as one who should scaffold learning for children and a beginning recognition of how children were learning through interactions with one another (Berk & Winsler, 1995).

The "Typical" Classroom—2005

Revisiting the 2005 classroom exemplifies the acceptance of commercial products that have now become a taken-for-granted part of early childhood education. The idea of environment as teacher lives as a didactic model in which the information on the walls exists for the child's consumption.

Curriculum documents published in the mid-1990s by my provincial government in Canada and similarly in the United States were illustrative of the time that placed a decreasing value on learning through play, and an increase in expectations that children are *taught* literacy and numeracy concepts. There is a shift as curriculum documents begin to be written in terms of learning outcomes and expectations for all children that give teachers less control over the content they teach or the topics they explore with young children. Teachers rely more and more on commercially produced materials and less on their own observations of children's interests. They have become silenced, just as these commercial materials, and the way they are used, silence children (Tarr, 2001, 2004).

Although classrooms may still have the centers that existed in the 1970s class, often the materials placed in the centers come with particular learning goals. For example, the goal of water play for one week might be to discover what sinks and what floats and to create a chart, or learning about the senses might be accomplished through specific activities that highlight a particular sense each day. It is *structured play* with an educational purpose. Many contemporary classrooms continue to operate in this way. Center time may be used as a reward for "good" behavior when academic work is finished. Teachers have replaced wooden unit blocks with foam blocks that lack the weight and substance of the maple blocks because foam ones are quieter. Safety and noise concerns have meant that young children may no longer have access to real tools and a woodworking bench, but must make do with plastic replicas. Recess and outdoors time has been shortened to 15 minutes a day or, in some cases, taken over by large blocks of academic time. What is the image of the child and what drives the creation of this educational environment? Is it fear that the child will not learn unless we teach? Is it fear about the capabilities of the child? Often, teachers tell me that they must use particular materials or programs because their school or district has purchased them. Is it fear about the capabilities of the teacher? The child and the teachers have both become consumers. These classroom environments now reflect the aesthetic of commercialism with simplified and colorful materials such as containers of plastic teddy bears used for counting, predetermined themes of the week with accompanying posters, and packaged literacy programs (Tarr, 2001).

The Reggio-Inspired Classroom

Now let us return to the North American Reggio-inspired classroom described previously. It is grounded in a view of the child as "a competent, active and critical child," constructor of meanings from complex environments (Rinaldi, 1998, p. 117). It is based on a belief that the child is a citizen from birth with the right to be a full participant in creating the culture of the school, rather than a recipient of the culture. Its design is based on a value that children have the right to the best possible schools.

It follows that the North American classroom reflects an awareness of the Reggio design principles and values described in Chapter 1 (this volume), even though it exists within a typical elementary school context. We can see that there is attention to the visual and aesthetic qualities of the environment, a softness created by the living and natural materials, the relationships of outdoors to inside, and the variety of textual qualities created through the use of fabrics, wood, cardboard, and other materials (Ceppi & Zini, 1998). Although there is not a central *atelier*, or art studio, in the school, there is a mini-*atelier* within the classroom. This has its roots in the art center of the past, but its boundaries are more permeable and its impact can be felt across the classroom in the drawings, paintings, clay, wire, books or digital stories, dance, puppetry, and movies that children have used to represent their thinking and understanding through their "hundred languages" (Malaguzzi, 1993, p. vi; Forman & Fyfe, 2012, pp. 257–258). The term "hundred languages" is a metaphor for the many ways children can be supported to express their thinking; each medium has the potential to become a vehicle for communication.

Place this classroom in contrast to the one-size-fits-all approach exemplified by commercial educational products, highly saturated colors, and stereotyped designs typical of so many North American classrooms. Ceppi and Zini (1998) argue that these primary colors present a simplified image of the child, as does a palette of pastel colors that suggest infancy. Increasingly, commercial toy companies are using color to reinforce stereotypic gender activities. Visit your local toy store, and it is easy to spot toys for girls by the walls of pink boxes and toys for boys in the blue or darker colors of superheroes and action figures. So to avoid gender stereotyping, it becomes even more important to carefully consider the colors that we introduce into our classrooms through wall colors, furnishings, equipment, and toys.

It is easy to fall in love with the aesthetics and beauty of the classrooms in Reggio. It is not so easy to probe beneath the surface to understand the complexity and deep ways in which these environments embody an evolving philosophy grounded in an ongoing process of research about children's thinking and meaning-making in a context of social interactions. It requires attention to notice the obvious, subtle, and layered ways that the values of the school, community, parents, teachers, and children are embodied in the environment. There is danger in trying to simply replicate these classrooms without considering how you will teach in them or how children will actually use the spaces. There are useful and well-conceived books that provide examples of beautiful classrooms, such as *Designs for Living and Learning* (Curtis & Carter, 2003), with textual content that goes beyond simple how-to books. It is easy to "decorate" a classroom, copying the inclusion of light tables, overhead projectors, mirrors, and transparent containers without examining the philosophy and values that underpin the selection of these items. The process must begin with a personal examination of your image of the child and an image of the child held by the social and cultural context surrounding your classroom. Return to Malaguzzi's statement that a school should reflect "the ideas, values, attitudes, and cultures of the people who live within it" (Gandini, 2012, p. 339). This applies equally to the culture of the children as well as the culture of the adults. For example, I have seen superhero action figures incorporated into projects in Reggio Emilia, while frequently these action figures are banned from the North American early childhood classroom. A school on the island of Crete cannot look the same as a school in southwest Australia, Arizona, Maine, or the Pacific Northwest. Each school must reflect the natural, manufactured, and human/cultural environments in which it exists. That is not to say that classrooms should replicate these values mindlessly, because classrooms, as demonstrated by the municipal preprimary schools in Reggio Emilia, can also become models of new visions of the potential of children and possibilities for education.

IF THE ENVIRONMENT IS THE THIRD TEACHER, WHAT IS IT TEACHING US?

I now return to the question "If the environment is the third teacher, what is it teaching us?" This is the opportunity to step back to look carefully and critically. Your environment mirrors back to you your assumptions, values, and beliefs about education for young children.

- What is the image of the child reflected in the materials, room organization, and items on the wall?
- Does the space reflect the diversity of the people in the class and school?
- Does the space suggest that social interaction and group learning is valued?
- Are children's voices visible?
- Are there elements of the classroom that are there because they represent an unexamined part of early childhood history?
- Do you need centers or desks or tables for each child?
- Do they permit border crossings of materials and disciplines that provide opportunities for children to participate fully in creating the culture of the classroom?

Vecchi (1998) observed, "Children are nomads of the imagination and great manipulators of space: they love to construct, move, and invent situations" (p. 131). What might a rich, intentionally organized space look like within this flexibility?

Louise Cadwell (1997) reminds us that we must examine all of the spaces: "No space is marginal, no corner is unimportant and each space needs to be alive and open to change" (p. 93). Are there spaces that you take for granted, or that are unexamined, such as bathrooms, entries, a corner of the room that is piled high with unused materials?

In conclusion, through descriptions of classrooms in which I have taught, I have tried to demonstrate that environments reflect particular values and beliefs about children and learning. How might some be worth revisiting, such as the workbench with real tools or the flexible, open-ended, and physically challenging play yard in the university lab school? How might this type of outdoor play space influence thinking about indoor spaces: the availability of flexible, open-ended equipment and natural materials, a value for learning through social interaction and play? I have explored how my image of the child has changed to a more complex image of the child as a meaning-maker from the rich complexity of the environment. Children have the right to be protagonists in their learning, including the right to express these learnings through their hundred languages. I have learned to continually question my assumptions, to create classrooms based on listening with all of my senses as children and educators research together, and to place aesthetics at the core of creating environments for young children.

Discussion Questions

- How have educational environments influenced you as a person and as an educator?
- What is the image of the child reflected in the materials, room organization, and items on the walls? Are children's voices visible?
- How do the school and classroom reflect the individuals who live in the space and the community in which the school is situated?
- Are there neglected or taken-for-granted spaces? What might you do to make them into invitational spaces?
- What can we learn from the classrooms of the past? What elements might we keep? Why? What do we need to rethink and then do to create a classroom that supports children as partners in their own learning?

REFERENCES

Berk, L., & Winsler, A. (1995). *Scaffolding children's learning: Vygotsky and early education*. Washington, DC: National Association for the Education of Young Children.

Brosterman, N. (1997). *Inventing kindergarten*. New York, NY: Harry N. Abrams.

Burke, C., & Grosvenor, I. (2008). *School*. London: Reaktion Books.

Cadwell, L. (1997). *Bringing Reggio Emilia home: An innovative approach to early childhood education*. New York, NY: Teachers College Press.

Ceppi, G., & Zini, M. (Eds.) (1998). *Children, spaces, relations: Metaproject for an environment for young children*. Reggio Emilia, Italy: Reggio Children.

Curtis, M., & Carter, M. (2003). *Designs for living and learning: Transforming early childhood environments*. St. Paul, MN: Redleaf Press.

Day, C. (2004). *Places of the soul*. Burlington, MA: Architectural Press.

Forman, G., & Fyfe, B. (2012). Negotiated learning through design, documentation and discourse. In C. Edwards, L. Gandini, & G. Forman (Eds.), *The hundred languages of children: The Reggio Emilia experience in transformation* (3rd ed., pp. 247–271). Denver, CO: Praeger.

Gandini, L. (1993). Educational and caring spaces. In C. Edwards, L. Gandini, & G. Forman (Eds.), *The hundred languages of children: The Reggio Emilia approach to early childhood education* (pp. 135–149). Norwood, NJ: Ablex.

Gandini, L. (2012). Connecting through caring and learning spaces. In C. Edwards, L. Gandini, & G. Forman (Eds.), *The hundred languages of children: The Reggio Emilia experience in transformation* (3rd ed., pp. 317–341). Denver, CO: Praeger.

Kritchevsky, S., & Prescott, E. (1969/1977). *Planning environments for young children: Physical space* (2nd ed.). Washington, DC: National Association for the Education of Young Children.

Malaguzzi, L. (1993). No way. The hundred is there. (L. Gandini, Trans.). In C. Edwards, L. Gandini, & G. Forman (Eds.), *The hundred languages of children: The Reggio Emilia approach to early childhood education.* Norwood, NJ: Ablex.

Malaguzzi, L. (1994, March–April). Your image of the child is where teaching begins. *Child Care Information Exchange*, 52–61.

Olds, A. R. (2001). *Child care design guide.* New York, NY: McGraw-Hill.

Read, K. (1976). *The nursery school: Human relations and learning* (6th ed.). Toronto, Canada: W. B. Saunders Company.

Rinaldi, C. (1998). The space of childhood. In G. Ceppi & M. Zini (Eds.), *Children, spaces, relations: Metaproject for an environment for young children* (pp. 114–120). Reggio Emilia, Italy: Reggio Children.

Rinaldi, C. (2006). *In dialogue with Reggio Emilia: Listening, learning, researching.* New York, NY: Routledge

Rudolph, M., & Cohen, D. (1964). *Kindergarten: A year of learning.* New York, NY: Appleton-Century-Crofts.

Tarr, P. (2001). Aesthetic codes in early childhood classrooms: What art educators can learn from Reggio Emilia. *Art Education 54* (3), 33–39. Available at www.design-share.com/Research/Tarr/Aesthetic_Codes_1.htm

Tarr, P. (2003). Reflections on the image of the child: Reproducer or creator of culture. *Art Education 56* (4), 6–11.

Tarr, P. (2004). Consider the walls. *Young Children 59*(3), 88–92.

Vecchi, V. (1998). What kind of space for living well in school? In G. Ceppi & M. Zini (Eds.), *Children, spaces, relations: Metaproject for an environment for young children* (pp. 128–135). Reggio Emilia, Italy: Reggio Children.

Vygotsky, L. (1978). *Mind in society.* Cambridge, MA: Harvard University Press.

CHAPTER 3

No Bad Weather, Only Bad Clothing

Lessons on Resiliency from
Nordic Early Childhood Programs

Megina Baker
Judith Ross-Bernstein

This chapter investigates Nordic values around environmental design for young children and the relationship to children's development of resilience. Drawing upon examples from Sweden, Norway, and Denmark in particular, we examine how the furnishings and arrangement of typical Nordic preschool classrooms communicate values of the good childhood: independence, democracy, and freedom from adult control (Wagner & Einarsdottir, 2008). We note how these values cluster to situate the young child's foundation for resiliency. We also address unifying Nordic values that underpin these practices, attending to wider "environments" such as adult beliefs, practices, and policies that support the development of resiliency in children. The chapter concludes with a discussion of resiliency and what can be learned and applied in the American context.

Both of us consider ourselves "knowledgeable outsiders," having spent more than 35 years in the United States within the field of early education and care, and 20 of those years visiting, studying, teaching, and living in Sweden, Denmark, and Norway. Far from claiming to be Nordic childcare and early education experts, we comfortably speak to the joyful provocation of living and working outside of one's own culture. Developing resilience in children stands out to us as a Nordic cultural imperative and a rising challenge in the American context. We are curious about whether there is something we can learn, adapt, or bring home. Here is a slice from Judith's experience.

No Bad Weather, Only Bad Clothing

First impressions last a lifetime. It is November and my first visit to Sweden; low sun and thick hanging clouds make the dusk-like afternoon light an accomplice to the cold and bone-chilling dampness. Two days' worth of heavy rain has finally stopped and wide puddles mark the play area of this eight-division day care center. An outdoor play area with durable and colorful wooden equipment for climbing, swinging, rocking, and socializing lines the length of this rectangular-shaped day care structure interspersed with natural areas of sand, large boulders, and grass. Areas of blacktop for bicycle riding, push toys, and ball play are carefully planned as well.

In one shallow puddle, a lone toddler, nearly 3 years old, kneels on one knee and leans on a railroad tie while playing. The boy is dressed in what look like red rubber pants, striped rubber boots, a blue plastic coat, cotton mittens, and a matching wool/cotton hat. The amount and size of his clothing dwarf the shovel, bucket, and small metal car that hold his attention for what seems like at least 20 minutes. As I watch the child absorbedly scoop and dump water, and fly and crash the car between bucket and puddle, the favorite Swedish expression *"Inga dåliga väder, bara dåliga kläder,"* or, "No bad weather, only bad clothing," rings in my ears.

ENVIRONMENTS THAT SUPPORT RESILIENCE

Almost simultaneously, my American-ness flares up like the discomfort of a slow-growing heartburn. A silent series of inner questions bombards my observations: Why is he sitting there alone; is the child's safety at risk? Where are the other adults? What if he loses his footing and can't get up? How can he be so content without an adult nearby? Do all Swedish toddlers stick to one activity for so long? What will his parents say about wet clothes? Will his experiments in the cold and wet eventually lead to illness?

In hindsight, this particular cluster of questions is a familiar one, as is each culturally defined answer. We acknowledge that calibrated risk runs through the line and lens of American questioning. Looking back, my own hyper-vigilant, risk-averse perspective provides a stark contrast to the multi-dimensionality of Nordic trust made explicit in an Organization for Economic Co-operation and Development (OECD, 1999) childcare review:

> The team was profoundly impressed by the omnipresent spirit of respect and trust that characterized Swedish early childhood services. There was trust in children and in their abilities, trust in the adults who work with them, trust in decentralized

governmental processes, and trust in the state's commitment to respect the rights of children and to do right by them. (p. 38)

Trust permeates the above vignette of our wet toddler. Yes, Scandinavians do trust: that the clothing will keep this toddler comfortable and dry; that the child will be safe and not drown in 1 inch of standing water; that the child can discover what interests him, test ideas, and learn without adult intervention; that outdoor air keeps the child healthy; that parents share these ideas of well-being on the part of the child and most likely want the child to "get wet" with the world, and so do the day care director and the governing bodies at both the local municipality and broader state levels for children's early care (Christensen & Clausen, 2004).

Throughout this chapter, we construct a relationship between trust, children's experience with the environment, and their incremental development of resilience. Further, we wonder what the view of the child is in this context: one that is expected, or groomed, to be resilient? Are there culturally shared assumptions (implicit or explicit) of children's resilience that transcend international boundaries?

We recognize that the relationship between observed environments and behaviors is rather complex, as are the meanings we make of them. In order to consider play-environment relations, one must take into account micro- to macro-level factors (Bronfenbrenner, 1992). Micro-level factors "zoom in," focusing the lens on the daily activities of the child, or on immediate interactions between the child, teacher, and environment (as in the initial vignette). To understand these micro-level examples, one must "zoom out" to consider macro-level factors such as: how teachers plan for children, what constitutes their expectations for learning and development, what parents want for their children, how a national curriculum is implemented, and what certain policies are regarding children and their care.

In this chapter, we "zoom in" and "zoom out" to assemble a systemic picture of the relationship between resiliency, the environment, and cultural factors that support it. We begin with reflections on resiliency in American children, continue by digging deeply into the Nordic context, and conclude with implications and suggestions for practice at home in the United States. The following interrelated questions remain central throughout:

- How does the environment shape children's experiences and support the development of resilience?
- How does the shared Nordic concept of the good childhood define play and learning and engender the development of resilience?
- How are Nordic national policies and cultural values reflected in planned environments for young children?

ARE AMERICAN CHILDREN RESILIENT?
RECENT CONCERNS

Our journey as outsiders has provoked us to question our own cultural assumptions about resilience in American children. We find that we are not alone; instead, we are in very good company. "We've become a nation of risk-averse, safety-obsessed, Purell-loving freaks," warns Belkin (2011). Her dire commentary on the American bubble-wrap generation (Malone, 2007) is alarming; as parents and educators, have we failed our children? Are they less resilient than the children in other corners of the world, raised with a different set of expectations and in a different, perhaps more challenging, environment? With Belkin's public outcry runs a parallel academic concern regarding the upbringing of our nation's children at both ends of the socioeconomic spectrum (Tough, 2012). From Tough's perspective, Paul succinctly summarizes Tough's argument, explaining that we are witnessing the "extremes of American childhood: for rich kids, a safety net drawn so tight it's a harness; for poor kids, almost nothing to break their fall" (Paul, 2012, p. BR19). Tough explains that children who grow up in stressful environments with no safety net generally have difficulty with self-regulation, while children with too tight a harness have no threshold for adversity or skills to combat challenge, often experiencing intense feelings of shame and hopelessness and demonstrating unusually high rates of depression beginning in middle school.

Seligman (2007) concurs, writing that America is in the midst of an epidemic of pessimism as parenting and education goals fail to address children's developing sense of optimism, from the very young through the adolescent years. Optimism as a positive explanatory style ("habits of thinking about causes" [Seligman, 2007, p. 52]) can indeed be nourished. Following Seligman, research by Reivich and Shatté (2002) has shown each person develops an explanatory style (a way of looking at the world and understanding life events) during childhood. This explanatory style is the primary determining factor in the development of resilience, more significant than other factors such as genetics, childhood experiences, or economic opportunities.

Taking a life-long perspective, Galinsky (2010) argues that teaching very young children to take on challenges is one of seven essential life skills that every child needs:

> When I first began contemplating this skill, I saw it as managing stress. As I thought about it more deeply, I saw it as the skill of resilience. But now it's clear to me that the real essential skill is taking on challenges—being proactive rather than reactive when difficulties arise. My mother always called it 'getting back on the horse after falling off.' (p. 283)

Engendering a disposition of resilience in children means cultivating optimism, the ability to take on challenges, grit, persistence, self-control, and curiosity—a daunting task that is somehow, mysteriously, commonplace in Nordic environments. How can this be?

HOW DOES THE PHYSICAL AND SOCIAL ENVIRONMENT SUPPORT THE DEVELOPMENT OF RESILIENCE?

INTO THE WOODS

Wednesday morning is forest morning for the mixed-age group of 1- to 5-year-olds in Vitsippans förskola in Härlanda, Sweden. Undeterred by wet weather, the group gathers in a large hall, where each child has his or her own cubby stocked with extra clothing, indoor slippers for use inside the preschool, and a set of rain gear and boots for outdoor use.

As the teachers assist the youngest children with their rain gear, the older children in the group support one another with snaps and zippers. As soon as the children are dressed, they exit through the hallway door directly onto the adjoining playground, although the teachers are not yet present outdoors.

Once the whole group is outdoors, a teacher opens the gate at the back of the fenced playground. Immediately beyond the playground is the forest, with a familiar path toward boulders and fallen logs, spaces for building forts out of tree branches, and opportunities to gather the treasures of the wood. Children run ahead of the teachers, reminded to stop when they reach the clearing ahead. The rain has left behind fantastic puddles, and along the way, several children test out the efficacy of their rain boots, stomping, splashing, or even sitting down in the puddles to explore the properties of water. The group will remain in the forest for the duration of the morning, returning to the preschool for midday lunch and rest.

Do you find yourself, as we did during our initial journeys to the north, surprised as you read this vignette? This culture shock is to be expected; the picture of the children in the forest here may be strikingly different from what one could expect to see in an American preschool. Our forest scene might warm the heart of the American naturalist and educator Richard Louv (2005), who warns that children who do not spend enough time outdoors in natural spaces suffer from "nature deficit disorder," and are at risk for developing a host of problems including attention deficit/hyperactivity disorder, obesity, and mental health issues. In contrast, access to and activity in natural spaces typify Nordic childcare programs.

The physical and social environments both support this excursion to the woods, allowing the cultivation of mastery, optimism, and resilience. According to Levine (2012):

> Mastery of the world is an expanding geography for our kids. For toddlers, it's the backyard; for preteens, the neighborhood, for teens the wider world. But it is in the small daily risks—the taller slide, the bike ride around the block, the invitation extended to a new classmate—that growth takes place. In this gray area of just beyond the comfortable is where resilience is born. (p. SR8)

This consideration of mastery provides an appealing lens with which to examine the forest vignette. Outdoors, daily risk is provided, and these experiences extend to children's encounters indoors, with spaces designed to anticipate and encourage children's experience with mastery.

In the foyer of the preschool, for example, children tackle the potentially overwhelming task of dressing for inclement weather, accomplishing as much as possible on their own (independence), yet supported by peers (collaboration), by teachers, and by the physical environment of the school. Plentiful space for hanging outerwear enables parents to leave extra rain gear at the school, and children can easily reach these items, which are stored at their eye level. A special piece of furniture provides children with a handle to grip while prying their own boots off using a bar below. The foyer is equipped with drying cupboards, special heated cabinets with racks to manage wet items when the children return from the woods (see Figure 3.1). In the event of a particularly muddy cleanup, some schools (especially in Norway) have two foyers, one for removal (and rinsing) of muddy wet garments and an inner room for changing into dry clothing and slippers. Perhaps the knowledge that one can easily become warm and dry again after swimming in a puddle alleviates some anxiety among the children, and enables them (and their parents) to feel more comfortable trying out a cold splash. Children develop mastery over the process of preparing for their trek outdoors, cultivating both independence and interdependence along the way.

The architecture of the school is intentionally designed for easy access to the outdoors as well. Doors that open directly onto the play yard mean children can easily move outside as they are ready. This is acceptable in the Nordic context, as the adults in the preschool are able to see the children through the window. It allows some privacy even to young children, something that is encouraged and even supported at the policy level. And the physical location of the school, situated next to a green area and with a gate at the back of the play yard, makes access to the forest seamless. The presence of green spaces,

Figure 3.1: View from Outer Foyer to Inner Coatroom; Rain Clothes Are Stored in the Outer Room

even in urban Nordic locales, makes this accessibility pervasive rather than exceptional.

Into the woods now. As children scramble over wet logs, climb boulders, and run ahead of their teachers down the forest path, risk is inherent (see Figure 3.2). In contrast to Tough (2012), Belkin (2011), and Malone's (2007) discussion of the dangers of overly cushioning childhood, children *do* fall in the forest, scraping their knees and palms—although older ones offer hands of support to smaller peers as they navigate steep inclines. In fact, according to Sandseter (2009), high degrees of physical risk are acceptable to Norwegian educators, who see risky play as an opportunity for children to develop mastery over their physical bodies and to cope with recovering from small injuries. Could this be the "grey area" of which Levine (2012) speaks? When the environment encourages risk-taking, children have opportunities to go beyond their limits, and it is through this opportunity that mastery can be developed over time. As Seligman (2007) writes, "Masterful action is the crucible in which preschool optimism is forged. Your child's task, aided by informed parenting, is to make a habit of persisting in the face of challenge and overcoming obstacles" (p. 12). In Sweden, Norway, and Denmark, regular time spent outdoors in natural spaces provides countless opportunities for the habits of persistence and optimism to be developed.

**Figure 3.2: One-Year-Old Child Climbing on a Rocky Slope
in the Forest**

Let's now consider experiences in the indoor environment, and take a
look at how the "good childhood" defines play and learning. Here we explore
how resilience is further engendered by adult ideals and practices.

HOW DOES THE SHARED NORDIC CONCEPT OF THE GOOD CHILDHOOD DEFINE PLAY AND LEARNING AND ENGENDER THE DEVELOPMENT OF RESILIENCE?

THEY CAUGHT A FISH!

The pedagogue (Danish early childhood professional) leads us to a
group of 22 5- to 6-year-olds. The children have just finished lunch and
are starting a free-play period. We walk upstairs to find two connected,
large, sparsely furnished rooms. At the end of the second room is a four-
stall bathroom. The first bright room has large windows that make the
clean linoleum floors shine. A few round tables with matching adult-
sized chairs and a small shelf with fine-motor materials complete the
sparse furnishings. The second room has a full-sized couch near a

bookshelf. The walls are somewhat bare but have a few selected child drawings posted.

A foursome of 5-year-old boys plays with a very thick rope, about 6 feet long. Three of the boys have tied the rope around the legs and waist of the fourth boy. The laughter is loud among the three holding the rope, amid shooting dialogue exchange in Danish. The fourth boy (the one tied up) bucks with the rope around him, squealing with energetic laughter and grunts. While the three boys grab the rope in unison, they begin to drag their friend, mostly by the legs and feet, zigzagging through the length of the two school rooms, stopping to talk and laugh.

Other children watch as the group passes by. Some read books on the couch, while others sit quietly at tables with pegboards. A few acknowledge the boys' dragging game with a nod, but others remain focused on their own activity. The pedagogue observes the play, but says nothing to the boys.

Forty-five minutes into the tour, the squealing from the boys increases in volume and tempo. They are out of the hallway and have dragged their friend into the bathroom and into a toilet stall where there is heated dialogue. The pedagogue calmly walks toward them, and the three report excitedly in Danish, ending with the exclamation *"Fisk!!!"* The pedagogue looks at me, quietly smiles, and says, "They caught a fish!"

Our "catching-fish" vignette portrays a typical episode of rough-and-tumble play reported from Nordic early childhood program settings but that commonly may provoke discomfort in the American reader (Carlson, 2011; Tannock, 2008). Are the boys disruptive? Is it safe to have a rope in the classroom? Should the children be playing in the bathroom? Can someone get seriously hurt? One might have litigious concerns; can this risky play constitute grounds for a lawsuit if someone gets hurt?

We can humbly attempt to unpack our pedagogue's perspective, her quiet delight with the physically and emotionally charged episode above. She likely does not see the catching-fish play as dangerous, and most certainly the potential of a lawsuit would not cross her mind.

Instead, from her perspective, the children's experience is valuable in and of itself. Themes of risk and trust reemerge. We see examples of small daily risks embedded in the rope play and the children's many decisions. We also see that the teacher, in her hands-off approach and quiet acknowledgment, trusts that the children, taking a chance in this rough-and-tumble play, will learn their own limits and those of their peers. Allowed by the pedagogue, these indoor experiences with mastery afforded by the physical, social, and temporal environment engender resilience in the children.

In the physical environment, less is more (see Figure 3.3); the lack of substantial materials directed at teaching academics (as one may expect in

Figure 3.3: Interior Environment of a Nordic Preschool

an American preschool setting) is notable. The walls are bare except for selected children's work. There are no commercially bought visuals, charts, or
pictures to teach alphabet, letter sounds, number concepts, or shapes. The
cleanliness of the bare linoleum floor is remarkable, as is the absence of rugs
with letters, shapes, or numbers, or squares for children to sit within. The
large spaces, unencumbered by furniture or rugs, are used flexibly, allowing
for child-initiated play that runs the gamut of quiet-sedentary (the children
reading together or playing with pegboards) to loud-mobile (playing *fisk*).

Here, the environment appears people-focused, rather than materials-
focused. Physical space and materials for interaction are provided through
large areas to gather and furniture that seats more than one child at a time.
Materials, such as the rope in the above example, tend to be open-ended, affording processes and products with the materials to vary as children choose
to play alone or together. In the *fisk* episode, choice and challenge arise from
each step of the self-initiated rough-and-tumble play: How will we move the
fish (lift, drag, push)? How far can we move the fish in one effort? How do we
reconfigure to make the moving easier (or more challenging)? What purpose
will the rope serve?

As with the children's explorations of puddles outdoors, indoors we see
the opportunity to meet incremental challenges. Here, children problem-solve,
negotiate, and move the story forward to its determined conclusion.

Temporally, uninterrupted play periods are typical in Nordic settings. The *fisk* episode lasted 45 minutes from beginning to end—just a part of the free-play period in Nordic settings, which can last for up to 2 or 3 hours at a time. The expectation is that children will choose their own activities and keep themselves engaged.

Let's dig a bit deeper into our pedagogue's values. Her first instincts are not to reinforce rules or to stop play—as might be the first responses from an American perspective. In truth, our teacher's perspective and the children's actions would be quite common in Nordic settings for young children. The catching-fish vignette and reflections speak to Nordic cultural expectations of what constitutes a "good childhood." According to Wagner and Einarsdottir (2008), "Deeply embedded and widely embraced, the concept of the good childhood (in Danish, *en god barndom*) is reified in public policy, reflected in teachers' pedagogical practices, and animated in children's everyday lives"(p. 265). It exemplifies the explicit high value that child-centeredness and play receives and serves as a central thread to broader Nordic underpinnings of the concept. As best can be conveyed in English, central constructs of a Nordic good childhood are as follows:

> Naturalness of childhood; equality and egalitarianism; democracy defined as lived daily experience for children; freedom, conceptualized as autonomy to play and to develop one's own self; emancipation, or liberation from over-supervision and over-control by adults; warm and cooperative social relationships with adults and peers; and solidarity with Nordicness, or connecting with Nordic heritage through consistent enactment of distinct cultural traditions. (Wagner & Einarsdottir, 2008, p. 265)

The good childhood frames our pedagogue's perspective in her day-to-day decisionmaking and teaching. In the catching-fish episode, our pedagogue likely believes that the children have the right to steer the direction of the play, with equal weight to, if not more than, the will of the adult. Children are seen as essentially competent. Therefore their play is respected as their own; it captures their own ideas and voices as their imagination and creativity are exercised.

Expectations for collaboration via social demands are met, sustaining the positive feelings and enjoyment among the boys throughout the vignette. Perhaps each boy had a subtle vote in how their play goes forward, through nuanced nonverbal smiles, nods, and continuation of engagement. With no disruption by adult supervision, the boys have the freedom and control to claim the direction of the play. Here, we see that age-appropriate elements of democratic practices are evident throughout as we return to this idea in the next vignette.

We move now to examine how policies and norms impact aspects of the physical environment such as the architecture, furnishings, and materials in Nordic preschools.

HOW ARE NORDIC NATIONAL POLICIES AND CULTURAL VALUES REFLECTED IN PLANNED ENVIRONMENTS FOR YOUNG CHILDREN?

PASS THE POTATOES

It is nearly lunchtime, and children in this Gothenburg preschool come in from the playground for their meal. A few children set the tables family-style with simple white ceramic plates, silverware, and child-sized glasses, enough for one adult and four to six children at each table. The tables are at adult height, but the children's chairs are designed to allow them to climb up independently to sit comfortably at the tables. With the exception of the very youngest, the children serve themselves.

At one table, two children talk excitedly about their adventures in the forest that morning, and the slugs they found while walking on the path. Across the room, someone starts telling a silly story, and is quickly rewarded with laughter and attention from her peers. Undeterred by the social fabric of this meal, a particularly committed 2-year-old focuses intently on buttering her crispbread, gripping the bread firmly by pinning it to the table and dabbing her small wooden knife on the bread. She smiles as a large pat of butter adheres to the bread, decides this is enough for now, and promptly licks it off with a grin. Her teacher smiles too, reminding her to try some of the bread as well.

The leisurely meal draws to a close, and children begin to ask if they may be excused from the table. All of the children who are able to walk confidently carry their own dishes to the dishwasher across the room, receiving some support from a teacher to rinse their plates before placing them into the dishwasher racks. Then hands and faces are washed and dried with individual cloth towels that hang near the sinks before time for books and rest.

The mealtime vignette above, typical for a Swedish preschool group, is peppered with qualities that are distinctly Nordic: trust in young children as capable individuals, an emphasis on shared power (democratic practices), and the importance of a family-like environment for children spending time outside of the home. These qualities are influenced by broad, macro-level factors that pertain to the parental work environment (parental leave, work-life expectations, and so on) as well as directly shape environments for young children in these countries.

Swedish preschools, predominantly designed and constructed in the 1970s to meet the expanding needs for child care, tend to look very similar to one another. In order to make children feel at home, preschools were built to look like houses, referred to by the majority of the population as *daghem*, or "day homes." This mentality of hominess has impacts on the preschool environment; when entering the preschool, for example, children and parents alike remove their shoes and put on slippers for indoor wear. In the mealtime vignette, the notion of hominess is demonstrated through the adult-sized tables and chairs, as well as the family-style serving of the meal. In this environment, children are encouraged and supported to take care of their mealtime needs as much as they are able, a practice that encourages the development of motor skills as well as self-control (taking an appropriate number of potatoes) and independence (clearing one's own plates after the meal).

Each *avdelning*, or area for one group of children (typically 18 children with two preschool teachers and one full-time assistant), consists not of a single classroom, but as a series of small, connected rooms with doors that may be closed by adults or by children. Children are welcome to play in small groups in one of the little rooms, closing the door behind them (but always visible to teachers through small windows in the doors or walls at adult height). The very architecture of the preschool buildings has been designed with the trust of children's competencies in mind.

Democratic values are evident in our mealtime vignette as well as in the catching-fish vignette. The Swedish National Curriculum for the Preschool (Ministry of Education and Science, 1998), an elegantly slim 16-page document, opens with the words "Democracy forms the foundation of the preschool" (p. 3). The curriculum proceeds to voice the rights of the child to participate in decisionmaking in the preschool and to select materials and activities over the course of the day, as is evident in the decision to take one more potato at lunch, or in the choice to use a rope or a pegboard. The national curricula of both Norway (Norwegian Ministry of Education and Research, 2012) and Denmark (Pædagogiske Læreplaner for Dagtilbud, 2004) echo these same democratic principles.

The environment outside of the preschool's walls matters as well: The Nordic penchant to embrace a harsh climate plays a significant role in the physical environment, the furnishings of the schools, and the way in which spaces are used. In fact, the Norwegian curriculum for the preschools (Norwegian Ministry of Education and Research, 2012) ensures the practice of spending time outdoors daily, in all types of weather, as one of the rights of the child. In Norway, special sleeping porches in the preschools allow young children to nap outdoors, even in the winter. This practice is considered healthy and is desired by most parents (M. Waaland, personal communication, August 6, 2012).

A principle of acceptable risk is apparent here, in which the society expects children to develop some resilience and, in this case, immunity perhaps, through getting dirty, by offering opportunities to handle real and breakable materials, and by literally bringing the child up to the level of the adult with adult-sized furnishings. Policies at the national level are broad and unconcerned with lawsuits and penalty, allowing for a more optimistic view of risks.

BRINGING IT HOME:
POSSIBILITIES FOR PRACTICE IN THE UNITED STATES

Do you find the Nordic interplay between the environment and the child appealing? Baffling? Does the idea of embedding and allowing risk in the environment with the intention to develop resilience cause you to wonder if this could ever be possible in the United States? Although there are many contrasts that you may have perceived between cultures, we focus here on two broad dichotomous themes: trust as opposed to litigious worry, and risk-taking as opposed to bubble wrapping. Both affect the potential to develop an early disposition toward resiliency.

American avoidance of risk in the context of our heavily litigated society is well documented (Greenman, 2005; Laudan, 1997; Ropeik & Gray 2002). In contrast, resiliency permeates at multiple levels in Scandinavian childcare environments. The undercurrent of trust that we have witnessed, and the OECD team affirms, enables Nordic childcare environments to offer children more exposure to gradual risk, and in turn, we argue, enable them to become more resilient. The arguments of Seligman, Tough, Louv, Galinsky, Belkin, and Levine, which we have explored in this chapter, add more voices to the conversation, suggesting that we need to pay more attention to cultivating resiliency. If we take these experts seriously, it seems that some of the lessons provided by Nordic early childhood environments would be well applied to our own practices.

Despite the chasms of difference between cultures, there *are* small but significant ways in which we might begin to bring some of the Nordic values home to reconsider our early childhood environments with an eye on the early development of resilience. Inspired by our Nordic encounters with resilience, we propose eight concrete adjustments to the social and physical early education environment that could enhance American children's encounters with trust, mastery, choice, and risk. We begin with the social environment, because as early childhood teachers, what we think, what we say, and what we do are inseparable, inextricably linked in practice. We then conclude with several concrete suggestions for the physical environment.

Shifts in the Social Environment

In order to foster resiliency, adults can shape the social environment for children by:

1. *Stepping back before stepping in,* as our Danish pedagogue did. This means acting as an observer before leaping to protect children, thereby allowing space for discovery and a chance to develop self-regulation. When adults monitor their own responses to children's risk-taking, they can consider their own stress levels and the messages that they may be sending to the children in their care.

2. *Trusting young children,* viewing children as competent individuals capable of sharing in some age-appropriate decisionmaking.

3. *Forming authentic adult-child partnerships* around children's individual stories and capabilities. Knowing children well allows adults to provide explicit and reasonable expectations, demanding that they stretch and explore but setting attainable challenges.

4. *Making the language of resilience explicit,* communicating trust, respect, fostering a growth mindset, and offering encouragement. For example:
   - Communicating trust on the playground by saying, "You can climb to the top of this structure; I've seen you climb up the first three steps."
   - Respecting the child's ideas while working with clay, by asking, "What can you do to make this thinner?"
   - Fostering a "growth mindset" (Galinsky, 2010, p. 10) by acknowledging, "That looks frustrating, but you can try it this way next time, and see if that works."
   - Offering concrete encouragement, such as, "I see you spent time folding that paper, you made it flat. See if it can tear now."

Shifts in the Physical Environment

As we have seen throughout this chapter, this fabric of the social environment interacts with the physical environment to foster resiliency. The following practices could translate to American early childhood settings:

- *Offering open-ended materials* that invite child-directed, creative, and self-regulated play (Drew & Rankin, 2004). Carter and Curtis (2003) refer to a "loose parts" curriculum, offering children large pieces of fabric, hollow blocks, cardboard tubes, and the like for dramatic play, indoors or outdoors. Art materials could also provide for freedom of expression. For example, we suggest that children and teachers use found materials as "beautiful stuff" (Weisman Topal & Gandini, 1999) that children can gather and transform into sculptures or props for play.

- *Providing real materials,* such as ceramic plates and glass drinking glasses, entrusting children and embedding the "small daily risks" of which Levine (2012) speaks.
- *Allowing rough-and-tumble play* as a kind of valuable play. It promotes active trust, a sense of belonging, supports the establishment of empathy, and builds the capacity to handle exclusions and humiliations. When adults allow it, it fosters the skills of friendship—negotiation, setting workable rules and limit setting— and establishes many of the foundations that allow later adult communities to flourish (Carlson, 2011; Tannock, 2008).
- *Spending time in natural spaces,* following Louv's (2005) advice to get off the rubberized playground once in a while. Finding green, natural spaces gives children time and space to interact with nature. Yes, there might be some scraped knees as children climb over logs and gather leaves, but a sense of wonder could also be cultivated, along with resiliency.

These concrete shifts in the environment are intended as a provocation for practitioners. By looking to the Nordic countries and their environments for young children, we open space for discussion and reflection, for considering ways to bring Nordic early childhood values home and infuse the social and physical environment with a bit more trust, and a hint of risk. In doing so, we might offer children a "good childhood" of our own, allowing them to be challenged, and through challenge, to develop resiliency.

Discussion Questions

- Examine your teaching and learning environment. What opportunities for daily risks and mastery are provided?
- What might be the American version of the good childhood? How do you think we could provide this for children?
- How could you collaborate with parents and administrators around fostering resiliency in young children?

REFERENCES

Belkin, L. (2011, September 19). Teaching kids to fail. *New York Times.* Available at parenting.blogs.nytimes.com/2011/09/19/teaching-kids-to-fail/?_r=1

Bronfenbrenner, U. (1992). Ecological systems theory. In R. Vasta (Ed.), *Six theories of child development: Revised formulations and current issues* (pp. 187–249). London, UK: Jessica Kingsley.

Carlson, F. (2011). Rough and tumble play: One of the most challenging behaviors. *Young Children 66*(4), 18–25.

Carter, M., & Curtis, D. (2003). *Designs for living and learning: Transforming early childhood environments.* St. Paul, MN: Redleaf.

Christensen, M. N., & Clausen, S. W. (2004). Pædagogiske Læreplaner i Dagtilbud. Naturen og Naturfænomener. Available at uvm.dk/Uddannelser-og-dagtilbud/Dagtilbudsomraadet/Fakta-om-dagtilbud/Paedagogiske-laereplaner-for-dagtilbud

Danish Ministry of Education. (2004). *Pædagogiske Læreplaner for Dagtilbud.* Available at uvm.dk/Uddannelser-og-dagtilbud/Dagtilbudsomraadet/Fakta-om-dagtilbud/Paedagogiske-laereplaner-for-dagtilbud

Drew, W. F., & Rankin, B. (2004). Promoting creativity for life using open-ended materials. *Young Children 59*(4), 38–45.

Galinsky, E. (2010). *Mind in the making: The seven essential life skills every child needs.* New York, NY: HarperCollins.

Greenman, J. (2005). Places for childhood in the 21st century—A conceptual framework. *Beyond the Journal, Young Children 60*(3). Available at www.naeyc.org

Laudan, L. (1997). *Danger ahead: The risks you really face on life's highway.* New York, NY: Wiley & Sons.

Levine, M. (2012, August 5). Raising successful children. *New York Times.* p. SR8.

Louv, R. (2005). *Last child in the woods: Saving our children from nature deficit disorder.* Chapel Hill, NC: Algonquin.

Malone, K. (2007). The bubble-wrap generation: Children growing up in walled gardens. *Environmental Education Research 13*(4), 513–527.

Ministry of Education and Science. (1998). *Curriculum for the preschool—Lpfö 98.* Stockholm, Sweden: Fritzes. Available at www.skolverket.se/fakta/faktablad/english/index.shtml

Norwegian Ministry of Education and Research (2012). *Framework plan for the content and tasks of kindergartens.* Available at http://www.regjeringen.no/upload/KD/Vedlegg/Barnehager/engelsk/Framework_Plan_for_the_Content_and_Tasks_of_Kindergartens_2011.pdf

Organisation for Economic Co-Operation and Development (OECD). (1999). *OECD country note: Early childhood education and care policy in Sweden.* Paris, France: OECD.

Paul, A. M. (2012, August 26). School of hard knocks. Review of *How Children Succeed: Grit, Curiosity, and the Hidden Power of Character*, Paul Tough. *New York Times.* p. BR19.

Reivich, K., & Shatté, A. J. (2002). *The resilience factor: 7 keys to finding your inner strength and overcoming life's hurdles.* New York, NY: Broadway Books

Ropeik, D., & Gray, G. (2002). *Risk: The practical guide for deciding what's really safe and what's really dangerous in the world around you.* New York, NY: Houghton Mifflin.

Sandseter, E. B. H. (2009). Characteristics of risky play. *Journal of Adventure Education and Outdoor Learning 9*(1), 3–21.

Seligman, M. E. P. (2007). *The optimistic child: A proven program to safeguard children against depression and build life-long resilience.* New York, NY: Mariner Books.

Tannock, M. (2008). Rough and tumble play: An investigation of the perceptions of educators and young children. *Early Childhood Education Journal, 35*(4), 357–361.

Tough, P. (2012). *How children succeed: Grit, curiosity, and the hidden power of character.* Boston, MA: Houghton Mifflin Harcourt.

Wagner, J. T., & Einarsdottir, J. (2008). The good childhood: Nordic ideals and educational practice. *International Journal of Educational Research, 47*(5), 265–269.

Weisman Topal, C., & Gandini, L. (1999). *Beautiful stuff! Learning with found materials.* Worcester, MA: Davis.

PART II

OUTDOOR SPACES

The notion of a "playground" conjures up many images. In this section we explore spaces outside classroom walls and invite readers to consider ways in which the outdoors promotes play and learning. Chapter 4 closely examines the relationship between the affordances of intentionally designed playscapes and the quality of children's social and physical activities. Lisa Kuh, Iris Chin Ponte, Clement Chau, and Deborah Valentine first offer a historical perspective of the origins of outdoor playscapes in the United States and define types of outdoor play spaces. The chapter highlights a particular play space that underwent a transformation from a traditional playground to a natural playscape, intentionally designed to include features of a natural outdoor environment. The authors conclude with guidance for educators in early childhood settings on how to improve their playgrounds to promote play experiences that support constructive and cooperative play.

In Chapter 5 Carley Fisher-Maltese takes up the school-gardening movement as a manifestation of the "greening trend" in today's society and traces the philosophy and history of school gardens. Applying the contextual model of learning to school gardening, the author emphasizes that school gardens are not merely a plot of land with plants growing, but a type of socio-constructed environment for student learning. Focusing on two particular school gardens, the author examines both teachers' enthusiasm for children's learning in school gardens and the obstacles to their utilization. The chapter concludes with recommendations for improving and sustaining the school garden as a component of an early childhood environment.

For Chapter 6 Morgan Leichter-Saxby and Anna Housley Juster merge the UK-based field of Playwork with U.S. early childhood education to help adults develop powers of "informed improvisation"—enabling them to respond fluidly and creatively to children's cues. The authors explicitly explore the roles of adults in supporting play environments. The chapter describes one expression of Playwork in the United States—the Pop-Up Adventure Playground, a free, public, child-directed play event where children and families come together to engage with everyday materials donated by local businesses and/or volunteers. The authors share implications for ways Pop-Up Adventure Playgrounds and the notion of "playground" can be expanded into children's greater communities.

CHAPTER 4

Take It Outside

Rethinking and Reclaiming Outdoor Play

Lisa P. Kuh, Iris Chin Ponte,
Clement Chau, & Deborah Valentine

When you think about playing out of doors as a child, what comes to mind? What are your memories of playing outside, both in and out of school? In our conversations nationwide with people about outdoor play spaces, we often show photographs of familiar, yet what could also be described as vintage, playground equipment and the response is generally the same. First, laughter; people remember the feeling of a conventional metal merry-go-round—the way it spun, how it made you sick, memories of your brother who would not stop spinning it, the heat of the metal on a summer day burning your backside right through your shorts, and jumping to the sand, gravel, or often concrete that usually surrounded it. Stories of skinned knees are remembered as badges of honor. Images of large, metal "jungle gyms" provoke similar responses (see Figure 4.1)—seeing how high you could climb, the feeling of power that came with that, hanging upside-down. Almost everyone knows of at least one child who fell and broke an arm.

Then, usually, people mention that when they played outdoors, even on a playground, they were often on their own or at least they felt on their own, whether in a city or in a rural area. People also have vividly personal yet very similar stories about games with rules they made up and dramatic play scenarios involving hiding, chasing, collecting, racing, and building.

As pointed out in Chapter 3, because we now live and work in a climate of highly regulated safety norms (Rivkin, 1995), it has become more crucial for educators to help children enjoy outdoor experiences where they can feel independent, create their own complex play narratives, and play in an environment that affords them open-ended connections with nature and

Figure 4.1: Vintage Playground Climber

with peers. School and societal contexts have evolved into highly structured blocks of time in which children are reliant upon television and computers for entertainment, have limited opportunities to play in cooperative community groups, and experience diminishing recess time in schools. "Recess," as a noninstructional time, has been reconceptualized to suit the high-stakes academic climate. Recess has been devalued and viewed as precious minutes stolen from otherwise productive academic endeavors. Educators and policymakers have resorted to terms such as "academic rest" to justify recess as part of the academic delivery block. More than ever, educators bemoan the loss of outdoor play periods and must explore new ways to legitimize recess and unstructured outdoor playtime. Although we laud such efforts to allow for periods of outdoor activity, we also want to promote outdoor time and children's play as crucial contexts for informal learning that warrant intentional thinking about design and more emergent curricular connections.

This chapter tells the story of one school's playground makeover. The Eliot-Pearson Children's School at Tufts University in Massachusetts transformed its traditional playground space into a natural play space that sought to give its children a unique and meaningful outdoor experience. The school's teachers and professors observed the shifts in children's play when the traditional playground was redesigned as a natural playscape.

We first take a brief look at the historical origins of outdoor play in the Progressive Era to uncover the roots of the playground movement in the

United States. Then we describe types of playgrounds to illustrate the range of possibilities for design, followed by the playscape renovation story and its implications for children's play, design, and teacher practices. We end with four key considerations for "taking it outside" that elucidate the importance of the outdoor environment in a climate of standardized curriculum, the elements of outdoor environments that promote complex play, and what teachers can learn from listening to and observing children's play outdoors.

HISTORICAL CONTEXT

The idea that a particular outdoor space should be designated and designed to support and promote children's play and early education is, in the scope of human (and American) history, relatively new. Its primary roots extend back only about 150 years, to the mid-19th century, arising alongside the concept of childhood as a distinct phase of life defined by innocence, play, and learning; the emergence of the field of developmental psychology; and the creation of the kindergarten. This era also saw the resultant proliferation of age-graded institutions, laws, policies, and practices that now shape much of the human experience, at least in the Western traditions. Prior to these developments, playgrounds were not expected features of early childhood programs, elementary schools, suburban neighborhoods, or urban parks (Frost, 2010; Valentine, 2004).

Our notion of the modern playground stems from three competing and complementary historical paths and influences—German theories of physical development, the parks movement of the 19th century, and the kindergarten movement's theories of play, which were later supported and expanded as children became the focus of study for developmental scientists. More broadly understood as a means of Progressive Era child-saving reform, 20th-century playgrounds were designed to solve social problems by structuring physical spaces to facilitate particular types of activities and discourage others (Beatty, Cahan, & Grant, 2006; Cavallo, 1981; Frost, 2010).

A focus on the importance of specifically equipped outdoor spaces dedicated to promoting physical exercise is most directly tied to German influences. In the early 19th century, a number of German educators began to address concerns about the potentially negative impact of urban life on the physical and mental health of the nation's children, leading to the creation of the outdoor gymnasiums and programs of instruction. The idea that physical education could and should be integrated into school curricula and reflected in the built spaces of the school began with these efforts (Frost, 2010; Mero, 1908). In the 1880s, German influence also led American play advocates to imitate the "sand garden" by placing large piles of sand in outdoor play yards.

Often affiliated with social settlement houses or other charity organizations, sand garden playgrounds usually consisted of "a sand heap or sand box with or without other apparatus such as swings or see-saws" and were limited to use by children under 12 (Rainwater, 1922, pp. 48–49). Other than "fresh air," other natural elements were not viewed as essential components of a sand garden playground or of the supervised playgrounds that followed.

Although German-influenced play advocates focused on providing space and equipment for particular kinds of outdoor play activities, parks-movement advocates in the latter part of the 19th century focused their efforts on the creation of urban green spaces. America's 19th-century parks were expected to address social problems through the passive influence of nature; active play was often restricted. Children's play was not a primary focus of this movement. However, there were important exceptions. Opened in 1888, the Women and Children's Quarters of Golden Gate Park was specifically designed for use by young children and their caregivers, as was the Children's Playground in Fairmount Park, Philadelphia, that opened in 1899. These were sprawling playscapes covering multiple acres and they contained not only unique play equipment, like the Children's Playground's wooden slide, now the Smith Memorial Playground, and the Golden Gate Park's Children's Carousel, but also provisions that would appeal to adult caregivers (Schenker, 1996; Valentine, 2013; Young, 2004).

Play within these contexts was constructed primarily as a means of producing pleasure, specifically for children, with an occasional reference to the physical (and vaguely spiritual) benefits provided by fresh air and nature. These were destination playgrounds, places that required caregivers to facilitate children's access to the space and to supervise play within it; they did not require professionally trained play supervisors.

Parks advocates might have paid little attention to children's play, but for the "kindergarteners"—a term that signified not primarily kindergarten students, but the professionally educated middle- and upper-class women who taught them—children's play was a central subject of discussion and thought. Based on the model created by German educator Frederich Froebel, kindergarteners posited that during the preschool years moral values and beneficial habits should be taught through play and contact with the natural world. Thus, they facilitated play by including elements from nature indoors and out. Foreshadowing future claims made by playground advocates, kindergarten advocates argued that children's play in these protected spaces had the potential to transform life beyond them.

Of particular importance here is the fact that the kindergarten required the creation of a specifically designed space for play, not previously understood to be necessary to classroom design. A special play area (preferably grassy) and a garden (outdoors if possible) were posited as important components of a kindergarten (Beatty, 1995). Though some British Infant Schools of the early 19th century and a few day nursery (childcare) programs included outdoor play space in their design, the inclusion of outdoor play space in programs for preschoolers was more of the exception than the rule (Prochner, 2009; Rose, 1999; Valentine, 2013). The kindergarten movement provided clear connections between children's play and a particular type of outdoor space that included elements from the natural world as well as space for active play.

Supported by increasingly popular evolutionary theories of development that presented childhood as a distinct phase of life within which play was understood as essential to developmental processes, late 19th-century play advocates began to present active play as essential to child development, a need that many urban children could not realize. By the early 20th century, school play yards, typically just bare lots surrounded by a fence, were often the location of supervised summer playgrounds, led by professional play leaders, most often kindergarteners. Practical challenges raised by the impact of crowded, unsanitary living conditions, and increasingly busy streets, on which children, especially boys, played among trolley lines and piles of trash, were powerful motivators for playground development.

Some 19th-century play leaders added a new dimension focused on supporting children's free choice in play as opposed to facilitating teacher-directed activities. Philadelphia's supervisor of kindergartens and playgrounds Constance Mackenzie (1897) painted a picture of the typical Philadelphia playground as one directed by children's choices, diverse needs, and goals:

> The playgrounds invite them in, provide them with material through which they may express themselves, offer them plenty of space for play, or pleasant, shady places in which they may rest with quiet work, singing, listening to stories, minding the baby if need be. (p. 164)

The American play movement was institutionalized in 1906 with the creation of the Playgrounds Association of America. Colleges began offering courses focused on play and physical education, and cities began establishing departments of recreation to oversee playground development, maintenance, and supervision. During this process of professionalization and nationalization in the field of play, new developmental theories, G. Stanley Hall's popularization of recapitulation theory in particular, emphasized adolescence rather than early childhood as the most crucial period of development. This shifted early childhood from a central priority of development studies to the sidelines of the American movement (Bederman, 1995; Castañeda, 2002; Hall, 1906/2006).

As the American Playground Movement became the Recreation Movement in the 1930s, preschoolers and preschool play spaces affiliated with early childhood programs received less attention or support from national play advocates. Playgrounds served a widening age range within divided and specialized spaces and programs.

In the 20th century, youth recreation developed into a wide variety of distinct applications, including camping, physical education classes, community recreation programs, vocational education, and organized youth sports. The rise of the materials industry (see Chapter 1 in this volume) also spawned outdoor equipment manufacturing and the ubiquitous climbing structures seen in almost every playground—be it a schoolyard or public playground. However, today the lack of recess in schools, awareness of obesity issues, and concern for children's health have created a resurgence of thoughtful playground designs that offer children exposure to nature, healthy risk, and places that promote development (Kuh, Ponte, & Chau, 2013). In the sections that follow, we highlight one school's attempt to replace traditional structures with what is known as a natural playscape, first discussing types of playgrounds that influence current design and that in many cases are prevalent globally in parks and schools.

TYPES OF OUTDOOR PLAY SPACES

There exists a range of outdoor play venues, from naturally wooded areas to intentionally designed spaces containing prefabricated structures and grassy areas to constructed spaces with asphalt surfaces. Outdoor spaces specifically designed for children's play continue to undergo transition, from highly structured play spaces to more open and flexible settings.

An impetus for this change has come from both the architecture community, whose interest in design has resulted in structures that are interesting and visually pleasing (Pellegrini, 2005), and the education community, whose interest is in providing places for children to engage in constructive and prosocial activity. Although playgrounds vary, there are a few primary types worth noting. Their characteristics provide us with a vocabulary for talking about the elements of outdoor spaces we want to preserve, promote, and integrate into our work with children. As social scientists, we are interested in what children do in these play spaces. We ask questions such as:

- What effects do playground elements have on children's play?
- Do children play differently in certain contexts?

These questions guide readers and researchers in their thinking about play spaces and children's development, and we invite you to think about them as you move through this chapter.

Traditional Playgrounds

Traditional playgrounds are typically made up of fixed metal structures such as swings, slides, jungle gyms, merry-go-rounds, and seesaws, and they usually feature concrete "flooring." A description from Perry (2003) may bring to mind a playground you remember:

> The climbing structure is located in the periphery of the yard. It is marked by a ground covering of tan bark, which separates it from a cement portion of the yard. The climbing structure includes a seven-foot high, two-tiered deck supported by brightly painted poles from which attach a number of slides, chutes, sliding poles, and ladders. (p. 27)

The modern traditional playground design dates back to the early 1900s and is still among the most common type in America today (Brett, Moore, & Provenzo, 1993).

Traditional playgrounds offer few adaptable materials in that all of the toys and climbing structures are fixed to the ground. The climbing equipment is often "one-size-fits-all" with climbing structures too high for kindergarten children to reach. Many adults have fond memories of these play structures. There are some advantages such as mass manufacturing, ease of establishment, factory-fabricated equipment, quick installation, and consistency across playgrounds. The equipment serves a very particular purpose, as each is designed for a specific type of play, eliciting specific movement and social interaction (Kuh, Ponte, & Chau, 2013). However, as our own research has demonstrated, there are limitations as children tend to play *with* the equipment rather than *folding* the space into their own play narratives.

Contemporary Playgrounds

These playgrounds emerged in the early 1960s as designers and architects experimented with a variety of materials such as wood, stone, railroad ties, and recycled materials in an attempt to blend the playground into the natural environment and provide more flexibility for play. More attention was paid to include open-ended materials or equipment that afford children agency to appropriate these materials into their own play experiences. A child might encounter a complex wooden castle structure with cargo nets, tunnels to crawl through, and a zip line. A wooden plank on a structure might serve as a boat sailing across a sea of grass.

Adventure Playgrounds

Unlike traditional and contemporary playgrounds, adventure playgrounds have an abundance of loose materials for children to use. "Loose parts" refer to items that are not fixed in place and can be manipulated in open-ended ways (Nicholson, 1971). These items may or may not be found in nature. Adventure playgrounds offer a variety of materials, such as sticks and pinecones or prefabricated wooden blocks that children can use to create their own play spaces.

Adventure playgrounds had their beginning in postwar Denmark. Experienced playground architect C. Th. Sørensen noticed that children enjoyed playing with materials left from his construction sites. This observation led him to create the first "junk" playground. These playgrounds are flexible, employing open-ended materials such as sand, water, large wood blocks, and woodworking tools. Open-ended materials can be used in many different ways, not in fixed ways as is the cases for swings and seesaws. Such playgrounds were often described as places where children could be free and play unrestricted by lack of space or opportunity. Issues such as upkeep, need for a play leader to help manage loose parts, perceptions of a messy aesthetic, and concerns about safety risks make such playgrounds a rare site, especially in the United States (Frost, 1992).

Natural Playscapes

The term *natural playscape* describes intentionally designed playgrounds inspired by natural landscape features including elements found in nature (Keeler, 2008). Designs vary and can include features of traditional, contemporary, and adventure playgrounds such as swing sets, wooden climbers, and movable planks. Common features of natural playscapes include vegetation for creating play habitats; terraces, slopes, and flat landscapes to promote varied physical movements; and organic elements such as water, sand, stones and rocks, pinecones, acorns, and wooden sticks to foster play, investigation, and fine-motor activities (Fein & Rivkin, 1986; Fjørtoft, 2004; Rivkin, 1997). Open-ended circuitous pathways and play areas and the presence of loose parts promote exploration and discovery (Nicholson, 1971).

The natural playscape movement has contributed to the hybridization of playgrounds. However, traditional design elements persist, as the ease of catalog items and the prevalence of safety regulations dominate the choices we make. Theoretically, these features provide important contexts for children's play in some way; and how well pathways, landscape features, and loose parts attract children, hold their attention for extended exploration, and impact the quality of children's play is the focus of the study discussed in the following section.

THE PLAYGROUND MAKEOVER

The students of the Eliot-Pearson Children's School decorated the playground with streamers and messages of love. It was time to say good-bye. The old playground was thought to be progressive for its time, but that was the late 1960s. The old climber had seen better days; it was starting to rust and the tube slides were beginning to lose their bolts. The licensor for the school said that the equipment was no longer to code and had to be removed. The planning began for a new playground.

The task was daunting, but the core philosophies related to natural playscape design were part of our vocabulary. We wanted something flexible that provided opportunities with natural materials, areas for gross-motor challenges, beautiful landscaping, spaces for small and large groups to gather, and flexible materials. After many meetings we finally had a design we were happy with—a natural playscape.

The makeover of our traditional playground to a natural playscape led effortlessly to a research project. We wanted to closely examine various playground features and their impact on children's play experiences—in particular, those associated with the replacement of the climbing structure with a tree house and the addition of a large unbounded sand area with a water feature, pathways connecting play elements, and landscaping. We observed children over the course of a year pre- and post-construction, and also interviewed children about their play. We developed the Outdoor Play Inventory© (Chau, Kuh, & Ponte, 2010), a time-sampling observation protocol that coded for social and physical play behaviors. The following sections describe changes to particular areas of the playground (see Figures 4.2 and 4.3 to see overall changes). What could we learn from our playground makeover that might help other schools and teachers? A closer look at some of the specific areas of our natural playscape may inspire shifts in your own settings or in your thinking about outdoor spaces.

Climbing Structure to Tree House

The old climbing structure, like many of its kind, had multiple access points that encouraged repetitive climbing in a circuit-like pattern. Children used the structure as a climbing circuit with clear entry and exit points, replaying the

Figure 4.2: Old Playscape with Climbing Structure

Figure 4.3: New Landscaping, Paths, Treehouse

same themes. For example, children would typically run up an access ramp and down the slide repeatedly, saying things like, "I'm an army (guy) and my armies are trying to fight me so I go down the other slide." It was not unusual to find children on the platforms on the climber looking down on other children and calling out, "This is our ship! You can't come up here."

When the climber came down, it was replaced by a "tree house" composed of a series of short wooden staircases leading to a platform that was elevated just below the lower branches of a nearby pine tree, a place rarely used as a play hub. In contrast to play scenarios that tended to be limited to the climber itself, children moved in and out of the tree house briskly, engaging in play activities that spanned the playscape. Initially, many children visited the tree house. It had a novelty that attracted children to the platform in the branches. As the year went on, fewer children visited this area and those who visited spent less time. Did they not like this space? Why the quick visits? Our interviews and observations revealed a new play pattern.

"I'll show you what I get first. I bring a bucket, get some water and sand, and then carry it up here. We leave it up here a few minutes and then take it back down."

The same pattern of carrying items in and out of the tree house occurred with large hollow blocks taken into the tree house via to the nearby bridge.

"We get the blocks, put them on the bikes. We drive them all the way to the bridge [near tree house steps]. Then we come back and get some more blocks and do it again and again."

Children's play shifted from territorial play on the climber to using the tree house as an important destination as children entered the tree house to drop off blocks or buckets, and then left for another area to gather more materials and extend the play narrative.

The pine tree also served another purpose as an endless supply of natural loose parts in the form of pinecones and pine needles. Children carried buckets full of pinecones and pine needles in and out of the tree house area, promoting cross-area play experiences that connected tree house activities to locomotor play and nature play in other areas. "Family" games involved bringing materials such as pine needles and buckets of sand to the tree house "home" as well as large blocks to act as props for home furnishings. Natural loose parts and materials became crucial artifacts connecting children's play experiences in the tree house area to other play areas using the new pathways for transport.

"No Children Allowed" to Accessible Shed Area

Accessibility proved to be an important component of the new space. Prior to construction, the children always wanted to get into the shed where tools, materials, sleds, sports equipment, and the large hollow blocks were stored. However, children were not allowed into the shed for safety reasons.

It was not a child-friendly space, and teachers had to take blocks and materials out of the shed for the children. More often than not, the materials went unused. In the new space, a child-friendly door and dividing wall allowed access only to the large wooden blocks, and a new construction platform was installed nearby.

We observed a significant increase in constructive play in this area. As with the tree house, activities in this area were brief and tended to span across adjacent areas. The shed area was a primary location for accessible loose parts as children transported materials from one area to another by riding tricycles or pulling wagons via the pathways. In one typical scenario, children designated a wagon as the "Super Car," pushing and pulling a wagon full of blocks. Sometimes the car would "break down," and the children would cry, "We can do teamwork!" The new building platform was a convenient venue for picking up and dropping off blocks via the pathways that were busy with tricycle activity moving to and from the tree house or sand area.

Children adopted assigned roles and tasks, such as block retrievers and builders. This seems to have been an important strategy to accommodate more children in the overall play experience, given the limited space for construction. Although only one or two children might have been acting as "block retrievers" in the shed area, they were also collaborating and cooperating with children on the pathways. For example, a "yard sale" game involved loading blocks and natural materials such as pinecones into a wagon or onto a tricycle, traveling along the pathways to "sell" wares and make deliveries to the tree house and sand areas, and then traveling back to the shed where blocks were kept. Sellers would yell, "Junk for sale!" and conduct transactions along the paths adjacent to other areas.

Dry Sandbox to "Beachfront" Sand Area

A small, contained sandbox was transformed into a sprawling "beach" that blended into the landscape bordered by grass and woodchip surfaces. Large boulders set into the existing hillside created a climbing feature. A water pump activated by pushing a button attached to a post at the bottom of the hillside caused water to flow out of the top of the boulder climb and down into the sand. This feature attracted more children to visit the new sand area for longer periods of constructive play and nature play. Before the playground makeover, children rarely mentioned sand play as a focus of activity in the area containing the small, bordered sand box. Preconstruction play was represented by a few children digging a large hole, and activities mainly involved moving in and out of small alcoves near the sandbox. When asked specifically about sand play, a typical comment was, "We dig."

After construction, cooperative and constructive activity grew in sophistication, with more children engaging in the play. The new water pump afforded a unique play experience that prompted children to engage in coordinated constructive play to keep water flowing, keep dams from breaking, and dig channels to hold the water during play. The distance between the water pump button, the top of the boulder climb where water emerged, and the sand area below required children to adopt roles and coordinate with one another to monitor the flow of water. One child would operate the push-button pump, others noted when water began and stopped flowing from the top of the rock climb, and others assessed their construction of dams, rivers, and bridges and made necessary amendments based on their observations. Children routinely called out, "Push the button!" to signal a child to activate the water feature. This was often followed by, "Okay, now get back and let's dig!" During interviews, children reported activity such as taking "some dry sand over wet sand, with rocks." Or, "Some kids mostly like to make a dam and do chef stuff." Another child described, "They just like get sand and sand and sand, and water and water, and they stick it together and it makes a strong wall."

The operation of the water pump highlights the affordances offered by the distance between elements that may require joint effort, promoting coordination in movements and roles leading to more collaborative, constructive play experiences. Children's play involved traversing the playground to access building materials such as wooden planks and blocks, and moving them within the sand area. Accessibility to loose parts materials, such as blocks, stones, pinecones, and planks from other areas, offered the perfect ingredients for the kind of constructive play that educators value (Dalhberg, Moss, & Pence, 1999; Wilson, 2009).

Pathways for Purposeful Locomotion and Expanding Play Narratives

One of the largest additions to the new playscape was a pathway designed to connect all areas of the playground. The new pathway (largely rubberized surfacing with some areas of cobblestone) included varied terrain, tunnels, and bridges, and prompted children to take up the opportunity to traverse with intention. Before construction, when children moved from one area to another, the play theme or intention generally ended and children shifted to a new endeavor. However, postconstruction, children's play narratives were connected all over the playground and included teamwork and joint effort. For example, natural materials such as pine needles, pinecones, woodchips, sand, and water were put into buckets from the sand area, transported into the adjacent tree house, and then transported to the shed area on tricycles. The new pathways provoked sustained cooperative, constructive, and dramatic play scenarios by contextualizing the children's movements in play narratives, rather than simply promoting movement as a fixed-path, repetitive, static exercise.

"TAKE IT OUTSIDE": CONSIDERATIONS FOR EDUCATORS

From our almost daily observations of this playscape and our empirical research, we identified four important practices for "taking it outside." We consider practices related to the role of "loose parts," the importance of guided discovery and care of materials, designing spaces to promote challenges and risk, as well as teacher moves that support children's endeavors.

The Role of Loose Parts and Natural Materials: Offering Choices for Discovery, Cooperation, and Construction

One way of thinking about outdoor spaces is that playgrounds are small-scale replicas of the world. They offer options for social, physical, cognitive, and sensory experiences. For example,

- Rough and smooth objects to touch
- Heavy and light objects to lift and move
- Wet materials as well as dry
- Cool materials in the shade as well as hot materials in the sun
- Soft and hard surfaces to run and jump on
- Things that make sounds (running water, chimes)
- Smells of all varieties (flowers, bark, mud)
- High and low places and materials natural, synthetic, thin, and thick

Crates, buckets, or baskets filled with sticks; slices of logs, large smooth stones, shells, pinecones; or large cardboard tubes can give teachers and children an arsenal of materials to choose from. Planks of smooth wood, an old set of wooden unit blocks, large hollow blocks, stumps, or even cardboard boxes complement children's play. Of course, children will bury things in the sand and materials will have to be replaced over time, but they can be treasures for future children to discover.

This does not mean inundating the environment with options, but rather choosing elements wisely and intentionally. (See also Chapter 6 for a discussion of offering children loose materials to support spontaneous play experiences.) In our new playground, providing children with independent access to play materials, as with the large hollow blocks in the shed, was an important facet of the philosophy of the natural playscape, as it fostered independent exploration and peer collaboration (Heft & Chawla, 2006).

Sand and water in combination proved to be powerful materials that promoted complex construction techniques and provided problem-solving challenges not often encountered indoors. The ever-changing nature of wet sand, combined with children's ability to manipulate this material as they build, provided a built-in troubleshooting experience that drew children into a collective constructive experience. Roles came naturally as children controlled the flow of water and collapsing sand structures. An old-fashioned hose, bucket brigade, or more complex water pump can each fit this need.

The Prepared Environment: Guided Discovery for Respect and Care of Spaces

Once the stage is set and there are plenty of materials to see, touch, smell, hear, and taste, children must feel invited to interact with the space. The playground needs to be accessible, open, inviting, and, most important, must make children feel comfortable and in control. If children feel that they have ownership over the space, they will be more likely to have a positive experience. For example, the ability to move over, under, around, and through provides children with the control to choose which direction to go.

The introduction of and preparation for experiences on playgrounds can take various forms. Teachers and schools who see outdoor space as disconnected from daily experiences are often puzzled by children's behaviors and approach to materials outside, leading to teacher involvement as "policing" rather than as active guides for children's play. Schools and educators must make a commitment to introduce and maintain the playground so that children have respect for the outdoor environment and treat materials carefully— be they things from nature or prefabricated loose parts.

Engaging children in guided discovery where spaces and materials are gradually introduced is an oft-missed strategy (Denton & Kreite, 2000). Walking around the playground as a group, introducing outdoor materials inside at circle time, or having a guided discovery meeting outside before playing helps children brainstorm possible uses of materials and establishes guidelines for play appropriate to the context of the space, school, and community. Equally important is modeling cleanup and having adequate and accessible storage for materials. All this can greatly increase chances that spaces will be used effectively.

Designing for Challenge: The Road to Cooperative Play and Healthy Risk-Taking

Choice and Cooperative Play. A successful playground should provide children with choices. Individual children should be able to decide whether they would prefer to play alone or in a group. Options can be created by the spaces such as sheltered areas for solitary play, more ample space for small groups, and a large open space for a bigger group. Multiple entrances and exits to climbing structures as well as varied routes through structures also provide an element of choice. Such elements support play encounters that foster socialization and cooperation among children, motivate them to explore with nature, encourage them to interact and build with natural materials, and provide the possibility to actively move from one setting to another (Churchman, 2003; Rivkin, 1997). These types of behaviors are all components of children playing cooperatively. The development of cooperative play is an important benchmark in children's growth, and outdoor spaces can help children as they move from solitary and parallel play endeavors, to those that require organization toward a common goal (Frost, 1992; Parten, 1932).

Range of Experiences and Time. The playground should contain challenges, ranging from those appropriate for toddlers to those that challenge older, more experienced children. By doing this, the play space provides children with the option of experiences that they know they have mastered as well as the ability to attempt harder ones. We found that children, when introduced to new playground components, made repeated, short visits to different elements before developing games and play patterns that became part of the social fabric of play in a given space—a testament to the time it takes for children to develop play themes and "take up" certain environmental affordances.

Pathways and Destinations. Pathways and destinations were key factors in children's self-scaffolding of challenge and development of complex play narratives that spanned the play space. The new pathways resulted in changes in locomotor activity. Children could now ride in a circuit that had multiple options for travel and surfaces. The pathways attracted children to engage in cooperative play as they took on roles in a larger constructive play narrative that involved the retrieval and delivery of loose parts to various locations as others constructed and built. Prior to the new pathways, children mainly engaged in functional play along the pathway, and riding tricycles and walking back and forth were the primary experiences.

Open-Ended Elements. Designing for challenge also means that preconceived notions of play themes that are stereotypically "child-friendly" are actually counterproductive to children's play. Like the colorful activity rugs discussed in Chapter 1, playground equipment built in the shape of fire engines, horses, submarines, rocket ships, and other such objects from the real world may seem enticing to children for a short period of time, but they are actually too confining. Children can create their imaginary world from simpler, cheaper things, such as a mound of dirt or a branch of a tree. The more general the form or object, the more freedom it allows the children to impose their own meaning to it.

Teacher Moves to Support Challenge and Risk in Play

Natural playscapes offer a variety of gross-motor opportunities that are important for young children's development and can emerge in relation to objects in the environmental landscape (Pellegrini, 2005). As outdoor environments vary, the extent to which a playscape fosters locomotor play is dependent upon the particular environmental affordances that children take up and the extent to which teachers guide and allow certain types of play.

Supporting play outside can challenge teachers' thresholds of safety and risk. Children are likely to engage in gross-motor rough-and-tumble play or take physical risks that make teachers uncomfortable. They can ameliorate some of this fear by collaborating with children to codesign play experiences and narratives. This practice offers children the freedom to imagine and discover while giving teachers some assurance that they have some control over the children's activities.

Teachers' skills as "stage managers" allow them to provide tools and materials for play, intentionally populating play spaces with props to promote creative play (Jones & Reynolds, 2011). Observers of young children can learn to be respectful guides who support and scaffold—not hover—and of course stand by in case help is truly needed (Denton, 2007). (See also Chapters 3 and 6 for discussions of safety and risk related to spontaneous play.)

VALUING OUTDOOR PLAY

In the context of children's school experiences, the outdoor environment is generally situated as an entity separate from activity that happens inside the schoolhouse. School playgrounds are not necessarily designed or used in concert with best practices for supporting children's development. When early childhood educators create spaces for children, they must understand how children may play in a given space.

Many view experiences with nature as a key venue for exploration that offers possibilities for children to be critical thinkers and co-constructors of their play experiences, with adults as respectful guides who take children's endeavors seriously (Dalhberg, Moss, & Pence, 1999; Gandini, 1998; Heft & Chawla, 2006). The first step is to go outside. Value outdoor time and make it a priority. Although classroom time has become more precious, the outdoors can open the possibility for projects, investigation, and increased social opportunities that positively impact development.

We are not advocating that everyone replicate a forest in a playground, but attempts to replicate elements that afford children certain play opportunities are worth pursuing. There are benefits to loose parts, pathways, and natural features such as sand, water, and trees. Those considering natural playscape features might carefully choose some of these elements as they conceptualize new spaces for children. Educators want children to develop the ability to problem-solve, cooperate, observe, and navigate complex environments. These views are in keeping with constructivist principles that are the foundation of best practices in early childhood education (Devries, Zan, Hildebrandt, Edmiaston, & Sales, 2002). Access to elements of natural playscapes promotes exploratory and investigative play that helps children develop beyond isolated, overly repetitive, and constraining experiences on monodimensional equipment.

Discussion Questions

- How can I bring elements such as sand and water to my playscape on a small or large scale?
- What loose parts can our school collect from our families and our community, and how can they be stored and accessed at our site?
- What is an educator's role when outdoors with young children?
- What is my comfort level with different types of children's play and why is it so? Can I allow children to play beyond my comfort level?

REFERENCES

Beatty, B. (1995). *Preschool education in America: The culture of young children from the colonial era to the present.* New Haven, CT: Yale University Press.

Beatty, B., Cahan, E. D., & Grant, J. (Eds.). (2006). *When science encounters the child: Education, parenting and child welfare in 20th-century America.* New York, NY & London, UK: Teachers College Press.

Bederman, G. (1995). *Manliness & civilization: A cultural history of gender and race in the United States, 1880–1917.* Chicago, IL: University of Chicago Press.

Brett, A., Moore, R. C., & Provenzo, E.F. (1993). *The complete playground book.* Syracuse, NY: Syracuse University Press.

Castañeda, C. (2002). Developmentalism and the child in nineteenth-century science. In C. Castañeda (Ed.), *Figurations: Child, bodies, worlds* (pp. 12–45). Durham, NC & London, UK: Duke University Press.

Cavallo, D. (1981). *Muscles and morals: Organized playgrounds and urban reform, 1880–1920.* Philadelphia, PA: University of Pennsylvania Press.

Chau, C., Kuh, L., & Ponte, I. (2010). *The outdoor play inventory.*

Churchman, A. (2003, June). Is there a place for children in the city? *Journal of Urban Design,* 8, (2), 99–111. Available at http://www.tandfonline.com/doi/abs/10.1080/13574800306482#.UzCVq84OotE

Dahlberg, G., Moss, P., & Pence, A. (1999). *Beyond quality in early childhood education and care: Postmodern perspectives*. London, UK: Falmer Press.

Denton, P. (2007). *The power of our words: Teacher language that helps children learn*. Greenfield, MA: Northeast Foundation for Children.

Denton, P., & Kreite, R. (2000). *The first six weeks of school*. Greenfield, MA: Northeast Foundation for Children, Inc.

Devries, R., Zan, B., Hildebrandt, C., Edmiaston, R., & Sales, C. (2002). *Developing constructivist early childhood curriculum*. New York, NY: Teachers College Press.

Fein, G., & Rivkin, M. (Eds.). (1986). *The young child at play: Reviews of research* (Vol. 4). Washington, DC: National Association for the Education of Young Children.

Fjørtoft, I. (2004). Landscape as playscape: The effects of natural environments on children's play and motor development. *Children, Youth, and Environments, 14*(2), 21–44.

Frost, J. L. (1992). *Play and playscapes*. Albany, NY: Delmar G.

Frost, J. L. (2010). *A history of children's play and play environments: Toward a contemporary child-saving movement*. New York, NY: Routledge.

Gandini, L. (1998). Educational and caring spaces. In C. Edwards, L. Gandini, & G. Forman, (Eds.) *The hundred languages of children* (2nd ed., pp. 135–149) Westport, CT: Ablex Publishing.

Hall, G. S. (1906/2006). *Youth: Its education, regimen and hygiene*. Middlesex, UK: Echo Library.

Heft, H., & Chawla, L. (2006). Children as agents in sustainable development: The ecology of competence. In C. Spencer & M. Blades (Eds.), *Children and their environments: Learning, using, and designing spaces*, (pp. 199–216). Cambridge, UK: Cambridge University Press.

Jones, E., & Reynolds, G. (2011). *The play's the thing: Teachers' roles in children's play* (2nd. ed.). New York, NY: Teacher College Press.

Keeler, R. (2008). *Natural playscapes: Creating outdoor play environments for the soul*. Redmond, WA: Exchange Press.

Kuh, L. P., Ponte, I. C., & Chau, C. (2013). The impact of a natural playscape installation on young children's play behaviors. *Children, Youth, and Environments, 23*(2), 49–77.

Mackenzie, C. (1897). Playgrounds in cities. The work and words of the National Congress of Mothers: First annual session, held in the city of Washington, DC, February 17, 18, and 19, 1897. Journal of proceedings, the addresses and discussions, and other miscellany of the meetings (pp. 155–164), D. Appleton & Co., New York, NY, 1897.

Mero, E. B. (Ed.). (1908). *American playgrounds*. Boston, MA: American Gymnasia Co.

Nicholson, S. (1971). How not to cheat children: The theory of loose parts. *Landscape Architecture, 62*, 30–35.

Parten, M. (1932). Social participation among preschool children. *Journal of Abnormal and Social Psychology*, 27: 243–269.

Pellegrini, A. (2005). *Recess: Its role in education and development*. Mahwah, NJ: Lawrence Erlbaum Associates.

Perry, J. P. (2003). Making sense of outdoor pretend play. *Young Children, 58*(3), 26–30.

Prochner, L. (2009). *A history of early childhood education in Canada, Australia and New Zealand*. Vancouver, Canada: UBC Press.

Rainwater, C. E. (1922). *The play movement in the United States*. Chicago, IL: The University of Chicago Press.

Rivkin, M. (1995). *The great outdoors: Restoring children's rights to play outside*. Washington, DC: National Association for the Education of Young Children.

Rivkin, M. (1997). The schoolyard habitat movement: What it is and why children need it. *Early Childhood Education Journal, 25*(1): 61–66.

Rose, E. R. (1999). *A mother's job: The history of day care, 1890–1960*. New York, NY & Oxford, UK: Oxford University Press.

Schenker, H. M. (1996). Women and children's quarters in Golden Gate Park, San Francisco. *Gender, Place and Culture, 3*(3), 293–308.

Valentine, D. (2013). *Playing at learning and learning at play: a history of race, play and early education in Philadelphia, 1857–1912*. (Unpublished doctoral dissertation). Rutgers University, Camden, NJ.

Valentine, G. (2004). *Public space and the culture of childhood*. Aldershot, Hants, England & Burlington, VT: Ashgate.

Young, T. (2004). *Building San Francisco's parks, 1850–1930*. Baltimore, MD: Johns Hopkins Press.

Wilson, P. (2009). *The playwork primer*. College Park, MD: Alliance for Childhood.

CHAPTER 5

The School Garden

Fertile Ground for Learning

Carley Fisher-Maltese

Going green has become a mainstream term referencing everything from housing to politics. One manifestation of this greening trend is school-garden programs. I became interested in school gardens as an elementary school teacher
over the course of 7 years. I found that when I incorporated the garden into my
teaching practice, my students learned the required curriculum, and more, in
deep and meaningful ways. I have been exploring this topic ever since with the
hope of better understanding the gardens potential impact(s).

School gardens are more than a plot of land with plants growing; they are
a socio-constructed environment for student learning. Despite the resurgence in
the popularity of school gardens, neither the learning that takes place in them
nor the range of impacts associated with their use is fully understood. In fact,
there is little empirical research (and much intuitive and romanticized content)
on the impact of these gardens on learning and how children interact with and
conceptualize nature. Interestingly, in spite of the deeply held notion that it is
good for children to frolic in an A. A. Milne–inspired world and more reality-
based beliefs such as the idea that children learn science when they are out in a
garden or that getting children outdoors to exercise and to grow and eat healthy
food is good for them, teachers often report that they seldom use the school
garden, if their school even has one. Barriers, such as a lack of time and content
knowledge in the areas of science and gardening, have been reported among
teachers (Fisher-Maltese, 2013; Fisher-Maltese & Zimmerman, in review). These
barriers are perhaps related to a policy context that requires teachers to ad-
minister high-stakes tests and adhere to curriculum that excludes a thoughtful
understanding of what kinds of environments might be most conducive to learning. This is unfortunate for *all* children, especially those who attend struggling

schools and often already have little opportunity to interact with nature and growing things.

This chapter will delve into difficult questions such as

- How can the school garden be seen by teachers as a part of the regular, daily school environment?
- What do teachers and administrators perceive as barriers to incorporating the school garden into practice?
- Why is sustainability so difficult to achieve in spite of myriad academic and social affordances?

This work is grounded in the Contextual Model of Learning—a framework that posits learning is a contextually driven effort to make meaning (Falk & Storksdieck, 2005). According to the Contextual Model, learning is not abstract, nor does it occur within a vacuum. Instead, the Contextual Model describes learning as the complex interactions between an individual's personal, sociocultural, and physical contexts (Falk & Dierking, 2000). First, the personal context encompasses an individual's knowledge, interests, motivations, perceptions, expectations, and prior experiences (Falk & Dierking, 2000; Falk & Storksdieck, 2005). For example, experiences gardening at home or during the previous school year would fall into the personal realm.

Next, the sociocultural context takes into account how learning is affected by individuals' social relationships and/or their position within a social group. This refers to within-group social interactions in the garden setting, as well as mediation by others outside of the social group (e.g., teacher, researcher, school garden coordinator). For example, the sociocultural context would include how a pair of students interact together to capture a butterfly or learn how to use a field guide to identify an unknown plant in the garden with the help of a teacher.

Last and particularly applicable to school gardens, the Contextual Model privileges the physical environment as an integral component of learning (see Figure 5.1). The physical context is comprised of large features of the setting, as well as fine details. Macro and micro aspects of the school garden such as the location of the garden in relation to the school, raised or in-ground beds, seating for students, and signs identifying plants or butterflies that frequent the garden would fall into the physical context.

In the following sections, I present a historical and philosophical perspective, followed by a brief introduction to school-gardening research and the current policy context. Finally, I will share my own explorations in researching school gardens as environments for learning and offer recommendations for improving and sustaining school-garden use.

Figure 5.1: Contextual Model of Learning Applied to a School-Garden Context

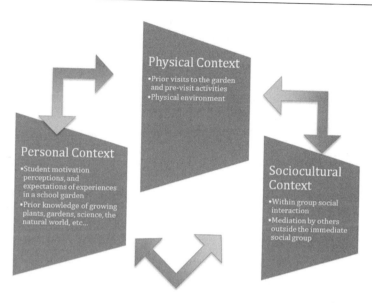

Source: Adapted from Falk & Dierking, 2000

PHILOSOPHY AND HISTORY OF SCHOOL GARDENS

School gardens have their roots in child development and educational philosophy highlighting the importance of a child's connection to the natural world. In the 1700s at the birth of the Enlightenment period, Jean-Jacques Rousseau was one of the first to discuss the importance of nature in the growth and development of children. In his semi-fictitious novel about the growth of a young boy, *Emile*, Rousseau makes the conscious decision of rearing Emile in the countryside as opposed to the city to help him develop righteous ideals. According to Barbara Beatty (1995), his criticism of education led to new teaching practices: "In place of formal instruction in reading or book learning, he prescribed informal learning experiences in which children explored the physical environment, observed objects in nature, and played games designed to enhance their sensory abilities" (p. 9).

Later, in the second half of the 18th century during the period of Romanticism, Johann Pestalozzi, a Swiss pedagogue, further developed Rousseau's idea that children should learn amid activity in nature. One of his pupils was Friedrich Froebel, who in 1840 developed the first kindergarten (literally "children garden"), putting Rousseau's and Pestalozzi's nature ideals into practice, with gardens being an integral part of the curriculum. Froebel (1826) was a great proponent of "natural education," positing that children would gain insight from studying nature directly in "the garden, the farm, the meadow, the forest, the plain." The first kindergarten involved activities that were part of the everyday life of the child, such as gardening.

At the turn of the 20th century, Maria Montessori, an Italian educator, also emphasized the importance of nature in education and recommended gardening as an activity for all students. She believed classrooms should be designed so that children could move from the indoor environment to the outdoors fluidly. She observed that gardening had many psychosocial benefits in that it could lead children to intellectual contemplation as well as an awareness and appreciation for their environment where they could learn from real experiences in real settings (Alexander, North, & Hendren, 1995). She developed detailed curricula for botany and instructed, "Children love flowers, but they need to do something more than remain among them and contemplate their colored blossoms. They find their greatest pleasure in acting, in knowing, and in exploring, even apart from the attraction of external beauty" (Montessori, 1967, p. 72). In sum, all of these educators—Montessori, Froebel, Pestalozzi, and Rousseau—were committed to experiential learning, and the garden provided an ideal setting for active learning to take place. Instead of learning about botany by reading textbooks or through lecture, students observed, inquired, and investigated in the garden.

At approximately the same time that Maria Montessori was having an impact on early childhood education in Europe, school gardens were enjoying the height of their prominence during the earliest days of Progressive education in the United States (Dewey & Dewey, 1915).

> The progressive period had a wide agenda, but one priority was an explicit attempt to change the core of schooling from a teacher-centered, fact-centered, recitation-based pedagogy to a pedagogy based on an understanding of children's thought processes and their capacities to learn and use ideas in the context of real-life problems. (Elmore, 2004, p. 15).

An ideal setting for children to observe and explore these real-life problems was a school garden. One of the Progressive Era's central figures, John Dewey, and his daughter, Evelyn, detail several experimental schools in *Schools of Tomorrow* (1915) that incorporate active learning through nature study and working school gardens. They suggest that schools be reorganized in such a way as to remedy what is wrong with public schools, specifically that learning has become too indirect, abstract, and bookish (Dewey, 1916). The Deweys, as well as school-garden advocates today, assert that school gardens are a way to incorporate best practice pedagogy into instructional practice because they enable students to participate in real-life activities. However, this pedagogical trend encountered resistance and then experienced resurgence.

Although gardens were being introduced at many schools and residential victory gardens were being planted to provide homegrown food during World War I, with the advent of "scientific techniques," such as the popularity of intelligence testing in the 1920s, school gardens began to lose momentum. As progressives lost favor and were severely criticized for their lack of academic rigor, school gardens, too, came under fire. With the launch of Sputnik in 1957, school gardens all but disappeared as the rise of the standards movement and the country's focus on academic excellence and being competitive in a global economy took precedence. Only in the past 20 years have school gardens reappeared in the United States. Presently, more than 2,000 gardens located throughout the United States are registered on the National Gardening Association's website for its Adopt a School Garden Program (National Gardening Association, 2010), and those are only the few that have applied for funding. In California alone, there are more than 3,000 gardens being used for academic purposes (California Department of Education, 2007). Southern states (e.g., Florida, Louisiana, South Carolina) now have school-garden programs (Emekauwa, 2004; Smith & Mostenbocker, 2005; University of Florida, 2006), and Northern states (e.g., New York, New Jersey, Vermont) do too, in spite of the cooler climate and shorter growing season (Faddegon, 2005).

CURRENT RESEARCH AND POLICY ON SCHOOL GARDENS

Reap What You Sow: Developing Nutrition Awareness in Schools

Recent interest in school gardens is at least partially due to concerns about the childhood-obesity epidemic in the United States. Most school-garden studies have focused on nutrition and health effects on children and have found gardens to be an effective means to teach children about nutrition and making healthy choices (Graham & Zidenberg-Cherr, 2005; Morris & Zidenberg-Cherr, 2002). Instructional gardens have been incorporated into mandated school district wellness plans, according to the Child Nutrition and Women, Infant, and Children (WIC) Reauthorization Act of 2004. In line with federal policy, instructional gardens provide an opportunity for nutrition education, with their direct connection to growing and eating healthy food. Studies found that garden-enhanced nutrition education programs increased the consumption of fruits and vegetables in 1st-grade children (Morris, Neustadter,

& Zidenberg-Cherr, 2001), 4th-grade children (Morris & Zidenberg-Cherr, 2002), and 6th-grade adolescents (McAleese & Rankin, 2007). Indicative of a national agenda to promote health is the planting of First Lady Michelle Obama's White House Kitchen Garden, which is aimed at targeting childhood obesity. A vegetable garden had not been planted on the White House lawn since Eleanor Roosevelt planted a victory garden during World War II.

Healthy Environmental Attitudes: Schools as Green Spaces

In February 2010, President Obama advocated that environmental literacy be included in the U.S. Department of Education budget for the first time (NCLI Coalition, 2010). Project GREEN (Garden Resources for Environmental Education Now) is one example of a program that uses the garden to teach about the environment and sustainability. Evaluation of this project found that 2nd- and 4th-grade students from four Texas elementary schools who participated in the garden program exhibited more positive environmental attitudes than students in a control group (Skelly & Zajicek, 1998). Another study from Project GREEN, involving 589 2nd- to 8th-graders from seven elementary schools in Texas and Kansas, showed statistically significant gains in environmental-attitude scores on pre- and posttests (Waliczek & Zajicek, 1999). Other qualitative school-garden studies have found that school gardens provide a variety of environmental stewardship opportunities, including composting and recycling that may be carried over into life outside of school (Brynjegard, 2001; Faddegon, 2005; Thorp & Townsend, 2001).

Gardening and Academics

Although research on the academic effects of school gardens is limited, it is thought that school gardens have potential direct and indirect effects on academic performance (Ozer, 2007). A recent synthesis of garden-based learning research, in fact, showed positive impacts on direct academic outcomes, with the highest positive impact on science, followed by math and language arts (Williams & Dixon, 2013). Garden-based education advocates argue that a school garden provides an authentic site for experiential, inquiry-based learning to take place (Corson, 2003; Kellert, 2002; Rahm, 2002). Inquiry-oriented instruction is considered best practice according to the National Science Education Standards (National Research Council, 1996). School gardens can be considered informal learning environments, which are seen as an important means to improve science literacy (American Association for the Advancement of Science, 1993; Bell, Lewenstein, Shouse, & Feder, 2009; National Research Council, 1996). Tiffany Lee and Leah A. Bricker, in Chapter 7, this volume, point to children's prior science knowledge and direct experiences with science content as a key context for learning science.

Policy Tensions

Federal policy has been responsive to research that shows the affordances of outdoor learning opportunities (Dillon et al., 2006). The No Child Left Inside Act was passed in 2011 and is being included in the reauthorization of NCLB. For example, several states (e.g., Vermont, Connecticut, Tennessee, Michigan) have developed programs to get children outside to learn and play through No Child Left Inside initiatives. In addition, some states (e.g., California and Washington, D.C.) have passed policies that directly support school gardens by providing funding for which schools can apply. For example, in August 2010, the Healthy Schools Act of 2010 was unanimously passed by the city council of the District of Columbia to "improve the health, wellness, and nutrition of the students of the public and charter schools" (Healthy Schools Act, 2010). Building on the momentum for urban agriculture, local foods, and school gardens, the act formally establishes a school garden program for schools in the District, including the distribution of competitive grants that support the creation and maintenance of school gardens. To date, the program has distributed 45 grants throughout the District.

In spite of such supportive policies, school gardens represent a critical tension in programming. Federal education policy dictates that children need to play outside more and be healthier, yet recess is disappearing in many schools, access to the outdoors is limited due to lockdown policies, and food grown in school gardens is often not allowed to be eaten due to food security fears. Moreover, because students (and teachers) are expected to meet curriculum standards and test-score benchmarks, indirect academic effects do not provide the hard assessment data that are required in a high-stakes climate. This may explain why teachers and administrators may have difficulty justifying the time for students to work in the garden. The fact that gardens often go unused implies that teachers are not able to balance this tension.

PLANTING THE SEEDS: EXPERIENCING SCHOOL GARDENS UP CLOSE

I was fortunate to spend extended time in school gardens as part of my research. Pond View Elementary School (a pseudonym), a K–5 elementary school located in New Jersey, has a long-established garden and I observed garden use and interviewed teachers and students. At Penns Neck

Elementary School (a pseudonym), also in New Jersey, I created and evaluated a garden-based science curriculum on insects in four 2nd-grade classrooms using multiple forms of complementary data. Both schools provide examples of successful school gardens and important insights on how to successfully navigate the barriers to implementing a school-garden program. Descriptions of these school gardens, as well as student and teacher experiences with them, help unpack the importance and challenges of school gardens as a viable learning environment for students.

The School Garden at Pond View Elementary School

Since the time of the school garden's inception in 1994 when the school's science labs had been dismantled due to a lack of resources, Pond View has maintained a strong gardening mission to provide authentic outdoor classrooms. School principal Richard DePalo explained, "They could take away my science labs, but they couldn't take away a plot of land." Committed to teaching science and with a personal interest in botany (he runs an orchid club for students after school), he decided to build the first of many gardens at the school. Initially, the school invited a landscape architect to be their artist-in-residence and to design a garden of native plants as an outdoor classroom in the school's inner courtyard. Approximately 7 years later, Shirley Miller, an energetic parent with extensive knowledge about gardening, approached Mr. DePalo about building another garden where students and teachers could grow vegetables and herbs. The garden would consist of in-ground beds and paths enclosed in a deer-proof fence and a border of pest-resistant plants. In the past 12 years, it has grown to incorporate several different gardens at the school: a heart-shaped memorial garden, a butterfly garden, an herb garden, a rainbow garden, and a garden to grow food for local businesses. The gardens are located next to the school and are visible from several classrooms. Students can explore the gardens during recess, and they have the choice to opt out of gym class and work in the gardens instead.

The School Garden at Penns Neck Elementary School

I taught 2nd grade at Penns Neck, a K–3 school, and initiated a school garden there in 2005. The garden consists of four large and two small raised beds surrounded by mulched paths and a deer- and rodent-proof fence. Vegetables (e.g., peas, tomatoes, carrots), herbs (e.g., basil, dill), fruit (e.g., blueberries, strawberries), and flowers (e.g., zinnias, marigolds, cosmos) are typically grown. The fence is lined with an internal and external border of perennial plants. One section of the border contains perennial plants that are food sources for local butterflies. The garden is located on the school's property, although it is a distance from the school building and across a parking lot. Access to water was a challenge for the garden in its earliest days, but since then, the local water department has run a line from the street free of charge. Students primarily use the garden during class time, accompanied by a teacher.

KEY ISSUES FOR SCHOOL GARDENS

Importance of Bolstering In-House Leadership

Leadership has been an important factor in the implementation of the school gardens at both schools. At Pond View, while it was Ms. Miller's driving force to expand the existing gardens at the school, the principal, Mr. DePalo, was responsible for clearing a path and sustaining the garden. In addition to creating a supportive school culture, the principal supported the garden financially. His commitment to keep gardening in the budget was an important move.

At Penns Neck, it was not only the leadership of the last two principals at the school, but the leadership of teachers that has made this instructional reform lasting. While I was a teacher at Penns Neck Elementary School, I initiated the school garden with the support of the principal at the time, as a means to improve science instruction and to provide a sense of school community, which had waned over the past few years. Together, we laid out the necessary steps to initially get the project off the ground: writing a formal proposal, presenting the idea at a whole-school staff meeting, starting a school-garden committee, researching garden programs at other schools, and planning the space for the garden to be built. The garden committee grew and made important decisions regarding designing and building the garden and how it would be used. Mr. Agnosto, the principal when I returned to the school as a researcher, describes his view of the garden's sustainability:

> I think any initiative that really builds from within is going to be the most successful. And what I mean by that is when you have a small group of teachers that start a project and then you have other teachers who are excited about it. Kids are excited. Parents are excited . . . then it's sort of contagious and other people want to find out about it, especially if it's something that appears to be successful.

Indeed, Hall and Hord (2006) tell us that teacher participation in project decisions is a facilitator to educational changes. However, leadership attrition can be a barrier. During the short history of the school garden at Penns Neck, I left the school to pursue doctoral studies, the former principal accepted a job as superintendent in another school district, and another teacher-leader was stepping down from heading the garden committee because she was going to be teaching a new grade level the following year. Just who would lead the school garden the following year had not been determined at the conclusion of my research. However, Mr. Agnosto seemed confident that finding someone to step up would not be difficult because the leadership role of the school garden now receives some financial compensation in the form of a stipend from the district for the individual's time and efforts. Back at the time of the school garden's inception, all of my efforts were on a volunteer basis, which is the case for many school-garden programs.

Importance of External Resources

The Pond View school-garden coordinator, Ms. Miller, represents an important element in the sustainability of school gardens—a knowledgeable person who can guide teachers and students in an area they may not know much about. One of the 5th-grade teachers explained, "I'm not a gardener *at all* so I really rely on Shirley. . . . *I* learn things when I'm outside. I personally rather that Shirley lead the way and help us get through." A 2nd-grade teacher described a session for teachers lead by Ms. Miller, saying, "Here you were going out with your kids and you're like, 'Great! I have no idea what to do.' She explained the whole process, how it was planted, how it's composted." Similarly, Penns Neck teacher Ms. Emilio noted that my input as an external resource and "local expert" helped make the implementation of the school garden less intimidating. Some schools that are not lucky enough to have a teacher on staff or parent willing to be school-garden coordinator have addressed this issue by recruiting individuals in Master Gardener programs from university extension programs who may need to fulfill volunteer or internship hours toward a credential or degree.

Involving parents who volunteer to assist with lessons and cleanup days throughout the school year and take over the responsibility of care of the garden during summers is another external resource (see Figure 5.2). At both schools, parents sign up as an opportunity to support the school, participate in an activity with their child, and enjoy picking rights of any ripe fruit, vegetable, or herb in the garden during their volunteer week. School-garden leadership organizes a sign-up schedule and trains parent volunteers before the summer recess.

Embedding Gardening in the Curriculum

At Pond View, Ms. Miller quickly learned that, although her primary goals were to improve the nutritional habits of students, the garden needed to have meaningful ties to curricula and state standards to be successful. Linking gardening directly to standards and to the curriculum can ensure that gardening

Figure 5.2: Teachers, Parents, and Students Volunteer on a Garden Work Day at Penns Neck Elementary School

is not simply an "extra" thing teachers do if there is time. The school-garden coordinator and teachers at Pond View worked together to create a garden-based program, which consists of individual curricular units from the district's standard curriculum. The program at Pond View is not a singular curriculum but an amalgamation of cross-curricular content and concepts the teachers are already teaching. It connects at least one curricular unit to the garden at each grade level (see Table 5.1 for examples of Pond View's garden-based lessons). The result is a multitude of lessons and activities in the school garden around planting, harvesting, and eating what they grow.

One Pond View 1st-grade teacher's comments were reminiscent of John Dewey as she explained why she bought into using the school garden:

> We can go out to the garden and use it as an outdoor classroom. Really it has everything represented and the children can actually see it. It means real-life connections to what we're learning. The gardening curriculum also fulfilled standards requirements for many curriculum areas, especially science such as the 1st-grade unit, Plant Parts and Function.

Table 5.1: Pond View Garden-Based Lessons

Grade	Pond View Garden-Based Lesson	Garden and Related Classroom Activities
K	Growing Soup—Students plant vegetables that they later harvest and use to cook vegetable soup in the classroom.	Students learn plant parts and functions. Students plant and harvest vegetables. Students read (and are read to) books about vegetables and growing things. Students learn about healthy eating. Students participate in washing, peeling, and cutting vegetables to cook soup in a slow cooker in classroom.
1	Rainbow Garden—Students plant a rainbow of colorful flowers and plants.	Students learn plant parts and functions. Students use prisms to make rainbows. Students read *The Reason for a Flower* by Ruth Heller. Students write stories about plants and flowers in their fiction/nonfiction books. Students solve addition, subtraction, and multiplication story problems. Students sing, "I Can Sing a Rainbow."
2	Butterfly Garden—Students learn the life cycles of butterflies using Monarchs and Black Swallowtails.	Students plant and observe fennel, parsley, and Queen Anne's Lace for Black Swallowtail caterpillars to lay their eggs and different kinds of ascelepias for Monarch caterpillars. Students plant and observe several nectar plants that butterflies eat: Lantana, Heliotrope, Cosmo, Coreopsis, Echinacea, Joe Pye Weed, Redbeckia, Liatris, Buddlea, Salvia, Zinnias.

Table 5.1: Pond View Garden-Based Lessons (continued)

Grade	Pond View Garden-Based Lesson	Garden and Related Classroom Activities
3	*Stone Fox*—Students read this book about a potato farmer.	Students plant potatoes in spring that are harvested by the next year's 3rd-graders.
4	Heirloom Seeds— Cherokee Trail of Tears	Students plant and harvest green pole beans, which were carried by the Cherokee tribe during the forced march to Oklahoma in 1838 and are the botanical ancestors of the bean we plant today.
5	American Flag Grid Project	Students plant an approximation of the American flag. The flag consists of a 4x8 grid of red, white, and blue flowers.

Source: Pond View School Garden Cooperative, 2007

The school garden at Penns Neck is primarily science-focused. For example, the garden is used in the following science units: earthworms in 1st grade, insects in 2nd grade, and plant growth and development in 3rd grade. One of the 2nd-grade teachers, Mrs. Captree, summarized the affordances she believes the garden lends in teaching science: "I think to be able to see the insects out in nature really helps. It's just so isolated here in the classroom." Second-grade teacher Ms. Emilio reported her own surprise at how much her students learned during the garden-based curriculum on insects:

> I thought it might be over their heads, especially classifying the butterflies . . . because it was hard for *me* to grasp. But they've been bringing in all types of caterpillars and insects. And talking about their markings and everything. So they're excited about it!

Gap Between Perceived Affordances and Actual Implementation

Interestingly, under-use of both school gardens seemed to occur in spite of numerous perceived affordances. Specifically, teachers, administrators, and students reported the following affordances that were consistent with the research on school gardens: engaging, cross-curricular lessons that met state and district standards; science learning as well as learning about the environment; improved nutritional habits by eating herbs and vegetables; and a sense of school community that was fostered among students through teamwork, increased self-esteem, and leadership skills. Nevertheless, most of the teachers said that they rarely got out to the garden—only about four times a year.

This phenomenon extended to the children as well. Most of the students at Pond View reported using the garden infrequently, even during the peak of the spring gardening season. One kindergartner reported that he goes out with his class "very rarely." Three 5th-grade students shared that they, too, go out to the garden "rarely, maybe three times a year." However, even students who had not been out to the garden all year were able to recall things that they enjoyed from previous years, such as eating herbs, planting seeds, and learning how to compost. Students participating in the garden-based curriculum on insects at Penns Neck understood the benefits of gardening even with minimal use (see Figure 5.3).

Barriers: Lack of Content Knowledge, Competing Demands

The gap between perceived affordances and actual implementation is due to two significant barriers to operating and having a school garden: a lack of science and gardening content knowledge and a lack of time. One teacher at Pond View admitted that she is hesitant to use the garden with her students without the school-garden coordinator being present, saying, "I wouldn't go out on my own . . . ever." Some teachers reported that they did not know what the different plants were. "I still don't know what is what," a teacher who has been teaching at Pond View for over 10 years shared. At Penns Neck, three teachers at the school who have extensive content knowledge of science and gardens are considered human resources for the school garden. However, the less experienced teachers at Penns Neck still felt that their lack of content knowledge about gardening was a barrier to using the school garden and saw it as an extra, separate space where they were overwhelmed, nervous, and lacked the knowledge to participate.

Penns Neck's principal, Mr. Agnosto, who recognizes that a lack of content knowledge is a barrier to garden use, suggested team teaching as a way for teachers to overcome unfamiliarity with the garden. This is a challenging proposition because teachers have enough trouble arranging garden visits with their students' schedules (e.g., specials, pullout classes for students with special needs), let alone coordinating with another teacher's class. From what I observed, this team teaching had not come to fruition, contributing to under use of the space.

Despite the principals' financial commitment, almost all of the teachers and administrators reported "not having enough time" as a significant barrier to using the school garden. A majority of the teachers noted that they lacked the

Figure 5.3: Why Penns Neck Students Think Teachers Take Them to the School Garden

"I think that [teachers] need to take [students] out to the school garden because it helps us learn when we actually see the real thing."

"To actually see some butterflies outside and not just see them in the classroom."

"Well, instead of just, instead of looking at pictures of insects and plants and stuff, we could actually see them for real."

"The garden has lots of bugs so that's the way to *really* study them."

---

time to both take their students to the school garden and participate in garden-related professional development because of competing demands. "If there were 46 hours in the day, I'd take a workshop on everything, yes." Another teacher shared, "As an elementary school teacher, the in-class responsibility is tremendous. We teach *all* of the subjects. It's a full day." The school-garden coordinator at Pond View shared that especially when she first initiated the school garden she sensed some resistance, a little bit of hostility, and a perception that gardens were extra or that it would be more work. Penns Neck principal Mr. Agnosto explained how he tries to get buy-in from teachers who feel overburdened by explaining that the garden is not something extra, but rather it's just a different way of teaching required content:

> I think it's important to show teachers that you're still hitting these objectives in the curriculum, but you're doing it in a different way. So you don't have to do lesson 12-1, 12-2, 12-3, 12-4 in a science book, or whatever it is, because instead you're replacing those.

It is common knowledge that teachers are overburdened and must balance a tremendous number of responsibilities (Fullan, 2007; Knapp, Copland, & Talbert, 2003). A 5th-grade teacher at Pond View Elementary School who has been teaching for 9 years reported that she has seen a real change in how and what she teaches compared to when she started: "We have to weigh out what the state and the district want us to do and we have to weigh out what we know is best for kids."

Clearly, there is perceived pressure and a shortage of time among teachers and administrators. One important factor seems to be the policy environment in which schools exist. A poignant point that was brought up at Pond View was the effect of high-stakes testing, a signature of NCLB. Though the school, located in an affluent, suburban area, is not labeled in-need-of-improvement because the majority of students fall into the proficient category in the tested subjects (New

Jersey Department of Education, 2008), teachers are not immune to the pressures of testing and realize that increased testing pressure results in a loss of rich curriculum. Of course, the pressure to do well on tests could squeeze out any innovation that may be perceived as "extra" or more time-consuming in the race to cover content (Crocco & Costigan, 2007).

It certainly seems that children have a profound experience in the garden, even when they seldom use it. Children see gardens as different from their traditional, indoor school environments. Given the powerful experiences reported by teachers and children, limiting gardening experiences because of time constraints and lack of content knowledge seems like a missed opportunity in an important learning environment.

RECOMMENDATIONS FOR IMPROVING AND SUSTAINING USE OF SCHOOL GARDENS

My experiences with school gardens illuminated both the joys and challenges of this environment for children. From my observations and the current and historical contexts emerge two recommendations for teachers and school administrators aimed at improving and sustaining school-garden use.

First, schools must provide and support professional development to improve (1) garden-based instruction, (2) garden and science content knowledge, and (3) teacher investment. In addition, professional development could help develop a new set of leaders who could take the helm as teacher-leaders and school-garden coordinators leave the school (Knapp et al., 2003).

Second, policymakers, districts, administrators, teachers, and families must consider the garden and its use as an integral part of the school and school curricula. The physical placement of the garden should be central to the school so that it can be seen from classrooms and accessed easily. The garden should be left open so children can explore it independently as well as guided by a teacher. Gardening should be incorporated into children's daily experiences, as at Pond View Elementary School where the children can opt to work in the garden instead of taking gym class. School gardens can be used to teach standards and benchmarks that already exist. Presently, the school garden often tends to operate on the fringe of the school's consciousness, typical of innovative school changes after initial investment (Hall & Hord, 2006), but development of integrated curricula and pedagogy will improve its utility.

Discussion Questions

- John Dewey asserted that school gardens are an important venue for teaching and learning. How are school gardens a means to incorporate best practice pedagogy into instructional practice?

- How does the current policy context pose a barrier as well as a facilitator to school gardens?
- In the two schools described in this chapter, what moves did teacher-leaders and administrators make that opened the door to school gardens?
- What is your own comfort level with gardening and how would you incorporate it into your curriculum?

REFERENCES

Alexander, J., North, M. W., & Hendren, D. K. (1995). Master gardener classroom garden project: An evaluation of the benefits to children. *Child Environments*, 12(2), 124–133.

American Association for the Advancement of Science. (1993). *Benchmarks on-line*. Available at www.project2061.org/publications/bsl/online/bolintro.htm

Beatty, B. (1995). *Preschool education in America: The culture of young children from the colonial era to the present*. New Haven, CT: Yale University Press.

Bell, P., Lewenstein, B., Shouse, A. W., & Feder, M. A. (Eds.). (2009). *Learning science in informal environments: People, places, and pursuits*. Washington, DC: National Academies Press.

Brynjegard, S. (2001). *School gardens: Raising environmental awareness in children*. San Rafael, CA: School of Education, Dominican University of California. (ERIC Documentation Reproduction Service No. ED452085). Available at edres.org/eric/ED452085.htm

California Department of Education. (2007). *Catalogue listing of publications*. Available at www.cde.ca.gov./re/pn/rc/ap/pubdisplay.aspx?ID=001512

Corson, C. (2003). *Grounds for learning: Hope for America's derelict schoolyards*. Available at www.cherylcorson.com/publications/html

Crocco, M. S., & Costigan, A. T. (2007). The narrowing or curriculum and pedagogy in the age of accountability: Urban educators speak out. *Urban Education*, 42, 512–535.

Dewey, J. (1916). *Democracy and education*. New York, NY: The Free Press.

Dewey, J., & Dewey, E. (1915). *Schools of tomorrow*. New York, NY: E. P. Dutton.

Dillon, J., Rickinson, M., Teamey, K., Morris, M., Choi, M. Y., Sanders, D., & Benefield, P. (2006). The value of outdoor learning: Evidence from research in the U.K. and elsewhere. *School Science Review*, 87(320), 107–111.

Elmore, R. F. (2004). *School reform from the inside out*. Cambridge, MA: Harvard Education Press.

Emekauwa, E. (2004). *They remember what they touch: The impact of place-based learning in East Feliciana parish*. Rural School and Community Trust, Arlington, VA. Available at www.peec.works.org/PEEC/PEEC_Research/S0009D4FB-0084FE88

Faddegon, P. A. (2005). *The kids growing food school gardening program: Agricultural literacy and other educational outcomes.* Doctoral dissertation, Cornell University, Ithaca, NY.

Falk, J. H., & Dierking, L. D. (2000). *Learning from museums: Visitor experiences and the making of meaning.* Lanham, MD: AltaMira Press.

Falk, J. H., & Storksdieck, M. (2005). Using the Contextual Model of Learning to understand visitor learning from a science center exhibition. *Science Education,* 89, 744–778.

Fisher-Maltese, C. (2013). *Fostering science literacy, environmental stewardship, and collaboration: Assessing a garden-based approach to teaching life science.* Unpublished doctoral dissertation. Rutgers, The State University of New Jersey–New Brunswick.

Fisher-Maltese, C., & Zimmerman, T.D. (in review). Teaching science in a "living laboratory:" How an informal learning lens reveals new insights into the use of a school garden. *Journal of Research in Science Teaching.*

Froebel, F. (1826). *The education of man.* Available at members.tripod. com/~FroebelWeb/web7000.html

Fullan, M. (2007). *The new meaning of educational change.* New York, NY: Teachers College Press.

Graham, H., & Zidenberg-Cherr, S. (2005). California teachers perceive school gardens as an effective nutritional tool to promote healthful eating habits. *Journal of the American Dietetic Association,* 105(11), 1797–1800.

Hall, G., & Hord, S. (2006). *Implementing change: Patterns, principles, and potholes.* Boston, MA: Pearson.

Healthy Schools Act. (2010). Available at http://dcclims1.dccouncil.us

Kellert, S. R. (2002). Experiencing nature: Affective, cognitive, and evaluative development in children. In P. H. Kahn Jr. & S. R. Kellert (Eds.), *Children and nature: Psychology, sociocultural and evolutionary investigations* (pp. 117–151). Cambridge, MA: MIT Press.

Knapp, M. S., Copland, M. A., & Talbert, J. E. (2003). *Leading for learning: Reflective tools for school and district leaders.* Seattle, WA: University of Washington.

McAleese, J., & Rankin, L. (2007). Garden-enhanced nutrition education affects fruit and vegetable consumption in sixth-grade adolescents. *Journal of the American Dietetic Association,* 107 (4), 662–665.

Montessori, M. (1967). *The discovery of the child.* New York, NY: Ballantine Books.

Morris, J. L., Neustadter, A., & Zidenberg-Cherr, S. (2001). First-grade gardeners more likely to taste vegetables. *California Agriculture,* 55 (1), 43–46.

Morris, J. L., & Zidenberg-Cherr, S. (2002, January). Garden-enhanced nutrition curriculum improves fourth grade school children's knowledge of nutrition and preference for some vegetables. *Journal of the American Dietic Association, 102*(1)91–3.

National Gardening Association. (2010). Garden in every school registry. Available at http://kidsgardening.com

National Research Council. (1996). *National Science Education Council.* Washington, DC: National Academy Press.

New Jersey Department of Education. (2008). *NCLB Report.* Available at http://www.state.nj.us/education/reportcard/nclb.html.

No Child Left Inside. (NCLI) Coalition. (2010). *The problem.* Available at www.cbf.org/site/PageServer?pagename=act_sub_actioncenter_federal_nclb_problem

Ozer, E. J. (2007). The effects of school gardens on students and schools: Conceptualization and considerations for maximizing healthy development. *Health Education & Behavior,* 34(6), 846–863.

Pond View School (pseudonym). (2007). *Garden cooperative manual.* Available at http://www.psgcoop.org

Rahm, J. (2002). Emergent learning opportunities in an inner-city youth gardening program. *Journal of Research in Science Teaching, 39*(2), 164–184.

Skelly, S. M., & Zajiceck, J. M. (1998). The effect of an interdisciplinary garden program in the environmental attitudes of elementary school students. *HortTechnology,* 8(4), 579–583.

Smith, L. L., & Mostenbocker, C. E. (2005). Impact of hands-on science through school gardening in Louisiana public elementary schools. *HortTechnology,* 15, 439–443.

Thorp, L., & Townsend, C. (2001, December 12). Agricultural education in an elementary school: An ethnographic study of a school garden. *Proceedings of the 28th Annual National Agricultural Education Research Conference in New Orleans, LA* (pp. 347–360). Available at www.aaaeonline.org/conference_files/758901

University of Florida. (2006). *Florida school garden competition.* Available at hort.ufl.edu/ggk/comp.htm

Waliczek, T. M., & Zajicek, J. M. (1999). School gardening: Improving environmental attitudes of children through hands-on learning. *Journal of Environmental Horticulture,* 17, 180–184.

Williams, D. R., & Dixon, P. S. (2013). Impact of garden-based learning on academic outcomes in schools: Synthesis of research between 1990–2010. *Review of Educational Research,* 83, 211–235.

CHAPTER 6

Bridging Theory and Practice to Support Child-Directed Play in the Classroom Environment and Beyond

Anna Housley Juster
Morgan Leichter-Saxby

Imagine this. It is 10:30 on a Saturday morning and an urban library courtyard is filled with children and adults playing together. There are no brightly colored toys and no pretend kitchen sets with plastic zucchini and hamburger buns. Children are playing with cardboard boxes, paper tubes, and duct tape, and the kids are in charge—experts in their own play. When asked, parents and other adults help by cutting holes in boxes. These openings are secret passages for dragons, winding through castle walls, and then they are windows on a school bus. In the shade of an old elm tree, a father, mother, and 4-year-old boy play together inside of a refrigerator box, which they've transformed into a cozy living room. The family creates a chandelier out of two flowered paper plates, a handful of shiny gold perfume bottle caps, and string. Dad, reaching above his son's head, carefully tapes the chandelier to the cardboard ceiling. The new light casts an imaginary, yet almost perceptible, glow on the boy's upturned face. The boy holds up an egg carton he has filled with cotton balls so he and Dad can make dinner. Mom hands her son a real bagel with cream cheese. It's time for a late-morning snack.

This scene isn't imaginary. It is a Pop-Up Adventure Playground in action. A Pop-Up Adventure Playground, or Pop-Up, is a public celebration of child-directed play, best characterized by an abundance of loose parts (everyday materials such as cardboard boxes, fabric, tape, string, cotton balls, and so on). Through our Pop-Up Adventure Playgrounds, we showcase child-directed play in communities of supportive adults.

Trained Pop-Up Adventure Play staff and volunteers are available to supply an extra piece of tape, reach the top of a tall box, or cut materials with box cutters that are unsafe for children to use themselves. As staff and volunteers interact with children in this way, they are also modeling (for parents and other adults) ways to support children's play without taking over. Our Pop-Up model builds on core elements of the Playwork profession in the United Kingdom, combined with a strong foundation in the fields of developmental psychology and early childhood education.

Through our work as founding members of the nonprofit Pop-Up Adventure Play (www.popupadventureplay.org), we've helped create Pop-Ups in spaces such as schools, parks and playgrounds, libraries, museums, and block parties, always using materials provided by local businesses (e.g., paper plates, cardboard boxes, fabric samples, drinking straws, packing materials) and minimal purchased or donated supplies (e.g., tape, string, box cutters, markers, and glue). Our mission is to promote child-directed play for all children in communities of supportive adults. Why? Decades of research highlight the benefits of child-directed play. Yet current research indicates that many children (in the United States and elsewhere) do not have the play opportunities they need for healthy development (Ginsburg, 2007; Miller & Almon, 2011; Milteer & Ginsburg, 2011).

Although much discussion is dedicated to the obstacles affecting children's access to play (Goodenough, 2008), little attention is given to practical solutions. At Pop-Up Adventure Play, our efforts acknowledge obstacles, but focus on tangible practices that support child-directed play effectively in a variety of contexts. In the classroom, teachers may employ various strategies to draw out children's personal interests, allowing a child-initiated inquiry process to evolve as children learn at their own pace, explore materials, and draw their own conclusions. However, teachers are typically not trained in how to support child-directed play. In this chapter, we bridge this gap between theory and practice, highlighting specific practices and materials that teachers can use to support play for its own sake, in the classroom and beyond.

IMPORTANCE OF CHILD-DIRECTED PLAY

Child-directed play is so positively associated with children's cognitive, socioemotional, and physical development, as well as overall well-being (Bjorklund & Brown, 1998; Brown, 2009; Brown & Webb, 2005; Erickson, 1985; Ginsburg & Opper, 1988; Piaget, 1969/1970; Rogers & Sawyers, 1988; Vygotsky, 1978) that the United Nations High Commission for Human Rights declared it a right of every child (November, 1989).

Why Is Child-Directed Play Declining?

In spite of the many empirically proven benefits of play, including specific outcomes related to school success and children's well-being (Elkind, 2007; Piaget, 1962; Singer, Golinkoff, & Hirsh-Pasek, 2006), child-directed play appears to be declining in the United States (Ginsburg, 2007; Milteer & Ginsburg, 2011). In recent years, many schools have reduced or cut recess entirely from the school day, even in kindergarten (Pellegrini, 2005). An increased focus on standardized tests has forced teachers across demographic groups to *teach to the test* and, according to the Alliance for Childhood (AFC), child-directed play has even been reduced for many 2- to 5-year olds, as preschool and prekindergarten teachers experience pressure to focus on specific academic skill-building in order keep up with the increased demands of the formal school environment (Miller & Almon, 2011).

There is also evidence that many parents across income groups are currently not supporting child-directed play outside of the classroom (Anderegg, 2003; Elkind, 2001; Ginsburg, 2007; Luthar, 2003; Warner, 2005). For families living in poverty, a lack of safe outdoor play space may increase this problem (Milteer & Ginsburg, 2011; Goodenough, 2008), and low-income families are explicitly encouraged to focus on children's academic skills and school readiness through specific skill building (Dearing et al., 2009; Lareau, 1987; Prins & Willson Toso, 2008). Many families across income groups experience pressure to enroll children in numerous adult-directed activities (outside of school hours) in order to promote learning (Anderegg, 2003; Hirsh-Pasek & Golinkoff, 2003; Housley Juster, 2013). The American Academy of Pediatrics (Ginsburg, 2007; Milteer & Ginsburg, 2011) and many other experts argue that adults must do much more to support child-directed play for children across income and sociocultural groups both inside and outside of the classroom setting.

What Is Child-Directed Play?

In order for teachers and other adults to truly support child-directed play (also called *free play* and *unstructured play*), we need to begin with clear and consistent terminology. There are numerous definitions for play, which can cause confusion. We define *child-directed play* simply and clearly as play that evolves when children are allowed to choose what to play and make up their own rules for play.

The term *free play* can be confusing (*free* can be misunderstood as meaning "no cost") and also can lead some adults to imagine chaos, children out of control. The term *unstructured play* is also misleading, because children naturally create their own structure within their play. Anyone who has ever tried to break the rules when playing along in a game that children have invented will have experienced this structure firsthand! The play is self-structured rather than structured by adults, as it is *children* who create their own boundaries in the play and improvise as they see fit. We believe the term *child-directed play* is most useful, as it inherently describes the major difference between this type of play and adult-directed play or activities that, although potentially beneficial for children, are not child-directed (e.g., children playing an adult-refereed basketball game, creating a building with recycled materials as directed by an adult, attending a creative movement class). Child-directed play is a psychological necessity and a mechanism for self-healing, providing opportunities for children to explore and reframe problems and develop a sense of unique voice and relationship with the world (Axline, 1986; Miller, 2008; Winnicott, 2005).

What Does "Good" Play Look Like?

In any discussion about children's play, it is critical to get past the idea that there is a difference between *high-quality* play and *low-quality* play and instead consider the child's choice and depth of enjoyment to be the marker of play's value. Sometimes, a personal distaste for the dominance of superheroes or celebrities in play can lead to an underestimation of children's co-option of these narratives, and of the value of exploring common archetypes (Paley, 1981). Even the most repetitive forms of play can have profound therapeutic import (Sturrock & Else, 1998). Teachers, for example, don't generally need to be concerned about a child who pretends to be a dragon or Superman every day on the playground for 3 months . . . or more! Children choose their play narratives based on internal play, and repetition itself can be a clear indication that they are still benefiting from whatever it means to be a dragon or Superman. They are mastering something they need to master, dealing with a fear, or perhaps simply exploring an idea that needs to be explored. It is also likely that, even if play patterns seem identical (to the adult observer) from day to day, the young dragon or Superman is actually gaining something new from each repetition. Through our approach merging Playwork practices and early childhood education theory, we offer various strategies that adults can use to recognize and support children's play needs.

Sometimes, what may appear as destructive or aggressive behavior is misunderstood or represents distorted attempts by a child to engage in play (Russell, 2006; Sturrock & Else, 1998). Children who lack the skills and practice necessary to join, initiate, and maintain play narratives often appear withdrawn or aggressive—for example, smashing into games that they don't otherwise know how to enter. By creating rich environments for play with a range of entry points, teachers are able to support children in practicing the social and communication skills they need to play effectively both alone and with other children. Knowing that children are experts in their own play, teachers and other adults are prepared to recognize this process itself as valuable and allow children the opportunity to play through their ideas in their own time and for their own reasons.

FOUNDATION IN PLAYWORK

Beginning with the understanding that access to rich and varied opportunities for child-directed play is essential for all children, we bridge the tradition of Playwork (Brown & Taylor, 2008; Hughes, 2011; Playwork Principles Scrutiny Group, 2005; Wilson, 2010) in the United Kingdom with child-centered approaches to early childhood education and put these theories into practice. Playwork is a professional approach distinguished by its nonjudgmental, nonprejudicial, nondirective, and largely reflective approach (Brown, 2009), and playworkers support play in schools, parks, and a range of other settings. They view the problem of children's lost play opportunities holistically, impacted by pressures on school and home lives, as well as by large-scale changes such as the rise in car ownership and decline of face-to-face social networks.

In Playwork, a key method of improving environments for play is the introduction of ordinary, recycled materials that children are free to shape and change, also known as *loose parts* (Nicholson, 1971). Often referred to as *manipulatives* in education terminology (usually purchased through catalogs), this type of material can actually be as commonplace as cardboard boxes, string, and plastic containers. These everyday materials communicate that play does not require expensive toys and they are often more malleable than most commercially available materials. Because they are of little or no financial value, children (and adults) are able to use these materials freely, without a sense of being wasteful.

LANDSCAPES FOR INFORMED IMPROVISATION

Whereas teachers are typically taught to think of play as a means to learning, Playwork professionals in the United Kingdom and elsewhere have been working for decades to support child-directed play *for the sake of play itself.* At Pop-Up Adventure Play, our practices are grounded by two fundamental beliefs:

- Play is critical to children's overall well-being and healthy development.
- Children are experts in their own play.

By building on our foundation in Playwork and broadening the scope of Playwork practices into classrooms, home-school connections, and community settings, we have developed a set of practices, materials, and strategies for self-reflection, which can be adapted by teachers and other adults. We call this approach *informed improvisation*, as it offers teachers and other adults the ability to draw on theory and previous experiences, while still remaining present in the moment and adapting to constantly changing play frames.

Due to the numerous demands placed on classroom teachers, it is not reasonable to expect that teachers can allow children to direct their own play all the time. However, by adapting an improvisational attitude within the daily schedule, teachers are more likely to recognize and support child-directed play when appropriate. For example, consider the notion of the *teachable moment*. Usually, a teachable moment is an opportunity for a teacher or parent to draw a child's attention to something and naturally extend learning from that point. A child picks up a red leaf on the playground, and a teacher explains that it is red because the seasons are changing and there are fewer hours of sunlight. The teacher might then ask the child to look for more red leaves or find leaves in other colors.

Now, imagine this scenario. The teachable moment is sometimes reversed; instead of this moment being a chance for a child to learn something from his teacher, it is a moment for the teacher to learn something about the child. The teacher notices a child investigating a red leaf and says nothing. She simply watches. Maybe the teacher picks up her own leaf and turns it over in her hand, enjoying the moment for herself. Maybe she finds a green leaf and hands it to the child without saying anything at all. This redefinition of the teachable moment retains the possibility for something to arise from the child that surprises the adult—for example, an association made with neither the notion of *red* nor *leaf*, but instead the leaf's dry crunchy *texture*, or a story about things that fall to the ground. Sometimes, it is important to build children's understanding of certain content (in the context of a teachable moment). At other times, teachers can allow children to lead them toward new understanding.

Improvising takes practice and confidence, because at first, following children's lead can produce feelings of fear. Central to this approach is a faith in children to be experts in their own play and faith in oneself to navigate the changing landscapes the children create. Informed improvisation requires enormous empathy for children and families, as well as for oneself. All of us are continually learning, and by observing children at play, we discover more ways to enrich their environments, providing inspiration and permission if necessary and participating if invited. Remember, adults do not need to explicitly *teach* children to play, but children do need to be *supported* in their play, and the following broad strategies can help.

SETTING THE STAGE: ADAPTING TEACHER APPROACHES TO PLAY

There are several key strategies that adults can use to support children's play. First, teachers can create an environment for play, including open-ended materials that inspire exploration and creativity. In Playwork, creating an environment is not simply about setting up furniture and buying material; rather, it is a mindset, a stance, a way of thinking about play. Teachers also must be skilled in extending invitations to play and reflecting on the play process. Finally, thinking of play beyond the classroom walls and the school playground helps expand children's play landscapes, which is crucial to their development as active players and learners. The following four key strategies can help teachers support play in any context.

Value Play

When teachers value children's play, they value that which is individual, spontaneous, and handmade. In advocating for children's play opportunities to parents and other adults, we inevitably draw upon our own childhood experiences and those of the people we meet—this process can sometimes be challenging and is often surprising as we discover commonalities and differences.

Celebrate the Detail

When children share the details of their vision, they provide an invaluable window into their world. Listen carefully, and then consider whether to share some of these "play stories" with other students and even parents during pickup and dropoff. Rather than focusing only on the display of "finished projects" or on specific academic achievements, teachers can highlight the details and processes of play and learning. For example, rather than saying, "Look at this *amazing* castle that Eliza built," a teacher might focus on one or two details of the play, such as, "Eliza decided that there is a zebra in this door and the zebra only eats pizza." Ideally, teachers can share these play stories with parents, other family members, and caregivers while children are listening, thus celebrating the notion of "children as experts in their own play."

Analyze Risk/Benefit Balance

When making decisions that impact children's play, take care to consider all possible benefits, as well as the risks. For example, rather than having broad rules such as "We can never transport materials to the top of the slide," teachers can assess risk/benefit on a case-by-case basis and find ways to support child-directed initiatives in ways that diminish risk yet encourage play. If some children are excited about transporting a bucket full of wood-chips to the top of the slide and watching them flow down "like a big river" to the bottom, perhaps the teacher asks other children to temporarily move back from the slide to watch what happens. If the teacher is nervous about the child carrying the bucket to the top of the slide, maybe he hands the bucket to the child when she is already at the top. Children's ideas for how to use materials, equipment, and objects can test teachers' comfort zones, but considering the risks and benefits of each unique situation can help teachers become more flexible. (We will address the critical importance of materials later in this chapter.)

Reflection Play

We believe that the science of teaching is best expressed in the *practice* of teaching. Self-reflection is the key to good practice and is a fundamental tenet of Playwork. As teachers adapt the practices of informed improvisation into their typical classroom routine, they can begin to keep track of stories that emerge from play. For some teachers, this process of reflecting on play might start with a note jotted on a piece of scrap paper, and others may want to begin with a brand new notebook labeled *Playbook*. Begin by thinking back over the course of an hour of the day in the classroom and focus on memories of children at play:

- What themes evolve?
- What does it feel like to let children direct their own play?
- How does it feel to be invited into children's play?
- What is hard about allowing children to be the experts in play?

The playbook can help teachers identify vital details of children's evolving play in the classroom, and of their own learning. In her book *Wally's Stories: Conversations in the Kindergarten*, Vivian Paley (1981) beautifully summarizes the importance of teachers' approaches to play over time:

A wide variety of thinking emerges, as morality, science, and society share the stage with fantasy. If magical thinking seems most conspicuous, it is because it is the common footpath from which new trails are explored. I have learned not to resist this magic but to seek it out as a legitimate part of "real" school. (p. 4)

We recommend that teachers also reflect on what it feels like personally (as adults) to be *at play*. It is essential to understand what if feels like to be in a play mindset in order to support children's play effectively. *How did you play as a child? What is your play today?* Perhaps you like to sing while driving, or maybe you play the guitar or love the creative process of cooking. Maybe you like to write or relax with a good story. Consider what it feels like when you are directing your own experience, following your own lead, and then discuss these thoughts with other teachers.

CREATING AN ENVIRONMENT FOR PLAY

With a foundation in the four broad strategies (valuing play, celebrating play, weighing risks and benefits, and reflecting on the process), the following specific practices can allow teachers to create an environment for play for all children.

Give Permission

Teachers may need to explicitly invite certain children into child-directed play. Say, "It's okay. You can do whatever you'd like with these materials. I'm here to help you if you like." Or "It looks like you are trying to build that much taller; how can I help you to reach?" Some invitations are completely open-ended, while some involve a question or noticing something the child is doing.

Model Curiosity

Model a curious approach to novel contexts and ideas (rather than adopting a stance as the bearer of all information). Teachers can demonstrate the pleasures of exploration and experimentation for their own sake. By following children's lead as coplayers, and by listening carefully to the parents and caregivers they meet, teachers can open themselves up to learning through curiosity and experience.

Develop Your Empathic Imagination

Rather than teachers comparing the behaviors they observe with those they might wish to see, informed improvisers empathize, striving to understand better the positions and perspectives of all children and adults. It's very easy for teachers to assume that the people being observed have similar experiences and motivations to their own. For example, once, at a play site, Morgan saw a mother yank her child out of the mud where he had happily been playing. Morgan launched into a conversation about the benefits of messy play, only to be told by the mother that, after years of living in a refugee camp, the mother was not afraid of dirt, but of cholera.

Teachers can be sensitive to different perspectives in less extreme contexts as well. For example, some parents pride themselves on sending children to school in their best clothes. Providing old T-shirts to wear over clothing that is not meant to get dirty or gently encouraging parents to send in a change of clothes for playing outside in dirt, mud, or grass can help. It is important that teachers listen to parents carefully and work with them rather than against them, finding ways to support parents' beliefs and desires for children while also allowing children to feel comfortable in their play.

Support (Rather than Direct) Children's Play

Once children are engaged in play, there are many ways in which adults can continue to support their play, without interrupting or directing. This may be challenging for adults; for example, when a child struggles with a piece of tape, the adult's instinct is to fix it, unasked. But, by taking the tape, many adults also unwittingly deprive the child of opportunities to figure something out for herself and overcome obstacles she has chosen. Informed improvisers look for cues from the child before offering help, allowing the child to continue the play and enjoy her intrinsically motivated effort without interruption. When the child overtly *asks* for help, the teacher can offer assistance and then quietly withdraw.

Allow Time and Space

Allow play scenarios to develop. Teachers can designate one part of the classroom where children's play narratives are allowed to evolve over many days. Although the rest of the room will need to be cleaned each night, in this special space, children can leave block structures up to revisit over a series of days. Teachers can then add new loose parts to this space (or allow children to add other materials), which can encourage the play to continue and develop from day to day.

Become a Loose Part in Children's Play

Recognize that adults themselves can become loose parts in the classroom, changing and malleable, ready to improvise. In the same way that materials can be open-ended, teachers can support play by responding to children's direction (e.g., one minute a teacher is a bus, the next minute she is a tree, and then she is a doctor or truck driver). This is not to say that the teacher becomes the focus or the leader of play, but rather is a means by which children can extend their own play scenarios if they choose. Through informed improvisation, a teacher can adapt quickly to new situations (e.g., a teacher watches children building with blocks, realizes they are talking about telescopes, and hands them two paper towel tubes without saying a word). If teachers begin with these practices, nearly any environment can become an environment that supports play, but it is also critical to consider the materials offered children.

PROVIDING A RANGE OF MATERIALS

Almost anything can be considered potential *play material* with just a few simple questions. Is it available for free or very cheaply? Is it flexible, open to physical and imaginative change? Can it be struck and twisted without shattering? The main goal is to offer open-ended materials and objects for play that children can genuinely do with what they want. Think ahead of time about what that means for you in your classroom. If you're afraid children will fight with materials, provide cotton balls instead of pointy sticks. If you're afraid of a mess, use tape and crayons instead of paint and glue.

With these guidelines in mind, let your assortment of open-ended materials (or loose parts) reflect the place you're in and what you have on hand. That might include balls of yarn, wooden spoons and mixing bowls, or bags of leaves and acorns gathered in the park. The inclusion of real household items, rather than their fake plastic counterparts, can also help contribute to the variety of loose parts on hand (e.g., old computer keyboards or phones). A mixture of colors, textures, and scale ensures a range of play possibilities.

Teachers who are prepared with the materials of play have as much on hand as possible to help children overcome a range of barriers to play (e.g., smocks for children who aren't supposed to get messy at school). And, even when there is an assigned teacher-directed project (e.g., everyone working together to make lions for the jungle wall), the type and range of materials available makes a big difference. By including multiple open-ended materials and allowing children to choose what they'd like to work with in creating their own version of *lion*, teachers can create classroom environments that are generally more conducive to child-directed play and learning.

Keeping a constant supply of small cardboard boxes, paper towel tubes, magazines, tape, and string in a large bag makes it easier for teachers to bring these materials out for play during choice time or recess and then store them again. Teachers can also have fun by seeding surprises within classroom materi-als—for example, by mixing plastic forks and large bottle caps in with paintbrush-es at the easel or tucking large shiny buttons inside a small box. It is wonderful to hear children's gleeful questioning, "What is *that* doing here?" The incongruity of these objects and materials being jumbled together is in itself a prompt to children's curiosity, experimentation, and storytelling—to their play.

Teachers can showcase the importance of everyday, open-ended materials for children's play and learning by simply being cognizant of the materials that parents and others see in the classroom. If loose parts and everyday materi-als are displayed as useful and interesting, teachers can subtly begin to shift parents' views of materials and toys (e.g., a new pile of cardboard boxes and other everyday materials can be just as celebrated as a new stuffed toy or ac-tion figure).

PLAY BEYOND THE CLASSROOM

Sending Materials Home

With school-age children spending an average of only 20% of their waking hours in school across a full calendar year, parents play a critical role in de-termining how children spend the majority of their time. Part of what makes our work at Pop-Up Adventure Play accessible is the notion that we support play with everyday, easy-to-find materials that people of all economic groups are likely to have. Through play with everyday materials, teachers can break down numerous boundaries and create opportunities for play across the whole of a child's environment: home, school, and community.

The best stuff of child-directed play is often free. One simple way to help support child-directed play beyond the classroom is to send home bags containing, for example, some loose parts and a roll of tape. When Anna supported an after-school Pop-Up at a public elementary school, she allowed each of the 12 children to fill a bag with leftover materials at the end of the 8-week session. Children's eyes widened with the realization that they were going to be able to make and keep their very own bags of paper towel tubes, yarn, fabric samples, and cotton balls. They gathered materials excitedly, stuffing as much as they could into their bags. These take-home materials can become a play kit to prompt play and promote conversation about play outside of the classroom, and can be a great accompaniment to our Mini Pop-Up Kit, which can be downloaded for free at www.popupadventureplay.org. This resource includes important information about the benefits of child-directed play and tangible ways to promote play in everyday life.

Building Community Around Play

Recent changes in how public spaces (beyond schools) are used and controlled mean that the lives of children today are quite different compared with those of their parents and grandparents—even before immigration and relocation are taken into account. Public space has historically been open to children's roaming play in a way that it rarely is today. Internationally, parents cite such concerns as traffic, stranger danger, and a lack of safe provision as barriers to their children's play. These obstacles have increased in recent years. In the United Kingdom, 21% of children play outside every day, while 71% of their parents did as children (Playday, 2007). Children increasingly spend their out-of-school time inside playing video games, texting, or watching television (Rideout, Foehr, & Roberts, 2010), which is especially disheartening, as 89% of children rate *playing with their friends* as their favorite thing to do (Clarke, 2010). Even children as young as 3 (across income groups) spend numerous hours per week in adult-directed activities outside of school (Housley Juster, 2013). Although extracurricular, adult-directed activities (e.g., dance, violin, soccer, adult-directed playgroups or library story hours) can be very beneficial for children, the outcomes associated with adult-directed activities are not the same as the developmental benefits of child-directed play.

Pop-Up Adventure Playgrounds (public celebrations of child-directed play with open-ended materials) can fill the void in children's access to child-directed play in neighborhoods and broader communities (see Figure 6.1). Pop-Ups often attract material donations from community members (e.g., local business owners), involving whole communities in the process of supporting play. In organizing a Pop-Up, it is a good idea to make a wish list that explains what you are looking for (such as string, fabric scraps or samples, and clean plastic bottles or paper cups), as well as what you are not (such as things made of glass or other materials that shatter).

Organizers hosting Pop-Up Adventure Playgrounds often find that whole families (adults included!) seek the same permission, encouragement, and support as children do. Material donors may share stories of their own childhood play memories, and parents and grandparents often love to talk about where they grew up, what they most loved to do as children, and so on. Sometimes these conversations open up new levels of understanding, as parents share their hopes and dreams for their own children or grandchildren.

We often find that the greatest new material for play is the diversity of participants—adults often intermingle as children make new friends spontaneously through play. We are often surprised at how quickly people cross boundaries of age, background, and ability because play offers a shared vocabulary

Figure 6.1: Children Collaborate as They Engage in Self-Directed Play with Loose Parts at Pop-Up Adventure Playground

Photo credit: Suzanna Law

of verbal cues, facial expressions, and more. The abundance of free and accessible loose parts also allows children to make their *own social connections*—to *share their play.* After a Pop-Up Adventure Playground in Boston, Massachusetts, Anna's 5-year-old daughter Alex was playing with leftover boxes and other materials on the sidewalk in front of her house. A young girl and her father walked by and stopped, curious. Alex looked up at the girl and offered her a handful of giant green bottle caps. Without a word spoken, their story began. *Do you want to play?*

CONCLUDING THOUGHTS

Children are born ready to learn, ready to play. Through informed improvisation, including specific practices and open-ended materials, teachers can gain in-depth insights into children's thinking and learning and can understand better how to support play without directing. Child-directed play can be supported effectively in the most underserved classroom, in the narrowest hallway of the tiniest apartment, in stark, concrete-filled urban playgrounds, and in large public spaces where entire communities witness the power of truly child-directed play in action.

Adults in the field of education tend to understand play as *the work of children* and focus almost exclusively on the importance of play for learning in children's earliest years. However, it is critical to recognize that the need for play doesn't end in childhood (Brown, 2009). In the midst of the everyday demands of home, school, work, and all of life, *play on.* Please contact us at www.popupadventureplay.org to learn more.

Discussion Questions

- How are the children you work with "experts in their own play"? What have you observed them doing that points to their expertise?
- How do you "play" now, and what connections can you draw between your child-play and your adult-play?
- What are your memories of playing as a child? How might this impact your work with children?

REFERENCES

Anderegg, D. (2003). *Worried all the time: Rediscovering the joy in parenthood in an age of anxiety.* New York, NY: Free Press.

Axline, V. (1986). *Dibs in search of self.* London, UK: Ballantine Books.

Bjorkland, D. F., & Brown, R. D. (1998). Physical play and cognitive development: Integrating activity, cognition, and education. *Child Development, 69,* 604–606.

Brown, F., & Taylor, C. (2008). *Foundations of playwork.* London, UK: Open University Press.

Brown, F., & Webb, S. (2005). Children without play. *Journal of Education, 35*(Special Issue, Early Childhood Research in Developing Contexts), pp. 139–158.

Brown, S. (2009). *Play: How it shapes the brain, opens the imagination, and invigorates the soul.* New York, NY: Penguin Group.

Clarke, B. (2010). Playreport. Inter IKEA Systems B.V. Available at ikeafans.com/images/wordpress/uploads/2010/08/playreport.pdf

Dearing, E., Wimer, C., Simpkins, S. D., Lund, T., Bouffard, S. M., Caronongan, P., Kreider, H., & Weiss, H. (2009). Do neighborhood and home contexts help explain why low-income children miss opportunities to participate in activities outside of school? *Developmental Psychology 45*(6), 1545–1562.

Elkind, D. (2001). *The hurried child: Growing up too fast too soon* (3rd ed.). Cambridge, MA: Perseus.

Elkind, D. (2007). *The power of play: Learning what comes naturally.* Philadelphia, PA: Da Capo Press.

Erickson, R. J. (1985). Play contributes to the full emotional development of the child. *Education, 105,* 261–263.

Ginsburg, H., & Opper, P. (1988). *Piaget's theory of intellectual development* (3rd ed.). Englewood Cliffs, NJ: Prentice Hall.

Ginsburg, K. (2007, January). The importance of play in promoting healthy child development and maintaining strong parent-child bonds. *American Academy of Pediatrics.* Available at www.aap.org/pressroom/playFINAL.pdf

Goodenough, E. (Ed.). (2008). *A place for play.* Chicago, IL: Institute for Play.

Hirsh-Pasek, K., & Golinkoff, R. M. (2003). *Why Einstein never used flash cards: How our children really learn and why they need to play more and memorize less.* Emmaus, PA: Rodale Inc.

Housley Juster, A. (2013). *Child-directed play and the over-scheduling hypothesis: relationships among mothers' expectations for children's learning, parenting practices, and 3-year olds' time use.* Doctoral dissertation. New York University, United States. (Publication No. AAT 3567281).

Hughes, B. (2011). *Evolutionary playwork and reflective analytic practice.* London, UK: Routledge.

Lareau, A. (1987). Social class differences in family-school relationships: The importance of cultural capital. *Sociology of Education, 60,* 73–85.

Luthar, S. S. (2003). The culture of affluence: Psychological costs of material wealth. *Child Development, 74,* 1581–1593.

Miller, A. (2008). *The drama of the gifted child: The search for the true self.* New York, NY: Basic Books.

Miller, E., & Almon, J. (2011). *The crisis in early education: A research-based case for more play and less pressure.* College Park, MD: Alliance for Childhood.

Milteer, R., & Ginsburg K. (2011, December). The importance of play in promoting healthy child development and maintaining strong parent-child bonds: Focus on children in poverty. *Pediatrics.* Available at pediatrics.aappublications.org/content/early/2011/12/21/peds.2011-2953.full.pdf+html

Nicholson, S. (1971). How not to cheat children: The theory of loose parts. *Landscape Architecture, 62*(1), pp. 30–34.

Office of the United Nations High Commissioner for Human Rights. (1989, November). *Convention on the Rights of the Child. General Assembly Resolution 44/45.* Available at www2.ohchr.org/english/law/pdf/crc.pdf

Paley, V. G. (1981). *Wally's stories.* Cambridge, MA: Harvard University Press.

Pellegrini, A. D. (2005). *Recess: Its role in education and development.* Mahwah, NJ: Erlbaum Associates.

Piaget, J. (1962). *Play, dreams, and imitation in childhood.* New York, NY: Norton.

Piaget, J. (1969/1970). *Science of education and the psychology of the child.* New York, NY: Viking Press.

Playday. (2007). *Our streets too!* London, UK: Play England.

Playwork Principles Scrutiny Group. (2005). *The playwork principles.* Cardiff, UK: SkillsActive.

Prins, E., & Willson Toso, B. (2008). Defining and measuring parenting for educational success: A critical discourse analysis of the parent education profile. *American Educational Research Journal, 48*(3), 555–596.

Rideout, V. J., Foehr, U. G., & Roberts, D. F. (2010). *Generation M2: Media in the lives of 8-18-year-olds.* Kaiser Family Foundation Report. Available at www.kff.org/entmedia/upload/8010.pdf

Rogers, C. S., & Sawyers, J. K. (1988). *Play in the lives of young children.* Washington, DC: NAEYC.

Russell, W. (2006). *Reframing playwork: Reframing challenging behavior.* Nottingham, UK: Nottingham City Council.

Singer, D. G., Golinkoff, R. M., & Hirsh-Pasek, K. (Eds.). (2006). *Play = learning: How play motivates and enhances children's cognitive and social-emotional growth.* New York, NY: Oxford University Press.

Sturrock, G., & Else, P. (1998). *The playground as therapeutic space: Playwork as healing.* Eastleigh, UK: Common Threads Publications Ltd.

Vygotsky, L. (1978). *Mind in society.* Cambridge, MA: Harvard University Press.

Warner, J. (2005). *Perfect madness: Motherhood in the age of anxiety.* New York, NY: Riverhead Books.

Wilson, P. (2010). *The playwork primer.* New York, NY: Alliance for Childhood.

Winnicott, D. (2005). *Playing and reality.* London, UK: Routledge.

PART III

INFORMAL, OUT-OF-SCHOOL, AND VIRTUAL ENVIRONMENTS

While we tend to think of environments for young children in the context of schools, and perhaps outdoor or indoor play spaces, this section invites readers to consider a broader notion of environments. In Chapter 7 Tiffany R. Lee and Leah A. Bricker draw attention to young children's science learning across the settings of their lives (e.g., home, school, museums, outdoors). The authors emphasize the importance of teachers considering young children's science-related experiences, interests, and wonderings when designing science learning environments and activities to support their developing knowledge. The chapter showcases two pre-K units in which teachers created authentic science experiences in and out of the classroom for their young students. The authors conclude with recommendations for teachers including employing documentation strategies and connecting with students' families and other adults to create bridges between students' science-related experiences.

Chapter 8 focuses on the role of museums in the educational, social, and cultural lives of children. Through a social-constructivist and visitor-centered lens, Angela Eckhoff explores the ways in which children are encouraged to interact within cultural, historical, arts, science, and play-based museum environments. She discusses the ways that adults can support children's interactions before, during, and after museum experiences. The author encourages practitioners to utilize museums as sites rich in both content information and inquiry-based, pedagogical practices. The chapter concludes with suggestions for identifying on-site and virtual museums accessible for young children, preparing children for museum visits, and employing museum design principles in classrooms.

In Chapter 9 Laura Beals considers virtual environments for children known as virtual worlds. Their use by young children is increasing steadily, and although this environment can be important for the development of social, emotional, and cognitive skills, the author points to potential hazards of virtual worlds. This chapter denotes seven attributes that should be considered in critically examining virtual environments for young children, and focuses upon the ways in which these attributes can be used to scaffold successful experiences in the virtual environment. However, the author also raises concerns about the extent to which this technology should be used by children and the commercial nature of many of the most popular virtual worlds for young children.

CHAPTER 7

Connected Learning Environments

Bridging Informal and Formal Environments to Support Early Science Learning

Tiffany R. Lee
Leah A. Bricker

What counts as an authentic environment for science learning, and how can teachers design these environments using young children's science-related ideas and practices from their everyday lives? Throughout this chapter, we will explore these questions and showcase a few examples of how young children's science-related ideas, interests, and experiences can be integrated into prekindergarten science learning and teaching. Our goal is to broaden the concept of a "learning environment" to include not only spaces within early childhood classrooms and associated play areas, such as playgrounds, but also children's homes, neighborhoods, and the multitude of other settings in which they learn (e.g., electronic spaces, museums).

To support young children's development in science interest and learning, it is critically important for educators to

- Learn about children's experiences and interests associated with the various learning environments that children create and/or frequent
- Draw on these experiences and interests when designing activities and learning environments in early childhood classrooms and programs
- Develop ways of helping each child explore his or her personal interests and wonderings

In order to illustrate this agenda, we draw on past research and design work in prekindergarten and elementary school settings. Before we turn to these examples, we want to situate ourselves in the realms of theory and practice so that readers can better understand the lenses we use to view the examples we offer, and can think about using these lenses in their own contexts.

SCIENCE EDUCATION AND LEARNING

We are well aware that in many early childhood school settings, students do not have the opportunities to experience inquiry, exploration, and the various scientific practices that accompany those activities (e.g., data collection, presenting ideas, asking testable questions). If science is touched on, it is usually merged with English language arts and mathematics-related activities. One of our messages in this chapter is that it is worth engaging young children in authentic science-specific activity. In our collective experience teaching in formal pre-K–12 settings, conducting research to understand young people's science learning in and out of school, and using our research findings to design, implement, and study science-related curriculum and instruction, we adopt a stance that young people, including children in preschool, are capable science learners (see Michaels, Shouse, & Schweingruber, 2008). In addition, they have many experiences, wonderings, and interests that they count as science-related and that teachers can use to help foster rich science learning environments within classrooms.

For example, in a study of early elementary school students' conceptions of science, one of us (Lee, 2010) found that students enter kindergarten with a diverse set of science-related knowledge stemming from their everyday experiences, including backyard explorations of bugs, visits to zoos and science museums, books and television, and general activities with parents, siblings, and friends. In a follow-up study, Lee found that specific aspects of the experiences varied for students from suburban and rural communities of differing levels of socioeconomic status (e.g., students in the rural community had less frequent access to museums, but outdoor explorations were commonplace). Yet the overall findings held true—both groups of students spoke of a wide range of science-related experiences that they encountered outside of school. These types of experiences can serve as a strong foundation for engaging young students in science ideas and practices.

The type of activity represented in this chapter is grounded in Dewey's philosophies related to ensuring that formal school environments are connected to children's everyday environments. When school is more relevant, it can ensure deeper learning by fostering connections among experiences, interests, and ideas across the places children frequent. Dewey (1900/1990) wondered: "What can be done, and how can it be done, to bring the school into closer relation with the home and neighborhood life—instead of having the school be a place where the child comes solely to learn certain lessons?" (p. 166). There are many examples of projects that have built on this idea of fostering connections among the myriad of settings that children inhabit. For example, Luis Moll and colleagues (e.g., González, Moll, & Amanti, 2005) in their Funds of Knowledge project studied the knowledge and practices used in the homes of "working-class, Mexican communities in Tucson, Arizona" (p. 71). Moll and colleagues then used some of what they learned to design school curricula that drew on that knowledge and those practices. Maureen Callanan and colleagues (2001) designed a preschool science learning experience about animal life cycles and classification based entirely on student-generated questions about eggs, chicks, hens, and the children's roles as the caretakers of the chicks. Parents shared stories from home about how children were talking about their learning in school. In one example, a child picked up a ladybug at home and asked the bug about its day before telling his mother how he knew to classify the ladybug as a male.

Creating learning environments that bridge the many settings through which children travel is not simply a matter of ensuring better communication between home and school and ensuring a more comfortable and welcoming school environment, although both are without doubt important. Bridging these settings is critical to learning itself. Sociocultural learning theorists (e.g., Vygotsky, 1978) posit that learning does not take place solely in individuals' heads. Learning cannot be separated from our social, cultural, and historical contexts. Learning takes place within, and because of, practices situated in the routines and experiences of our lives. Often, however, learning in schools involves seemingly disembodied and abstract knowledge, with no apparent relevance to everyday life. This is the problem of practice that we seek to change through research that investigates learning across settings and through our subsequent designs of learning environments.

Life-long, Life-Wide, and Life-Deep Learning

Before we showcase a few examples of young children's science learning in environments that have been designed to bridge the various settings in which children participate, we wish to set the stage by discussing an example from our research that involved young people in 4th and 5th grades. Beginning in 2004, we participated in the Learning in Informal and Formal Environments (LIFE) Center, a National Science Foundation–funded Science of Learning Center (http://life-slc.org/). LIFE's mission is to explore the social foundations of human learning from infancy through adulthood. One representation of learning that emerged from LIFE's work involves life-long learning, life-wide learning, and life-deep learning (Banks et al., 2007). Figure 7.1 illustrates learning from birth though adulthood (life-long learning), as well as learning across settings—both formal and informal (life-wide learning).

Most people are familiar with the concept of life-long learning, or learning that takes place over long periods of time over the course of a life span. Life-wide learning refers to learning that takes place across settings. The "chicks and ladybug" example we presented earlier showcases life-wide learning because the young child was learning about animal life cycles and classification in preschool and then applied what he was learning to another living creature at home (and potentially in other settings as well). Life-deep learning refers to the idea that learning is undergirded by cultural practices, religious beliefs, values, and morals, the details of which are often left unexamined in many formal school environments and curricula.

Our first attempt to concretize life-long, life-wide, and life-deep learning took place as the result of a 3-year ethnography of young people's science and technology learning across settings and over time (Bell, Bricker, Reeve, Zimmerman, & Tzou, 2012). In this study, we followed the same 13 4th- and 5th-graders across the various settings of their lives (e.g., home, school, museums, houses of worship, parks, playgrounds, sports events, shopping malls) to better understand their science and technology learning. In order to get a deeper sense of these young people's learning, we observed and documented, through video and audio recordings, their interactions with peers, family members, and other significant adults in their lives (e.g., teachers, coaches). We interviewed the young people about a host of science and technology-related topics. In addition, we asked them to take digital photographs that represented their ideas associated with science and technology so that we had a better sense of what those words meant to them, what they counted as science and technology,

Figure 7.1: The LIFE Center's Life-Long and Life-Wide Learning Diagram

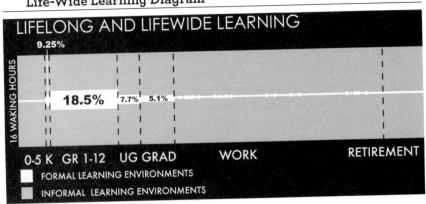

Source: LIFE Center: Stevens, R., Bransford, J., & Stevens, A., 2005.

who they thought participated in these enterprises, and whether they identified with the enterprises (and the people and practices therein). We also collected documents related to the young people's science learning in school and their interest-driven activities outside of school.

Through this study, we were able to document study participants' learning pathways related to science and technology. Some of these learning pathways encompassed activity that crossed a plethora of contexts in youths' lives (including school), and other learning pathways were examples of everyday activity and school activity being disconnected in ways that were problematic for career aspirations and continued expertise development (e.g., Bell et al., 2012). These latter examples represented missed opportunities primarily within the school setting to capitalize on young people's interests, experiences, and developing expertise, so that deeper learning could occur.

For example, one of the 4th-grade study participants loved to make perfumes at home that she created by mixing various scented oils included in an off-the-shelf science kit purchased at a museum (Bricker & Bell, 2014, for a fuller account of this particular case). She shared with us that she loved to mix things, which she related to chemistry (and at the time of her participation in the study, she wanted to be a chemist). Her mother reflected that this love of mixing started years earlier and was related to their family's Haitian cooking practices. Her mother told us stories of the study participant and her cousin using a mortar and pestle, a staple in Haitian cooking, to mix lotions and perfumes. The study participant's aunt was a chemist, so this 4th-grader also had a well-informed developing understanding about the practices that chemists use in a laboratory—practices that the study participant saw herself using when she recorded in a journal the various mixtures of oils that she used in her perfume making, labeled the different bottles of oils, and used measuring tools to ensure that the amount of oil she mixed was accurate given the perfume protocols.

During the designated science time in school, this same 4th-grader was seemingly not engaged, even when participating in activity that involved mixing (as part of a food chemistry unit, for example). We were initially perplexed by this observation and asked her about this. She shared that she was "bored" in school science because she did not perceive the activity in that environment as chemistry-related. In actuality, the school activity was very prescribed in the sense that there was no room for actual investigation.

These events we observed with this 4th-grade study participant took place across multiple settings (home, school, and potentially myriad others, the details of which we do not know)—life-wide learning. Additionally, these events spanned years—life-long learning—and were informed by various cultural practices (e.g., those associated with Haitian cooking)—life-deep learning. Because there was a disconnect between this participant's learning and activity across learning environments (a phenomenon that we documented with respect to several of our participants' science and technology learning pathways), and because one of those environments was the school environment (arguably a gatekeeper for many children and young people's continuing interest and competencies development, not to mention career aspirations), we had very similar questions to those that Dewey posed over a century ago about how to better align school with the other spaces in children's lives.

Through our research, we found many examples of life-long, life-wide, and life-deep science learning. Could the research methods that we used to document science learning also be used by teachers to support students' life-long, life-wide, and life-deep learning? How might we use our research (both findings and techniques) to help facilitate more robust science learning and teaching *in school* that builds upon and further extends students' science learning *outside of school?* Our next set of studies involved designing curriculum in collaboration with teachers to promote better connectivity among school and the interests and experiences of young people. We found that in most cases, when young people's interests, experiences, and wonderings are leveraged in school-based learning experiences, school-based learning becomes more meaningful and rigorous (see McIntyre, Rosebery, & González, 2001, for additional examples). We turn now to a discussion of one example of this curriculum work that took place in early childhood settings.

Laying the Foundation for a Science-Rich Environment

Building upon LIFE research findings about the importance of connecting science learners' everyday experiences with classroom learning, one of us (Lee) began a multiyear partnership with two prekindergarten classes to create science learning opportunities that recognized young children's developing science knowledge and skills (cf. Brown, Campione, Metz, & Ash, 1997; Eshach & Fried, 2005). This work built upon Lee's research described earlier in this chapter, in which she identified sources of science-related knowledge and experiences that entering kindergarten students develop through their everyday experiences. Through a multiyear design-based research partnership (cf. Bell, 2004), Lee collaborated with a prekindergarten teaching team (two lead teachers and two assistant teachers) to develop a year-long curriculum comprised of several units focusing on the life sciences. The overarching goals of the curricular design were to leverage young children's existing knowledge and interests about the natural world and to engage them in scientific practices (e.g., asking questions, planning and carrying out investigations, engaging in argument from evidence) as outlined in current national science education documents (e.g., National Research Council, 2012).

One shift that resulted from this codesigned curricular approach is the way the teachers introduced science at the start of the school year. Rather than using the same, preselected set of science units from year to year, the teachers began each year with an open discussion with the students to gain a sense of their science-related interests and experiences. Many topics emerged from these opening discussions with the prekindergarten students—apple trees, butterflies, birds, worms, spiders, dinosaurs, volcanoes—representing a wide range of experiences and interests that 4-year-old children may bring with them as they enter school. This initial sharing of ideas allowed the teachers to surface students' life-long, life-wide, and life-deep learning experiences, and guided the design of topical units within the classroom science curriculum for the year. Together with the teaching team, Lee developed units with weekly science lessons that emphasized age-appropriate engagement with scientific practices and core ideas and connections to students' existing knowledge of their surrounding world. Lessons included whole-group and small-group activities, and topics were often revisited during regular classroom time throughout the week. To preserve the authenticity of student-generated topics of study, the units were designed throughout the year to build upon students' emerging interests and questions.

Drawing upon the work with the 4th- and 5th-graders described earlier, the curriculum included lessons that emphasized the multitude of spaces where people learn about science throughout their lives. Curricular elements included connections to students' home activities, their outdoor pursuits, and the network of people who play a significant role in children's learning in and out of school. Lee and her team borrowed some basic design elements from other "connected learning environments" (see Ito et al., 2013) and curriculum work taking place across the larger research team, and modified them for the pre-K setting (e.g., a picture-taking activity with support from parents), while adding other curricular elements to further connect with students' life-long, life-wide, and life-deep learning (e.g., a field trip to the local science center, classroom presentations by parents and community members).

CREATING AUTHENTIC SCIENCE-RELATED ENVIRONMENTS IN AND OUT OF THE CLASSROOM

The following vignettes showcase curricular elements specifically designed to bridge informal and formal environments in these two pre-K science classrooms.

OBSERVATIONS AND REASONING DURING A NEIGHBORHOOD SPIDER WALK

In line with our goals of connecting school science with students' everyday lives, one of the pre-K science units focused on spiders and their ecosystems. Prior to this research partnership, the teachers had taught a unit on spiders that had very specific activities already identified.

Activities included reading books to teach students about spider-related facts (e.g., body structure, types of spiders, and habitats) and doing projects to demonstrate students' understanding of these facts (e.g., creating drawings to illustrate the parts of a spider). However, this time, the teachers used their students' spider-related interests to structure the introduction of the unit and to tailor specific lessons within the unit that addressed students' curiosities about spiders, which served to deepen students' engagement. This curricular redesign ensured that learning experiences for the children went beyond discrete activities, such as reading books about spiders.

The decision to develop a new unit on spiders emerged during the first several weeks of school. The classroom teachers reported that their students had been expressing an interest in spiders, noticing spiders and spiderwebs around the school, sharing stories about spider encounters at home (e.g., seeing spiders in the backyard or on the way to school), and asking a lot of questions about spiders (e.g., Do spiders bite? Are all spiders poisonous?). Lee and the teaching team decided to take advantage of this opportunity and created a modified unit focused on spiders that combined the students' interests with learning about a core idea in the life sciences, interdependent relationships in ecosystems. Given that it was fall, it was an opportune time to see spiders in their natural environment around the school building, playgrounds, and other nearby outdoor spaces.

During the whole-class discussion at the beginning of the unit, the students shared their knowledge about spiders and asked questions representing what they wanted to learn more about. For example, most students said they thought spiders lived outside, but they wanted to know what spiders ate. In another classroom activity, students had been learning about apples, so one student wondered if spiders could eat apples. Several students asked how spiders made their webs, and another student asked whether spiders lived on dirt or leaves. By starting the unit with this kind of discussion, students' interests drove the purpose for information gathering and the types of activities that would become part of the unit. Realizing that students could begin to develop answers to their questions by observing spiders in their natural environment, Lee and the teaching team identified the next activity that bridged in-school learning with a familiar out-of-school practice—an outdoor walk.

During this activity, referred to as the "spider walk," a teacher took a small group of five to seven students on a walk around the school buildings and the surrounding streets to look for spiders. On the walk, students found spiderwebs on neighborhood street signs, school fences, bushes and trees, and building windows. By observing the spiders and their webs in their natural environment, the students were able to begin thinking about the relationship among where spiders live, the location of their webs, and what they eat. The students noticed that the webs they saw were often connected between plants or structures, such as the metal fences or brick walls, but no one saw spiders on the ground or in the dirt.

When asked to think about the placement of the spiderwebs, one student said that she thought the spiders hid in the corner of their webs while waiting for bugs to fly into them. The teacher also reminded the class of a large web they saw in a building archway, and suggested that this might be a place where many bugs fly past and become stuck in the spider's web.

This example demonstrates how students' curiosities about their surrounding environments, spanning home and school, can be productively brought into science instruction. The spider walk activity required no special resources other than thoughtful planning time among the teachers, and there were clear learning opportunities afforded by going beyond the classroom setting to explore the topic, spiders, in a natural setting. By seeing spiders living outdoors and building webs around the school, students were able to begin thinking more deeply about the relationship between where spiders live and the food that they eat. This shared experience also served as a foundation to build upon throughout the unit while learning about interdependent relationships in an ecosystem—in this case, a garden ecosystem with plants, spiders, insects, rain, and so forth.

The emphasis on a garden ecosystem was another important component of this unit. Not only did this focus allow students to make connections between their spider-related learning at school and spider sightings in their own gardens/backyards (e.g., one boy recalled seeing a spider at home with a fly caught in its web, "so the spider could eat the fly!"), but it also gave students a chance to build upon their existing knowledge about the many relationships within a garden ecosystem (e.g., trees need sun, water, air, and dirt; birds live in trees; birds eat worms; and so on).

Harkening back to Dewey's call to build bridges between the classroom and other settings, authentic classroom activity is characterized by experiences where children explore their interests; see connections among their interests, experiences, and classroom activities; and have opportunities to learn new ideas and practices connected with their interests and experiences. With respect to STEM (science, technology, engineering, and mathematics)—related fields, these types of science-related learning environments are authentic because they provide opportunities for students to explore phenomena using scientific practices such as analyzing and interpreting data, formulating evidence-based explanations, and asking testable questions (cf. Edelson, 1997; National Research Council, 2012). Another feature of these learning environments that makes them authentic is that they provide opportunities for students to travel on the bridges among different settings (in real time, virtually, or metaphori-cally) in order to investigate and explore phenomena across these different settings. The pre-K spider unit described above showcased this feature of au-thenticity. Students' experiences with spiders and questions about spiders were the impetus for the unit and drove the design of the curriculum.

To provide another example of authenticity, we turn to another unit that emerged from students' interests. During the opening discussion about science interests at the beginning of the year, butterflies had come up as a topic within the group. Responding to that interest, the teachers created a unit in which the pre-K students could raise caterpillars in the classroom and learn about the caterpillar's transformation into a butterfly.

OBSERVATIONS AND EXPLANATIONS IN A TROPICAL BUTTERFLY HOUSE

The caterpillars had been purchased through a commercial supplier for science materials, and therefore arrived in plastic containers with a pureed food substance. This kit is similar to other butterfly kits for young children that are widely available across the United States. The instructions required the caterpillars to be transferred into a mesh cage once they formed their chrysalides, where they would stay until they were released as butterflies. This setup was very practical and easy to implement in a classroom setting, but it did not give students a chance to see caterpillars and butterflies in an authentic environment, where the caterpillars would eat leaves and the butterflies would drink nectar from flowers. Although books provided an opportunity for the students to learn about where caterpillars and butterflies live in natural settings, there was an obvious disconnect between the butterflies that would emerge and drink sugar water in the mesh cage and the butterflies that exist in the outdoors.

Seeing live caterpillars and butterflies outdoors was a rare occasion in this region, but the local science center had a tropical butterfly house as a permanent exhibit. Midway through the butterfly unit, the teachers planned a field trip for the two pre-K classes to learn more about the life of a butterfly. Though the exhibit featured tropical species of butterflies that would not live in the local region, the immersive quality of the butterfly house allowed students to see and feel a simulated version of the natural environment for these colorful butterflies. Upon entering, students immediately noticed the warmth and humidity in the space, and they were surrounded by lush plants and butterflies circling above their heads.

During the visit, the students observed butterflies flying high in the air, resting on leaves, and drinking from flowers and fresh fruits—experiences that would not have been possible without extending their learning opportunities beyond the classroom setting. Some students had visited the exhibit before with their families and shared what they had learned about how butterflies eat—by uncurling their long, thin proboscises—and why some were resting and slowly flapping their wings—to dry out their wings after emerging from a chrysalis. In addition to learning information from their peers, students also had the opportunity to learn from museum docents and parent chaperones, seeing people other than their teachers as important sources for information.

As described in both the spider and butterfly unit examples, a key component to this approach to science instruction is a switch from a preplanned curriculum to a curriculum that emerges from students' expressed interests and experiences. It is important to reiterate that this approach to instruction is not necessarily common practice in classrooms. With many competing priorities and explicit learning targets to address throughout the year, developing curriculum that is emergent and project-based is not always readily embraced or seen as possible by teachers. However, inquiry into student knowledge and experience is crucial to making connections between children's out-of-school experiences and school science learning. With careful planning, this strategy for science instruction can complement other curricular topics that teachers are required to teach. In this case, the prekindergarten teachers implemented this approach to science instruction and identified ways to address math and literacy learning objectives within the projects as well.

DOCUMENTING LEARNING EXPERIENCES TO CONNECT ACROSS SETTINGS

Incorporating activities such as outdoor walks or field trips can be beneficial for student learning. If whole-class field trips are not possible, teachers can also explore options for inviting an expert community member or classroom parent to visit the classroom, or might use resources such as videos or photographs to simulate a field experience without actually leaving the classroom. Whether students experience an actual or a simulated field trip, teachers often face the challenge of connecting these activities to typical classroom instruction. It is important that these activities do not become isolated, "special" events with little relevance to the curriculum (cf. Kisiel, 2006). In the two previous pre-K examples, the outdoor spider walk and the field trip to the topical butterfly house were critical for extending students' thinking and furthering their understanding of living creatures as part of an ecosystem. However, these two activities could easily have become isolated events had the teachers and the researchers not diligently thought about how to connect these cross-setting experiences with classroom experiences before and after the field trip.

Following both activities, the teachers led the students in an extended discussion about their observations and experiences. These discussions were strengthened by the incorporation of documentation of each activity. Digital photographs were projected onto a large screen in front of the classroom and served as documentation about the students' experiences in each of the settings (cf. Rinaldi, 2006; Wien, Guyevskey, & Berdoussis, 2011). If a projector is not available, this activity could be implemented using printed photos. Each photo should be large enough for the whole class to see, or several copies could be printed to share among students.

Viewing photos of the spider walk reminded students where they had seen spiderwebs and allowed them to think more deeply about the shape and placement of the webs without the distraction of being outside looking for spiders. Similarly, photos of their field trip to the butterfly house helped students see more detailed views of the butterflies and sparked conversations and questions about caterpillars and butterflies (e.g., Where were the caterpillars at the butterfly house?). These questions might have been missed if the students had not been given a chance to thoroughly revisit their field trip experiences upon returning to the classroom.

The photos served as reminders for the students and connected their out-of-classroom experiences with science activities in the classroom, recognizing the importance of life-wide learning. Furthermore, the photos allowed the students to take their experiences into their homes, and share their knowledge with their families. For example, many parents saw photos of the butterfly house field trip when dropping their children off at school or in the weekly parent letter, and the students were able to share their knowledge and experiences with their parents. Several parents reported having conversations with their children about the caterpillars in the classroom or the butterflies students saw on the field trip, and this led to further discussions about caterpillars and butterflies at home. One student later came to school with a newspaper article that her mother had shared with her. The article was from the local newspaper and described the Monarch butterfly's challenging migration through a very dry Texas, another example of how a student's home experience can be brought into the classroom. The teacher and the student presented the article to the class, resulting in a whole-class discussion about animal migration and the impact of weather.

IMPLICATIONS FOR PRACTICE

We started this chapter by asking two questions: What counts as an authentic environment for science learning, and how can early childhood educators design these environments using young children's science-related ideas and practices from their everyday lives? Consider this comment:

Often, people can competently perform complex cognitive tasks outside of school, but may not display these skills on school-type tasks. This finding indicates the importance of understanding learning in out-of-school settings, and how to build on this learning to support learning in school. (Nasir, Rosebery, Warren, & Lee, 2006, p. 491)

We know that this notion applies to even the youngest learners. Students at the pre-K level are more than capable of engaging in science-related practices (e.g., collecting data, generating testable questions) and learning important scientific ideas. (For ideas, see NGSS Lead States, 2013; National Research Council, 2012.) However, as educators we need to rethink what "counts" as science learning beyond scripted curriculum or a designated "science time" once a week. It is widely acknowledged that children are not "blank slates" or "empty vessels" when they walk into classrooms. Within their first few years of life, children have developed science-related interests, hobbies, passions, and experiences. It is important that we not only recognize their experiences and developing understandings of the world, but that we consider the opportunities to integrate them with aspects of school curriculum. How can teachers learn about and capitalize on the vast array of science-related resources (e.g., experiences, cultural practices, interests) that all children bring with them as they begin school?

First, we recommend that teachers employ a variety of documentation strategies when designing and implementing science curricula. An initial step, which all of our teacher collaborators took regardless of grade level taught, is to encourage the sharing of students' ideas, experiences, and curiosities, and then to record these so that teachers can use them to inform curriculum development. Capturing student dialogue, interests, experiences, and questions related to any given science topic and/or practice helps teachers plan, but can also be used to "play back" to students along with photographs during future conversations. As researchers, we use photographs to remind students of past experiences and encourage further discussion and reflection. This technique is also referred to as documentation in the Reggio Emilia approach as a way to make visible the process and products of learning, to reflect for children what they learned, and to share learning with other students, families, and the public (Gandini, 1998).

Second, we suggest that in addition to using children's developing science-related experiences, interests, and the like as resources, teachers also consider the role of children's families, community members, and/or significant others in children's lives when building a robust science curriculum. If they are willing, trusted adults can be engaged as volunteers in the classroom and on field trips, and can also take on the role of an expert if there is a match with the curriculum. For example, a parent may have extensive experience with gardening or farming and could serve as an expert during a unit on ecosystems. The parent could collaborate with the teacher to develop lessons and activities for the students, give a presentation to the class, or even invite the students on a field trip to visit his or her garden or farm in person. Connecting with students' families and other adults, as well as inviting them to share cultural practices and ideologies, provides an opportunity to leverage life-deep learning within science instruction.

In addition, this array of adults in children's networks can help shed additional light on the children's hobbies, interests, and experiences. Teachers can create two-way communication channels (e.g., blogs, journals), as well as artifacts (e.g., easy and inexpensive science activities that students and adults can do outside of school), to encourage life-wide activity. As in the butterfly-unit example earlier, activities that were happening at school often made their way into conversations between students and their parents during school dropoff, pickup, and at home. The one family's awareness of the butterfly unit at school led to a discussion at home on the newspaper article on the monarch butterfly's migration, and that article made its way back into a school conversation. Many teachers may already have regular communication with families, particularly in early childhood education. The next step is for teachers to build upon that practice and encourage communication with families around science, with the purpose of making life-wide connections that inform and shape the curricula.

Through the use of these suggested documentation strategies and collaboration with students' families and significant adult others, teachers can deepen their knowledge about their students and facilitate science learning across home, school, after-school, and other settings—creating bridges between children's science-related experiences. As we have noted, the first step that teachers need to take is to find out about students' questions, interests, and experiences. We return to Dewey's (1900/1990) wonderings about facilitating better connections among the various settings that children frequent, and we encourage teachers to create those connections in order to better engage children in their science-related learning, and to support *all* children's academic achievement.

Discussion Questions

- Looking back on your childhood experiences, what can you pinpoint that might, according to this chapter, count as science?
- What kinds of science experiences to you recall from your everyday/out-of-school life when you were a child?
- What kinds of science experiences do you recall from your in-school curricula across grade levels? How did the curricula connect to your everyday life as a child, if at all?

- As a teacher, with what kinds of science topics are you most comfortable?
- How might you connect those topics to the everyday lives of your students?
- Given those topics, how might you go about better understanding what interests, experiences, wonderings, etc. children have about those topics?

REFERENCES

Banks, J. A., Au, K. H., Ball, A. F., Bell, P., Gordon, E. W., Gutiérrez, K. D., Zhou, M. (2007). *Learning in and out of school in diverse environments: Life-long, life-wide, life-deep.* Seattle, WA: The LIFE Center and The Center for Multicultural Education (University of Washington).

Bell, P. (2004). On the theoretical breadth of design-based research in education. *Educational Psychologist, 39*(4), 243–253.

Bell, P., Bricker, L. A., Reeve, S., Zimmerman, H. T., & Tzou, C. (2012). Discovering and supporting successful learning pathways of youth in and out of school: Accounting for the development of everyday expertise across settings. In B. Bevan, P. Bell, R. Stevens, & A. Razfar (Eds.), *LOST opportunities: Learning in out-of-school time* (pp. 119–140). New York, NY: Springer.

Bricker, L. A., & Bell, P. (2014). "What comes to mind when you think of science? The Perfumery!": Documenting cultural learning pathways across contexts and timescales. *Journal of Research in Science Teaching, 51*(3), 260–285.

Brown, A., Campione, J., Metz, K. E., & Ash, D. (1997). The development of science learning abilities in children. In A. Burgen & K. Harnquist (Eds.), *Growing up with science: Developing early understanding of science* (pp. 7–40). Goteborg, Sweden: Academia Europaea.

Callanan, M., Coto, P., Miranda, L., Striffer, A., Allen, J., Crandall, C., & Murphy, C. (2001). Preschool science: Contextualizing curriculum with children's questions and family stories. In E. McIntyre, A. Rosebery, & N. González (Eds.), *Classroom diversity: Connecting curriculum to students' lives* (pp. 61–75). Portsmouth, NH: Heinemann.

Dewey, J. (1900/1990). *The school and society and the child and the curriculum.* Chicago, IL: The University of Chicago Press.

Edelson, D. C. (1997). Realizing authentic science learning through the adaptation of scientific practice. In K. G. Tobin & B. J. Fraser (Eds.), *International handbook of science education* (pp. 317–331). Dordrecht, The Netherlands: Kluwer Academic Publishers.

Eshach, H., & Fried, M. N. (2005). Should science be taught in early childhood? *Journal of Science Education and Technology, 14*(3), 315–336.

Gandini, L. (1998). Educational and caring spaces. In C. Edwards, L. Gandini, & G. Forman (Eds.), *The hundred languages of children. The Reggio Emilia approach—Advanced reflections* (2nd ed., pp. 161–178). Greenwich, CT: Ablex.

González, N., Moll, L. C., & Amanti, C. (2005). *Funds of knowledge: Theorizing practices in households, communities, and classrooms.* Mahwah, NJ: Lawrence Erlbaum Associates.

Ito, M., Gutiérrez, K., Livingstone, S., Penuel, B., Rhodes, J., Salen, K., . . . & Watkins, S. C. (2013). *Connected learning: An agenda for research and design.* Irvine, CA: Digital Media and Learning Research Hub.

Kisiel, J. (2006). Making field trips work. *The Science Teacher, 73*(1), 46–48.

Lee, T. R. (2010, May). *Young children's conceptions of science and scientists.* (Unpublished doctoral dissertation). University of Washington, Seattle, WA.

McIntyre, E., Rosebery, A., & González, N. (Eds.). (2001). *Classroom diversity: Connecting curriculum to students' lives.* Portsmouth, NH: Heinemann.

Michaels, S., Shouse, A. W., & Schweingruber, H. A. (2008). *Ready, set, science: Putting research to work in K-8 science classrooms.* Washington, DC: National Academies Press.

Nasir, N. S., Rosebery, A. S., Warren, B., & Lee, C. D. (2006). Learning as a cultural process: Achieving equity through diversity. In R. K. Sawyer (Ed.), *The Cambridge handbook of the learning sciences* (pp. 489–504). Cambridge, UK: Cambridge University Press.

National Research Council. (2012). *A framework for K–12 science education: Practices, crosscutting concepts, and core ideas.* Washington, DC: The National Academies Press.

NGSS Lead States. (2013). *Next generation science standards: For states, by states.* Washington, DC: Achieve, Inc.

Rinaldi, C. (2006). *In dialogue with Reggio Emilia: Listening, researching, and learning.* New York, NY: Routledge.

Stevens, R., Bransford, J., & Stevens, A. (2005). The LIFE Center's Life-long and Life-wide Learning Diagram. Available at life-slc.org/about/citationdetails.html

Vygotsky, L. S. (1978). *Mind in society: The development of higher psychological processes.* Cambridge, MA: Harvard University Press.

Wien, C. A., Guyevskey, V., & Berdoussis, N. (2011). Learning to document in Reggio-inspired education. *Early Childhood Research and Practice, 13*(2).

CHAPTER 8

Museum Spaces as a Provocation for Learning

Angela Eckhoff

Squeals of excitement coincide with an explosion of brightly colored scarves at the Sun Tubes exhibit at the Children's Museum of Richmond in Richmond, Virginia (http://www.c-mor.org/exhibits/central/sun-tubes). Sun Tubes is an interactive exhibit powered by solar panels on the museum's roof. The intricate design of the exhibit's maze of airway tubes through which the scarves move are attached to a large mural of the sun. The small group of children moves quickly to catch and gather the floating scarves. One child, acting as the unofficial group leader, quickly pushes the scarves handed to her by the other children into the opening in the maze. The group stands back in near silence and watches as the scarves are sucked into the tube and quickly travel throughout the length of the maze. "Here they come again!" shouts a child near the back of the group as all eyes are fixated on the tube's exit opening.

As the group rushes to gather the exiting scarves before they land on the floor, a new child wanders to the front of the exhibit and moves a lever at the opening of the tube entrance, and a new entryway to the tube maze is revealed. As the child puts a yellow scarf near the new opening, an air current moves the scarf into a new pathway. Children begin passing scarves to the front and excitement abounds when the children see that their scarves are taking a new path through the tube maze.

The Sun Tubes exhibit exemplifies the term *hands-on learning* within a children's museum setting. Children's museums are one type of museum environment where adults and children have come to expect hands-on experiences, but in practice, many museum environments encourage visitors to experience exhibits in a variety of ways. Hands-on-learning has become synonymous with children's use of manipulatives and object-centered learning activities in schools and in museum settings but it can involve much more than the mere physical manipulation of objects. In early childhood classrooms, children typically encounter materials because a teacher has put them at a learning center or, in some cases, children can choose materials from a shelf or area in the classroom. In museums, hands-on experiences are presented in the form of exhibits and are designed to encourage young children and adults to engage their cognitive capacities for rich, *minds-on learning* at their own pace.

At the turn of the 20th century, John Dewey argued that for society to flourish and for individuals to help society thrive, the educational experiences offered needed to be engaging and exciting, and had to foster curiosity and, perhaps most important, a desire to continue learning (Dewey, 1902, 1916, 1938). A century after Dewey emphasized the importance of experiential education as a way of life, cultural, historical, arts, science, and play-based museums stand at the educational forefront, poised to engage children and families in experiential learning. Experiential-learning theory highlights the central role of *experience* in the learning process (Kolbe, 1984). Placing primary importance on experience in learning brings the child and notions of playful, engaging learning to the forefront. In this regard, informal learning environments provide young children with the unrivaled opportunity to choose what, when, and how to engage and learn in an environment specifically designed to embody playful learning experiences. The variety of experiences encountered in one visit to a museum encourages all children to engage in firsthand explorations in a playful and memorable manner. Museums reveal treasures of antiquity; display the images, sounds, and experiences of ancient worlds and those only imagined; re-create the skeletal forms of extinct creatures that once walked our planet; and introduce or remind us of the many visual and auditory wonders of the present day. The visitor-centered approaches of contemporary museums invite children and adults to learn and experience in ways never before promoted within these dynamic spaces. The museum visitor, whether that person is a child or an adult, is central to the learning experience.

This chapter was written with the goal of expanding information on the pedagogical practices used in a variety of museum environments as they relate to young children. It is my hope that this chapter will serve to strengthen the connections between classroom learning and museum experiences for early childhood educators and students. The focus of the chapter is on making pedagogy come to life for early childhood educators working to incorporate children's experiences in museums into the everyday life of the classroom. Woven throughout the discussions of the conceptual and theoretical foundations of my work are vignettes selected from my observations at a variety of museums throughout the United States. In addition, my conversations with museum staff and educators are captured and presented to provide recommendations for teachers as they plan and implement on-site and virtual museum class visits.

CONTEXTS AND ELEMENTS OF MUSEUM LEARNING

Contemporary conceptions of learning emphasize the contextual nature of learning; a learning experience is always situated within a particular time and place (Lave & Wenger, 1991). Through this lens, learning involves the entirety of the experience and inextricably links the learner and learning environment. Meaningful learning in informal learning environments occurs as a result of individual experience and purposeful interactions within the cultural, historical, arts, science, and play-based learning environments. In these environments, children have opportunities to engage in hands-on experiences that are of a social nature. Contemporary research in the learning sciences supports a view of learning that emphasizes the role of context in learning experiences (Bransford, Brown, & Cocking, 2000) where the learning environment is a key element in the processes of knowledge construction. A rich learning environment is composed of physical, social, contextual, and cultural elements.

Importance of Interaction

Complementary views of learning, such as situated cognition (Roth, 1996; Greeno, 1998), distributed cognition (Cole & Engeström, 1993; Hewitt & Scardamalia, 1998), and sociocultural views of learning (Wertsch, 1991), stress the role of the learning environment through an emphasis on the interactions between learners and between learners and objects. Learning is not simply situated within the walls of the museum or cultural institution; it is distributed across the many elements that make up the learning environment. When individual visitors interact with museum displays, performances, and other people within the setting, they are engaging in the possibilities that exist for constructing new understandings or deepening existing knowledge (Hein, 1995; Jeffery-Clay, 1998). With this lens, the task for adults working with children is to assist them in negotiating their ways of making meaning and negotiating a learning experience (Gardner, 1985), communication (Tharp & Gallimore, 1988), narrative (Engle, 1995/1999; Taylor, 1993), and metaphor (Bruner, 1990).

In addition, it is important to keep in mind that an informal learning environment is in a constant state of flux as new visitors enter and bring their own ideas, understandings, and experiences to the setting. Because of the ever-evolving environment, no visit to a museum or performance center is exactly the same; each visitor has opportunities to craft an individualized experience, engaging as much or as little as he or she desires. Each visitor's motivation is another important aspect of informal learning. During a visit to a museum or a performance event, individuals may employ a variety of motivational processes to guide their experiences and learning. Motivational processes can include engagement in collaborative work, willingness to take on challenges proposed by the environment, and choice-making (Falk & Dierking, 2000).

In a museum setting, the process of knowledge-building is a conscious endeavor that can involve opportunities for problem solving, planning, experimentation, risk-taking, and reflection. Artistic, cultural, scientific, and historical museums support children's thinking skills in a number of ways:

- Providing school groups with docents and museum guides who can scaffold the experience in meaningful, developmentally appropriate ways
- Building on-site experiences that provide children with opportunities to practice relevant skills in such a way that all children achieve a measure of success
- Developing exhibits that provide visitors with visual, auditory, or tactile information so that they can successfully engage and be motivated to explore in greater depth
- Promoting opportunities for social interaction among museum visitors and staff centered around exhibits so that every visitor has opportunities to question, explore, elaborate, and reflect

Hallmarks of the museum experience—exploration of objects, opportunities to learn based on learner interests, opportunities for discovery and/or construction of meaning, and visitor-initiated activities—are routinely utilized in the educational programming of museum and cultural institutions. These environments are social in nature as visitors move between exhibits and interact with the artifacts, objects, or exhibits. The degree of interaction is determined by each individual visitor, but opportunities for discovery are available to anyone willing to engage, explore, and experience.

In museum environments, the approach to learning can require children to be physically active and to use their developing communication skills. Young children in informal settings can be engaged in active, self-directed discovery learning, or they can be engaged in a listening and looking experience. The exact approach will vary by setting, so it is important for the classroom teacher to determine the degree of discovery orientation that is best suited to each particular group of children. The educational philosophy guiding museum educational programming varies according to the affordances and aims of each particular site; however, a visitor-centered approach with young children typically draws from established educational philosophies and practices addressing the needs of the whole child and emphasizing the diverse abilities of children (Copple &

Bredekamp, 2009; Edwards, Gandini, & Forman, 2011; Gardner, 1985, 2006; Piaget, 1962; Vygotsky, 1978). These practices serve to encourage young museum visitors to become independent, self-directed learners.

Capturing Flight: A Museum Experience

The following vignette features the photographic efforts of a small group of preschoolers on their class trip to the Smithsonian National Air and Space Museum in Washington, D.C. In preparation for the preschool's class visit, Ms. Brown, the class teacher, recruited numerous parent and school volunteers to work with the 4- and 5-year-old students. This small-group approach enabled the children to move through the museum in small groups with their adult volunteer under the supervision of Ms. Brown.

PHOTOGRAPHING THE RED RACER

As Emma, Nicole, Griffin, and Cullen prepare to take a self-guided tour of the museum's flight galleries, Nicole's mom, Rebecca, asks the group what they plan to photograph today. Griffin quickly responds, "Fighter planes. I know there are fighter jets here." Emma quickly adds, "Just airplanes, all kinds of airplanes." The preschool class came to the museum armed with digital cameras to document the experience as part of their long-term project study of transportation. Cameras were shared by the small groups throughout the trip. The group decides that Griffin can be first to take a photograph as he quickly spots "a red fighter jet" housed in the Golden Age of Flight exhibit (http://airandspace.si.edu/collections/artifact.cfm?id=A19550104000). The group gathers underneath as Griffin captures the image of a Wittman Chief Oshkosh/Buster aircraft. Griffin shares his image on the camera screen, while Rebecca reads the name of the aircraft with the children. When she shares that the plane was a racer back in the 1930s and 1940s, Griffin responds by saying the plane "must have been the fastest of all because it is red, and red is very fast."

The group winds its way through the flight galleries, stopping to photograph planes that catch the eye of one of the children or Rebecca. As they are making their way through the *Legend, Memory and the Great War in the Air* exhibit, Griffin brings the group's attention to "another racer" that he's found. He points enthusiastically to a brightly painted aircraft hanging high above the group, the Albatros D.Va (http://airandspace.si.edu/collections/artifact.cfm?id=A19500092000). Rebecca asks why he thinks the plane is a racer. Cullen quickly points out that it has a propeller on the front like Griffin's "red racer." Nicole asks Rebecca to "read it to us," pointing to the information placard near the plane as Griffin takes the camera to capture the image of this new. Rebecca informs the group that this plane is even older than the red racer, and the children look closely at the captured image Griffin displays on the camera screen. Emma notes that this plane has a pattern on the wings so it "just doesn't look like a racer." "Well, you are on to something because it says here that this plane was really used during a war," states Rebecca. "Oh yeah, it just looks like it had to go fast but not as fast as a racer," Griffin replies. Rebecca suggests scrolling backwards on the camera to find the red racer image so that the group can see what is the same or different between the planes. The kids carefully peer between the red racer image and the Albatros D.Va, noting differences in color and size and similarities in structure (propeller, tires, and wings).

Following their museum visit, Griffin and his classmates returned to their classroom to download the images each group captured during the visit. The children used the images to extend their study of planes and flight by a point of research for the class as they explored the various types of aircraft used in human flight.

The experiences of Rebecca's group highlight the visual, aesthetic, and play-based nature of minds-on explorations that can occur during child-led interactions within a historical museum setting. The children in Rebecca's group followed their collective interests during their visit and worked together to build new ideas and understanding, thus making the children and their interests and ideas central to the museum experience. Prior to the class visit, Ms. Brown shared information with parent volunteers about the purpose of the class trip and emphasized that she hoped the children would take the lead in the exploration and documentation of their museum experience.

The vignette also illustrates how an experience in a hands-on learning environment taps into a multitude of experiential components and content areas, bringing to life the idea of an informal, teachable moment. The children's explorations were aided by the additional scaffolding tool, the digital camera, which served to support children's learning during the museum visit—in many ways slowing down their movement through the exhibit and enabling the children to "see" more deeply. Ms. Brown's original intention was to use the images captured during the field trip once the students returned to their classroom, but the cameras also helped scaffold children's observations during their visit.

CONCEPTUALIZING LEARNING IN THE MUSEUM

Learning experiences in cultural, historical, arts, science, and play-based museums can provide children with unique experiences to support their efforts to develop new information-gathering strategies, make observations, and build new ideas and understandings. In museums, learning tasks are often embedded in an inextricable way to the exhibit materials and experiences. As the experiences of Rebecca's group demonstrate, interacting with museum exhibits can be playful and inquisitive for all visitors. Though playful learning, these environments support young learners as they build language, social, creative, and cognitive skills. Museums also provide exciting possibilities for bringing children, parents, caregivers, and community members together to explore and learn in new ways.

Connections to Community

Early childhood teachers interested in utilizing museums environments as a part of the curriculum will find a wealth of expertly designed resources to support children's learning in a variety of content areas. These environments frequently offer teacher and classroom resources at no cost to educators working with young children. These resources have been carefully designed to promote age-appropriate content information based upon the recommendations and guidelines set forth in national, state, and early learning standards. Teacher and classroom resources are often designed around collections on display at the museum or feature exhibits or performances that travel from site to site around the globe. Drawing upon the wealth of information available from virtual or on-site cultural resources in the classroom is an important part of opening the doors of the community to all children.

Connecting to the community allows children to see beyond the walls of the classroom and links them to the unique learning opportunities available from museums and galleries. Because of cost, transportation issues, or family interests, many children do not have opportunities to visit their community's cultural resources outside of school-based visits. Bringing students to museums or bringing the museum to the children through virtual access allows teachers to integrate content knowledge, principles of experiential education, and cultural equity in the classroom to extend and bring meaning to educational experiences for all young learners.

Successful out-of-school learning opportunities in museum environments require careful planning and preparation by the classroom teacher and the institution. A great deal of time and effort goes into planning education and school experiences in museums. Museums receive approximately 55 million visits each year from students in school groups and also spend more than $2 billion a year on education activities; the typical museum devotes three-quarters of its education budget to K–12 students (American Alliance of Museums, n.d.). A carefully planned field trip can be engaging, educational, and fun whether the destination is a museum, performance venue, or a zoo. Learning to plan rewarding out-of-school experiences that facilitate and deepen classroom learning requires classroom teachers to expand their own understandings of when learning occurs and what learning looks like. Traditional understandings of teaching and learning become blurred when children and teachers learn and experience new concepts together in museums and other out-of-school settings.

Experience as Teacher

Informal learning experiences often arise out of the activities and interests of individuals and groups, but in forms not typically seen as traditional learning experiences. In informal settings, learning activities are flexible and may include hands-on experiences, discussion, presentations, and exploration. These activities are often provided in response to the specific needs and interests of a particular person or group. For example, when a group of preschoolers was touring the Denver Art Museum's American Indian collection, the class asked many "why" questions about the animals featured in the works of art. The "why" questions included inquiries about the location, color, and shape of those animals, as well as questions about animals that didn't appear in the collection artworks. The museum educator responded to the group's questions by providing information at a level appropriate for the children and encouraged the children to seek out more animal shapes as they continued their explorations of the art. Perhaps another group of children would have been more interested in the materials used in the creation of the artworks, asking the docent "what" questions instead of "why" questions. "What" questions could focus on the types of media used in an artwork or about the process of art-making. Educators at informal learning sites are skilled at responding to a wide spectrum of children's questions, comments, and curiosities but also rely on the classroom teacher to provide information to the museum staff about the needs of their individual group of students.

Classroom teachers can adopt the idea of child as central to the learning experience and take the lessons learned from a museum visit back into the classroom. At both the Children's Museum of Richmond's Sun Tubes exhibit and the Smithsonian National Air and Space Museum flight galleries, children were engaged in experiential learning that captured their minds and imagination bringing to life the concept of experience as teacher. The exhibit itself functions as a teacher—capturing children's attention, encouraging them to question what they know or are coming to know, and providing endless opportunities to question and explore. These ideas can be brought back to the classroom and put into action as teachers work to develop lessons and experiences for their students that build upon the hallmarks of high-quality museum experiences:

- Exploration of objects
- Opportunities to learn based on learner interests

- Opportunities for discovery and/or construction of meaning
- Visitor-initiated activities

The key to developing this approach within the classroom is to design learning experiences featuring media, artifacts, and materials that allow for exploration and learning at many levels.

VIRTUAL MUSEUM VISITS

Although this chapter focuses primarily on on-site museum experiences, many opportunities exist for children to explore museums virtually from their own classrooms or homes. The virtual world can, at various times, be exciting, intriguing, engaging, confusing, and overwhelming (see also Chapter 9, this volume). So, how can we introduce young children to virtual museum sites that build upon the strengths of the Internet while minimizing many of the challenges? One of the biggest benefits of virtual engagement is the opening of classroom doors to people and cultures across the globe. In recent years, many museums have developed digital programming for young children. The programming can be found on museum and gallery websites under resources for teachers, students, and families. The addition of virtual programming for young children is especially timely as limitations in school travel budgets for field trips are becoming more prevalent (Sabol, 2010).

Through high-quality programming and wide-reaching accessibility, the virtual museum stands to become the primary space for exposure to the world's artists and artworks. Using visitor-centered, active-learning designs, virtual sites have the potential to scaffold the youngest museum visitors' experiences with the visual arts. Virtual visitors can spend time planning for future visits and exploring artworks in the museum's collections. Virtual art learning environments are emerging spaces where museums are encouraging young children to interact, explore, and play with the visual arts, in a sense, promoting wonder and inquiry of the larger world of art. Well-designed, thoughtful virtual art learning sites afford unique opportunities for the young child, and adults who work with children, to explore the world of art and visual artists from their homes or school classrooms.

Museum Websites as a Learning Environment

Just like any learning environment, museum websites can vary considerably in quality. It is important for teachers to preview any site that will be accessible to children to ensure that both the content and approach to interaction are well suited to the students. The website should be "usable" for children and should balance high-quality images with limited text.

Young children enjoy interactive websites that encourage their participation through game play. For example, the Getty Museum's *Getty Games* website allows children to choose an artwork from the collection to turn into a puzzle that they can solve. Once the artwork is chosen, the child can choose the number of pieces they want to work with for their puzzle game. Many museum websites will allow children to print images or designs they encountered during their site visit. The National Gallery of Art's *Art Zone* allows children to explore and create a variety of artworks through an interactive design experience. Each piece created on *Art Zone* can be saved as a digital image or immediately printed as a paper copy.

In Figure 8.1 is a brief listing of 10 exceptional museum-based children's websites. Each website engages children through games and provides appropriate content information for early childhood students.

Virtual museum websites have the potential to bridge longstanding issues of access and help students and teachers transcend traditional barriers of time, location, or lack of funding to support broad exposure to museum experiences for all students. However, the sights, smells, sounds, and feel of a museum are not re-created in a virtual environment. Viewing two-dimensional, digital reproductions of multidimensional works of art or artifacts

**Figure 8.1: A Sampling of Museum-Based Virtual Websites
for Young Children**

- American Museum of Natural History—*Ology:* http://www.amnh.org/explore/ology
- Baltimore Museum of Art—*Matisse for Kids:* http://www.artbma.org/flash/F_conekids.swf
- The British Museum—*Museum Explorers:* http://www.britishmuseum.org/explore/young_explorers-1/discover/museum_explorer.aspx
- Denver Art Museum—*Wacky Kids:* http://www.wackykids.org/
- Getty Museum—*Getty Games:* http://www.getty.edu/gettygames/
- Museum of Modern Art—*Destination Modern Art:* http://www.moma.org/interactives/destination/
- National Gallery of Art—*Art Zone:* http://www.nga.gov/kids/zone/zone.htm
- The Science Museum of Minnesota—*Disease Detectives:* http://www.diseasedetectives.org/
- The Smithsonian—*Smithsonian Latino Center's Kids Corner:* http://latino.si.edu/KidsCorner/
- The Smithsonian—*Encyclopedia Smithsonian:* http://www.si.edu/Encyclopedia/Search/Kids%20Favorites

can result in the loss of key visual and aesthetic information, as variances in color, size, and texture may not translate clearly in the digital image. Although some museums have invested in advanced virtual imaging for key collection works, allowing the visitor to digitally handle the objects or view them in a 360-degree manner, the vast majority of digital objects are nonmanipulative, two-dimensional images. Ideally, students will have opportunities to experience both on-site and virtual modalities to enrich and inform their understandings. If using museum websites as a stand-alone experience, teachers will need to attend to issues of media, size, color, and texture with students as they explore to ensure that the students are developing grounded understandings of the artworks.

In the vignette that follows, a pair of kindergarten students explore a virtual museum website prior to an onsite class field trip. The vignette explores the use of a website prior to an onsite visit as a means to build students' prior knowledge and curiosity about their upcoming trip.

NAMING SCULPTURES: VIRTUAL EXPLORATIONS IN ART

Colby and Braden sit side by side in front of a computer screen playing a matching game designed by their kindergarten teacher. Their objective is to take a virtual walk through the online collection of outdoor sculptures at the Nelson-Atkins Museum of Art in Kansas City, Missouri. The class will be visiting the museum in a week and walking through the on-site Sculpture Park with more than 30 outdoor sculptures.

Colby and Braden are working together to give descriptive names to five images of sculptures on the museum website. The images, selected by their teacher, draw the children's attention to the shape, color, materials, and size of the five sculptures. Together, the boys have created names for four of the sculptures and are deciding on a name for a large bronze statue. The work they are examining, *Two-Piece Reclining Figure No. 9* (Henry Spencer Moore, 1968), is a large figural sculpture composed of two separate parts (http://nelson-atkins.org/collections/iscroll-objectview.cfm?id=10305). Colby notes that the statue looks like it's *lying down* as Braden clicks the online image to get a full-size view. Colby looks over the large image and points out the roundness of the piece. Braden pauses clicking for a moment to look at the posted image. Once satisfied with Colby's assessment, his attention turns back to the screen. After a moment, Braden suggests *Robot Sleeping,* and Colby quickly agrees. With shouts of "We're finished!" the pair draws their teacher's attention over to the computer area. After the boys talk about their titles, their teacher tells them what the artists actually named the sculptures that they will soon have the opportunity to see in person.

RECOMMENDATIONS FROM MUSEUM EDUCATORS

Colby, Braden, and all their classmates had the opportunity to virtually explore sculptures, which helped to support their later, on-site visit to the Nelson-Atkins Museum of Art. The virtual exploration of museum collections is one way to prepare children for their museum experience. In this section, museum professionals from around the United States share some suggestions to help teachers and parents make the most out of every museum experience. Advance preparation for visits is recommended by museum professionals and is seen as a major factor in the success of a trip to a museum or gallery. For example, at the High Museum of Art in Atlanta, museum educators advocate that early childhood teachers take some time before a museum visit to prepare children for the activities they will experience. In addition, showing the children a few images from the collection prior to the visit will help the children begin a conversation about the artworks in the familiarity and comfort of their classrooms. For tours with a specific focus, such as the High's Dikenga Tour and Workshop of West African artworks, it is recommended that teachers spend previsit time introducing background information on related cultures and traditions. Having advance knowledge of the museum's works can help support the connections children make during their tour.

Advance preparation can also help students become familiar and more comfortable with the sights and sounds of the museum before they arrive. At the Peabody Museum of Archaeology and Ethnology on the campus of Harvard University, visitors can watch welcome videos and videos featuring different collections on the museum's YouTube channel, http://www.youtube.com/user/peabodyharvard. Museum educators from the Peabody note that teachers who've used the YouTube videos report that they like being able to show their students spaces they will be visiting in advance of the on-site visit. Teachers can also share links to museum videos or YouTube channels with parents as a means to strengthen home-school connections.

Museum educators at the Museum of Modern Art (MOMA) in New York City recognize the challenge that many teachers and parents feel when they enter into a conversation about an artwork with a child. The MOMA has developed materials and tours that give teachers, students, and families a positive experience in the museum so they have ownership over their conversations about art, but the experiences are all based on interaction. In museum experiences at MOMA and other institutions that include studio time, adults are encouraged to work in parallel with the children, creating their own works of art in the studio or working together as a group to create a work of art. The emphasis of joint studio and gallery experiences is not to master a particular media or skill but to focus on the collection as inspiration and then to further explore those ideas in the studio.

Although visual art museums have long been focused on sharing works of art and their historical and cultural contexts, a visitor-centered approach allows museums to expand the reach of their focus. For example, museum educators at the Denver Art Museum are interested in exploring creativity. Specifically, the museum educators used the construct of creativity to design new programs for children and adults as well as web-based resources for teachers. As a result of their focus, the Denver Art Museum launched a comprehensive teacher resource website, *Creativity Resource for Teachers* (http://creativity.denverart-museum.org/), which presents lesson plans for early childhood, elementary, and secondary students. Each lesson plan is centered on an image from the museum's permanent collection and is designed to promote creative thinking as well as content-specific knowledge in the visual arts and language arts. Engagement with artworks in a museum and in the classroom builds critical cognitive, artistic, aesthetic, and creative thinking skills. Museums and galleries can be a great resource for classroom teachers as they work to bring the arts into the life of the classroom.

Communication is key to a successful on-site visit at a children's museum, according to staff at the Children's Museum of the Upstate (TCMU) in Greenville, South Carolina. Staff working with the booking and planning of school and class visits stress the importance of teachers asking questions as they make plans for the class trip. In particular, if any students have specific needs, the museum should be informed at the time of booking so a customized experience can be planned for the class. In addition, TCMU staff encourage teachers to take the time to read the previsit materials provided by the museum at booking and on the website and to follow up with the museum contact, listed in the preparation materials, before the day of the class visit. All chaperones and parent volunteers need to know that coming to a children's museum is a unique experience where chaperones and children will play side by side.

Tips for Teachers Planning a Museum or Gallery Visit

The comments of museum educators to teachers can be summarized as follows:

- When considering a museum visit, you should explore the museum's website to look at program options and get familiar with the museum collection.
- Programming for young children in large museums can typically be found on the museum website under the departments of School Programs or Family Programs.
- Most programming at the early childhood level will be focused on the elements of art and will work toward the encouragement of art-viewing skills.
- On-site museum programming may include a self-guided gallery tour, a gallery tour with a docent, or a combination of a gallery tour

and studio time, so be sure to select a tour that addresses the skills and experiences you wish to address.

- Gallery tours will typically focus on works in the permanent collection. If you'd like access to a special collection, be sure to inquire at the time you make reservations.
- Some programming for children may include access to the museum's studio classrooms for an art-making experience.

An important element of planning a trip to a museum or gallery is making decisions about the parent or adult volunteers needed for the trip. The number of adult volunteers needed for a museum or gallery trip will depend upon the needs of the students in each particular class. In addition, it is important to consider the experiences planned for the field trip. How long will the children be at the museum? Will there be an accompanying art-making experience in the museum studios? How many galleries will the students visit at the museum?

Answers to these questions will help determine how to plan for the necessary numbers of adult volunteers. In order to have a successful field trip, advance preparation of field trip volunteers is also an important consideration. A few areas to consider talking to all volunteers about prior to the trip are:

- Number of children each volunteer will be responsible for during the trip
- Behavior expectations for children during the trip
- Ideas for quieting and attention cues
- Expectations for small- and whole-group meeting times
- Emergency travel kits and plans

Tips for Talking About Appropriate Museum Behavior with Young Children

Museums are extraordinary places with irreplaceable treasures, so every visitor must take special care in treating the museum space with respect. Although museums welcome young children to come and explore visual media and artifacts, there are a few universal rules for appropriate museum behavior that both children and adults should be familiar with.

- *Explore with your eyes.* Please don't touch the objects or even get too close. Artworks and artifacts need to be protected from the dirt and natural oils that are on everyone's hands.
- *Stay together.* Please walk carefully and always stay with your group/ class.

- *Ask before taking photographs.* Not all exhibits can be photographed, so ask ahead and always remember to take photos with the flash off to help preserve delicate images and artifacts.
- *Pencils only.* Some museums will allow visitors to sketch in their galleries; check ahead to see if children can carry paper and pencils. Pens or markers should not be brought into any gallery space.

The temptation to touch gallery artworks or artifacts can be overwhelming for young children who have a natural desire to learn through touch. Providing young children with a task during their gallery visit can help children be successful in the gallery and curb the urge to touch the displayed objects. An easy addition to any museum visit is to have the children make viewfinders or observation glasses to take with them to their museum visit. These props serve two functions: They keep children's hands busy during their gallery tour and they help focus children's attention and observations. A viewfinder can be made by cutting a rectangle into a small piece of heavy cardstock or cardboard. Observation glasses can be made by attaching two cardboard tubes together and fastening a neck strap out of string. The use of props will promote appropriate gallery behaviors and create a fun, engaging environment for all students, encouraging them to attend to the many sites and sounds of the museum.

CONCLUDING THOUGHTS

Museums of every genre can be an important component of children's educational lives. Museums are charged with the task of collecting, preserving, exhibiting, and interpreting works of art, historical and scientific objects and events, as well as music, dance, and theatrical performances. These environments are designed to encourage engagement in interactive, dynamic learning experiences that are markedly different from the highly scripted lessons used in many classroom settings. Because of the nontraditional nature of teaching and learning in museum settings, teachers may begin to question the nature of learning in such spaces:

- What does learning look like?
- When does learning occur?
- What is the teacher's role in learning?
- What are outcomes of student learning in informal settings?
- What do tangible artifacts of student learning look like?

Each question is important for teachers to consider throughout the planning, preparation, implementation, and postvisit follow-up experiences connected to a museum visit. As the vignettes featured in this chapter demonstrate, children's experiences with museums are rich with possibilities for learning. Museum environments—both those especially for children and those with other audiences in mind, but that children can still access—are designed around particular goals. These goals are connected to attracting viewers and drawing them into the exhibit or artwork. In a museum, artworks, artifacts, and materials are displayed very deliberately, with expressed intentions for the visitor experience. The museum environment is carefully planned so that visitors of all ages, experience, and knowledge levels can engage with the exhibit in a personally relevant way. Classroom teachers can adopt this intentional approach to the learning environment by carefully considering the materials, lesson goals, and scaffolding provided within the classroom setting as children learn from and with the art, artifacts, and objects in their world.

Discussion Questions

- Which cultural, historical, arts, science, and play-based museum environments are located in your area? Do those environments have a website or online presence that you can access for resources?
- Looking at your long-range curricular plans, can you identify a time when a visit to a museum or gallery would complement the in-class curricula?
- What resources do you need to make an on-site or virtual visit a reality in your classroom?
- What are the most important planning elements to consider as you plan for an on-site museum visit with young children?
- In what ways is the approach to the visitor learning experience in museums similar or different from the approach to learning in your classroom?

REFERENCES

American Alliance of Museums. (n.d.). *About museums.* Available at aam-us.org

Bransford, J. D., Brown, A. L., & Cocking, R. R. (2000). *How people learn: Brain, mind, experience, and school.* Washington, DC: National Academies Press.

Bruner, J. S. (1990). *Acts of meaning.* Cambridge, MA: Harvard University Press.

Cole, M., & Engeström, Y. (1993). A cultural-historical approach to distributed cognition. *Distributed cognitions: Psychological and educational considerations,* 1–46.

Copple, C., & Bredekamp, S. (2009). *Developmentally appropriate practice in early childhood programs serving children from birth through age 8.* Washington, DC: National Association for the Education of Young Children.

Dewey, J. (1902). *The child and the curriculum* (No. 5). Chicago, IL: University of Chicago Press.

Dewey, J. (1916). *Democracy and education.* New York, NY: Macmillan.

Dewey, J. (1938). *Education and experience.* New York, NY: Macmillan.

Edwards, C., Gandini, L., & Forman, G. (Eds.). (2011). *The hundred languages of children: The Reggio Emilia experience in transformation.* Westport, CT: Ablex Publishing.

Falk, J. H., & Dierking, L. D. (2000). *Learning from museums: Visitor experiences and the making of meaning.* Lanham, MD: Altamira Press.

Gardner, H. (2006). *Multiple intelligences: New horizons.* New York, NY: Basic Books.

Greeno, J. G. (1998). The situativity of knowing, learning, and research. *American Psychologist, 53*(1), 5.

Hein, G. E. (1995). Evaluating teaching and learning in museums. In E. Hooper-Greenhill (Ed.), *Museum: Media: Message,* (pp. 189–203). London, UK: Routledge.

Hewitt, J., & Scardamalia, M. (1998). Design principles for distributed knowledge building processes. *Educational Psychology Review, 10*(1), 75–96.

Jeffery-Clay, K. R. (1998). Constructivism in museums: How museums create meaningful learning environments. *The Journal of Museum Education, 23*(1), 3–7.

Kolbe, D. A. (1984). *Experiential learning.* Upper Saddle River, NJ: Prentice-Hall.

Lave, J., & Wenger, E. (1991). *Situated learning: Legitimate peripheral participation.* Cambridge, UK: Cambridge University Press.

Piaget, J. P. (1962). *The language and thought of the child.* London, UK: Routledge.

Roth, W. M. (1996). Art and artifact of children's designing: A situated cognition perspective. *The Journal of the Learning Sciences, 5*(2), 129–166.

Sabol, R. (2010). *No Child Left Behind: A study of its impact on art education.* Reston, VA: National Art Education Foundation.

Tharp, R. G., & Gallimore, R. (1988). Rousing minds to life: Teaching, learning, and schooling in social context. *Cambridge University Press, 10,* 248.

Wertsch, J. V. (1991). *Voices of the mind: Sociocultural approach to mediated action.* Cambridge, MA: Harvard University Press.

Vygotsky, L. S. (1978). *Mind in society: The development of higher mental process.* Cambridge, MA: Harvard University Press.

CHAPTER 9

Think Before You Immerse

A Framework for Examining Virtual Environments for Children

Laura Beals

I start this chapter with a confession: Writing about technology for children is not an easy task, especially in a relatively short chapter such as this. Innovations in technology are moving at such a fast pace that what is current right now will be outdated perhaps in as little as a few months. In addition, there are many types of technology for children, each of which could be a chapter in itself. I do know, however, that it is essential to provide readers with a chapter about digital environments because so many children are exposed to technology on a daily basis—both in their homes and at school—as tablets, smartphones, digital toys, and computers become ubiquitous. To this point, Shuler (2007) writes:

> From virtual penguins to video games, there are a plethora of digital products on the market that target a new generation of digital natives—children growing up immersed in media that shape the way they live and learn. . . . Experts have documented and parents believe that the new interactive media developed largely in the past decade represent a vital opportunity to leverage children's interests to expand their skills and knowledge, but major concerns with the current market's overall quality, developmental appropriateness, and educational value persist. (p. 6)

I have decided to address these challenges in two ways. First, I will focus on a specific type of technology—virtual worlds. Virtual worlds allow children to simultaneously be present "in real life" while also immersing themselves in virtual environments. Why the focus on virtual worlds? KZero Worldswide—a consulting company that specializes in the virtual world, massively multiplayer online gaming, and social gaming sectors–produces a virtual world universe chart, segmented by target age, which is updated quarterly, and posted on their website (http://www.kzero.co.uk/universe-chart/). A few "stats" will help paint a picture of the prevalence of virtual worlds for children:

- KZero reported in 2012 that in the fourth quarter of 2011 there were 1.7 billion registered accounts in virtual worlds, 340 million were from virtual worlds targeted at children between the ages of 5 and 10 years (those for children ages 10 to 15 years had 787 million registered accounts). Of these 340 million accounts, 34% were from North American, 33% from Western Europe, 16% from Eastern Europe, 8% from South American, 6% from Asia, and 3% from other.
- More recently, according to KZero (2013), the top five largest virtual worlds for children under 10 had a combined total of over 600 million registered accounts in Quarter 3 of 2013, reflecting a growth of several hundred million new registered users between 2011 and 2013.
- In addition, KZero indicates that in the third quarter of 2013, the largest virtual world for children under 10 years old, Club Penguin, had 220 million registered users, having added 20 million accounts since the first quarter of 2013 (KZero Worldswide, n.d.). Their universe chart for this quarter also shows an additional five virtual world having more than one million. By comparison, the largest virtual world for adults (over age 20) has "only" 100 million users (Mitham, 2013).

Taken together, this small sampling of statistics related to children's use of virtual worlds indicates that there are, and will continue to be, many children for whom virtual worlds can provide an important environment for the development of their social, emotional, and cognitive skills, just as classrooms and playgrounds do. Sherry Turkle, a professor and the director of the Initiative on Technology and Self at the Massachusetts Institute of Technology, noted, "For young people, there is rather a kind of fluid boundary between the real and virtual world, and they can easily pass through it" (Richtel & Stone, 2007). Educators should be aware of children's use of virtual worlds so that they can better understand how this technology can be leveraged as a tool in their classrooms and be aware of the types of experiences their students may be engaged in at home.

The second way in which I am going to address the challenge is that I will not feature or highlight specific virtual worlds in this chapter. Instead, I will discuss virtual worlds in general as another environment in which children can learn and develop, providing criteria that both teachers and parents can use to reflect upon when deciding whether to use virtual worlds in their classrooms and homes. Finally, although virtual worlds can provide new means for children to learn, support their development in ways never before imagined, and connect them to other children instantly, they also raise new challenges for children's safety, privacy, and health. I will weave a discussion of these concerns throughout the chapter as well as conclude with some specific cautions about virtual worlds. Unlike the authors of other chapters in this book, I offer discussion questions at the ends of sections instead of at the end of the chapter. In sum, the three main goals of the chapter are:

1. To define select key terms regarding virtual world environments so that parents and educators have the vocabulary to talk about, think critically, and further their understanding of this technology.
2. To describe a framework of seven attributes to consider and key questions to ask when selecting and implementing a virtual world environment in a classroom or home setting—attributes that can also be applied to other forms of media and technology.
3. To provide resources where educators and parents can learn more about virtual world environments and technology more broadly.

KEY TERMS FOR UNDERSTANDING VIRTUAL WORLDS

Highlighting key terms is important both for framing further discussion throughout the chapter and for providing educators and parents with the terminology to use when, for example, thinking about implementation in a classroom, deciding whether a child should participate in a virtual world, or searching for additional information on the topic outside of this chapter.

Virtual Worlds

Virtual worlds are most broadly defined as computer-based simulated environments (Association of Virtual Worlds, 2010). The following definition explains virtual worlds more specifically as:

> Sites and applications that provide users with an online environment for interaction and socialization, typically through customizable avatars. Virtual worlds may include games, but are not games themselves. Typically, the virtual world is a graphically rendered 2-D or 3-D environment. Virtual worlds are distinct from massively multiplayer online games (MMOGs) such as World of Warcraft and from social network sites such as Facebook or MySpace. (Williamson, 2009, p. 2)

As described in the above definition, current graphical virtual worlds are often 3D, allowing graphical representations of the users, called avatars, to move around the environment and interact with other avatars. The first virtual worlds, which appeared in the late 1970s, were text-based (Damer, 2008; Glaser, 2007; Rheingold, 1993)—a user had to be able to read, write, and navigate only with words, in addition to understanding how to operate a complex computer system with an Internet connection. In 1986, one of the first two-dimensional graphically-based virtual worlds, called Habitat, was released by LucasFilm Games (Damer, 2008; Glaser, 2007), but it was still heavily text-based, especially for communication between users. These limitations meant that young children were not able to participate in virtual worlds.

Over the next 20 years, advances in computer hardware and programming capabilities resulted in the creation of more and more advanced graphical worlds. However, it was not until the early 2000s that Linden Labs released Second Life, one of the most well-known virtual worlds at the time. The media fury that surrounded the release of Second Life resulted in a surge of popularity of virtual worlds and a sense that they could be an important marketing and commercial platform. Even more recently, advances in Internet browsers, touchscreens, and mobile devices have significantly reduced the barriers to accessing virtual worlds, especially by young children. Young children now have the opportunity to participate in virtual worlds in ways that were not even conceivable 10 years ago.

Virtual worlds are not games. Richard Bartle (2004), creator of one of the first virtual worlds, writes that "even the ones written to *be* games aren't games. People can play games *in* them, sure, and they can be set up to that end, but this merely makes them venues. The Pasadena Rose Bowl is a stadium, not a game" (p. 282). He goes onto clarify that "virtual worlds are *places*. They may simulate abstractions of reality; they may be operated as a service; creating them may be an art; people may visit them to play games. Ultimately, though, they're just a set of locations" (p. 282).

Stand-Alone Virtual Worlds Versus Virtual World Programs

I believe that it is important to distinguish between what I call "stand-alone" virtual worlds and virtual world programs. I define *stand-alone virtual worlds* as worlds in which any child could find the virtual world on the Internet and request access—the world is not tied to or limited by a particular organization, such as a school or after-school program. Stand-alone virtual worlds are what a child would most likely access from home; however, teachers should still be aware of their existence in order to understand what their students may be experiencing during out-of-school time.

Virtual world programs, on the other hand, are those that are incorporated as tools in environments for children, such as classrooms. There are, and have been, several programs that do use virtual worlds as tools in classrooms, hospitals, and after-school settings—albeit for older children—including Indiana University's *Quest Atlantis* (Barab, Thomas, Dodge, Carteaux, & Tuzun, 2005), Harvard University's and Arizona State's *River City* (Dede, Ketelhut, Clarke, Nelson, & Bowman, 2005), and Tufts University's *Zora* (Bers, Beals, Chau, Satoh, & Khan, 2010).

Virtual Community

I would like to note that the term *virtual community* is often used in reference to work of this nature and sometimes is used interchangeably with the term *virtual world*, though for our purposes the two are very different. The term *virtual community* does not have a universally accepted definition. Barab, MaKinster, and Scheckler (2004) have described virtual communities as "a persistent, sustained social network of individuals who share and develop an overlapping knowledge base, set of beliefs, values, history, and experiences focused on a common practice and/or mutual enterprise" (p. 55). Virtual worlds are not necessarily virtual communities, and vice versa; for our understanding, virtual worlds *are a specific type of technology with which a virtual community can be formed.*

APPLYING DEVELOPMENTALLY APPROPRIATE PRACTICE TO VIRTUAL WORLDS FOR YOUNG CHILDREN

Virtual worlds are becoming just one more environment of which children today are part. For today's youth, media technologies are an important social variable and . . . physical and virtual worlds are psychologically connected; consequently, the virtual world serves as a playing ground for developmental issues from the physical world. (Subrahmanyam & Greenfield, 2008, p. 124)

As illustrated throughout this book, in the face-to-face world, environments for children are designed to accommodate their particular developmental level and age. A preschool classroom looks very different from an elementary school classroom, which looks different from a middle school classroom, which looks different from a high school classroom. Playgrounds, too, are designed to be best for the age level they are meant to serve. Virtual worlds should be no different—teachers and parents should critically examine virtual world environments to ensure that they are appropriately designed to support children's cognitive, social, and emotional development. As a tool, virtual worlds can support children's development and, as a component of a well-designed and thoughtful curriculum, can provide new opportunities for learning, as described below.

Though the phrase *developmentally appropriate* is one that is hotly debated, especially when combined with the words *practice* or *care* in the context of early childhood education, it is still an important framework for understanding environments for children. In this chapter, *developmentally appropriate* is defined using the National Association for the Education of Young Children's position statement on Developmentally Appropriate Practice (2009): "Practice that promotes young children's optimal learning and development" (p. 16). When applied to virtual worlds, educators and parents should reflect critically on whether a virtual environment supports children's development in an appropriate manner. Just as parents stand behind young children on playground climbing structures or steer them toward appropriately sized playground equipment, parents and educators need to apply the same thinking to virtual environments.

A FRAMEWORK FOR EVALUATING VIRTUAL WORLDS

To aid parents and educators in critically examining virtual environments, I offer a seven-attribute framework, based on the concept of developmentally appropriate design (Beals, 2011; Beals & Bers, 2009, 2010). Each of the seven attributes—purpose, communication, participation, play, artifacts, policies, and adult involvement—corresponds both to the virtual world itself and the real-life environment in which it is accessed. This real-life environment includes not only the physical environment but also the child's developmental trajectory at that point in time. Although these attributes can be applied to a larger context of examining children's environments, when applied to virtual worlds they take on a specific meaning related to what is developmentally appropriate for a particular child or group of children. In each of the sections below, I will provide a brief overview of each attribute and conclude with key questions that educators and parents should think about when deciding to include virtual world technology in their classrooms or homes.

Purpose

The attribute of purpose, at the most general level, refers to the reason, or reasons, why children would want to participate in a virtual world. Purpose also relates to the intent and goals of the program, though these may differ based on audience—for example, a child may believe that the purpose of a virtual world is to play games, but the purpose for the designers may be for children to purchase credits to play the games, resulting in financial gain. Parents and educators should consider whether the virtual world (or part of the world experience) requires payments; for example, some virtual worlds for children are completely free to use, some require payment or the purchase of a toy, and some are a combination (some aspects of the world are free, while others must be paid for). Even if a virtual world seems to be "free," parents and educators should be aware of any underlying marketing or advertising that may be used throughout the world (Common Sense Media, 2013), especially as young children may not be able to recognize advertising in the world. I will address the commercialism inherent in many of today's most popular virtual worlds for children at the end of this chapter.

The purpose of a virtual world may be the development of a virtual community. In general, there are two types of communities that virtual worlds can foster: bridging communities or bonding communities. "Bridging communities" bring together disparate members who have not met in real life, while "bonding communities" reinforce already-established networks of people. The distinction between these two concepts is not dichotomous; rather, it is more of a continuum, because often a community can have aspects of both but may have closer ties to one type (Norris, 2004). For example, one may create a virtual world program whose main purpose is to create a virtual community for children who are being treated for a particular chronic illness (Bers & Cantrell, 2012; Cantrell, Fischer, Bouzaher, & Bers, 2010). A bridging virtual community may be one in which youth experiencing that illness from all over the United States are invited to join, though they may have never met one another. A bonding virtual community, however, may be one in which only patients from a particular hospital who have already been meeting for face-to-face support groups are invited, allowing them to connect outside of the scheduled meetings (Bers, Gonzalez-Heydrich, & DeMaso, 2003).

Educators should consider the types of communities that virtual worlds can support, as a tool for supporting already-established classroom communities. Parents should be aware of the types of communities that are developed within the world and decide whether they are appropriate for their children, in the same way that parents are thoughtful about the types of playgroups in which their children participate. As another perspective, children often form groups based on affinity for a particular tool—for example, children who love to play with building blocks, children who watch a particular TV show, or children who own a particular toy. For young children, engagement with a virtual world can offer an opportunity to create a mindset about being part of a group. Parents and educators need to help children manage their participation in virtual communities—if managed well, there is an opportunity for real community-building in ways that may not have been possible without the use of the virtual world as a tool.

Key Questions

- What are the purposes of a particular virtual world? Who is hosting the world? How is the purpose of this world meeting the needs of my students/children?
- What features of the world are free? What features will require payment?
- What, if any, are the commercial ties of this virtual world?

Communication

The attribute of communication is defined as the means by which participants in the virtual world communicate with one another and with the administrators of the program. Communication can be electronic (e.g., through the virtual world's chat/messaging system, email, messaging-capable artifacts, and so forth), face-to-face (e.g., talk between a team of students in a classroom), or printed (e.g., curriculum materials).

Synchronous versus asynchronous communication. Electronic communication in a virtual world can take many forms depending on the features of the technology itself, but parents and educators should reflect critically about *how* communication occurs and *between whom*. In general, there are two main forms of communication within a virtual environment: synchronous and asynchronous. Synchronous communication occurs when users are online at the same time, as in the case of a chat system. Asynchronous communication occurs when users are not online at the same time; rather, they may, for example, leave messages for one another on bulletin boards or send emails (Preece & Maloney-Krichmar, 2003). Traditionally, means of communication within virtual worlds are text-based. However, depending on the literacy level of the young child using the virtual world, traditional text-based communication mechanisms may not be appropriate. Instead, alternate means of communication are necessary, such as by using symbols to convey feelings (e.g., icons representing different facial expressions), having messages spoken aloud, or using prescribed simple messages that can be read to the child if needed (Marsh, 2011). Virtual worlds can provide new and exciting opportunities to engage in learning both spoken and written words in order to complement real-life literacy learning.

Private versus public communication. Most likely, communication between users will be the most common type of communication, though users may include adult mentors, as described below. Communication can be *public*—when other users can see one another's chat, as in a public room—or *private*—when only the person to whom the communication is directed can see the message. Private communication in a virtual world is typically possible in one of two ways: using a "listening radius" for avatar communication or via private messages. The listening radius corresponds to how far away users can be in the world and still be able to "hear" one another. For example, if there is a small listening radius, users must be very close to one another in order to "hear" chats from the other users. On the other hand, if a very large listening radius is set, then all users, no matter where they are in the world, can "hear" one another.

Educators and parents should be especially cautious about private-communication features in virtual worlds. In many virtual world programs for classrooms, the private messaging feature is by default disabled or can be disabled. As public conversations within the world are considered public, adult mentors and project administrators can easily monitor the content of the conversations, whether in real time (i.e., as the chat is occurring) or after the fact (i.e., by examining the chat logs). Private conversations, however, are not so easily monitored for a variety of reasons. Furthermore, parents and educators should examine the virtual worlds' guidelines (policies) for users regarding expectations for communication—about language use, appropriateness of content, and so on.

Key Questions

- How do users communicate with one another in the virtual world? Is it available in a developmentally appropriate form for my students/children? Is private messaging allowed?
- What are the policies about communication? How is the communication monitored?
- How can you draw parallels between communication in virtual worlds and communication in other environments? How are the communication norms in other environments the same as or different from communication in virtual worlds? How can you help children understand and manage these similarities and differences?

Participation

Parents and educators should also reflect on the openness of the virtual world, as related to purpose. By openness, I mean who is allowed to participate. For example, is participation limited to a certain age? Members of a particular organization (as in the case of a virtual world program)? Members of a particular classroom or school? As you may imagine, the more open the world is, the more need for caution and adult supervision as, for example, it is difficult to confirm virtual identities (i.e., to prove that the person who seems to be a child user is actually a child). In closed situations—especially those tied to real-life environments, such as a classroom—there is a greater likelihood that the online avatars are "who they say they are."

Key Questions

- Who is allowed access to the virtual world?
- How are users' identities confirmed?

Play

> Play is to the child what thinking, planning, and blueprinting are to the adult, a trial universe in which conditions are simplified and methods exploratory, so that past failures can be thought through, expectations tested. (Erikson, 1964, p. 120)

The inclusion of play as a *necessary* attribute of virtual world programs for children is perhaps the most divergent from the literature about adult virtual worlds, as play for children serves a purpose that is very different from that for adults—as shown throughout this book, play is an important means by which children learn and develop. Play is a central aspect of healthy child development and is one of the main features of childhood. Therefore, virtual worlds need to support young children's need to play, with an emphasis on games and make-believe play, as this mimics their real-life cognitive, social, and emotional development.

Play in virtual world programs can take on many forms to support children's development, from interactions with pre-created games to free-form play devised by participants. Young children do not distinguish between "virtual play" and "real play"—to them, play in a virtual world is just an extension of the other forms of play in which they engage (Marsh, 2010). For example, very young children, who are still learning to play with others, cannot be expected to play collaboratively with others, and thus solitary or parallel games (games in which children can see others' progress through the game, but they do not have an impact on one another) should be present. For older preschoolers, games in which they can practice simple collaborative activities should be part of the world. As mentioned earlier, however, educators and parents should be cautious about games and other play opportunities, as they may require payment for all or part of the experience. With play and make-believe such integral components of a child's real-life development, the ability to extend this play to online technologies is one of the unique benefits of virtual worlds. (For more information about children's play in virtual worlds, see Bers, 2008b; Calvert, Strouse, Strong, Huffaker, & Lai, 2009; Kafai & Giang, 2008; Lim & Clark, 2010; Marsh, 2010.)

Key Questions

- What are the ways in which children can play in the virtual world? Are these options developmentally appropriate?
- What is gained and what is lost when children play in virtual worlds versus nonvirtual environments?
- Do any of the play features require payment?

Artifacts

I define artifacts as objects created by the users within the virtual world and/or within the program (i.e., users may create virtual objects or "real-life" objects to supplement the virtual experience). Today's graphic-based virtual worlds provide an outlet for children to share content that they create with others. The concept of constructionism, adapted by Papert (1980) from Piaget's concept of constructivism, asserts that people learn better when they are engaged in building personally meaningful artifacts and sharing them with others in a community. Bers (2008a) identified four pillars of educational experiences related to technology that are designed within a constructionist framework:

1. The potential of technological environments to help learners learn by doing, by actively inquiring, and by playing
2. The importance of objects for supporting the development of concrete ways of thinking and learning about abstract phenomena
3. The need for powerful ideas that span across different areas of the curriculum
4. The premium of self-reflection that engages learners in metacognition

Virtual worlds, when designed appropriately, can provide a unique opportunity for rich constructionist learning through artifact creation.

For young children, the ability to produce complex artifacts may be difficult because of the fine-motor skills needed to manipulate objects in the virtual worlds and the cognitive limitations of their age. However, this does not mean that they cannot create artifacts; it just means that the technology has to support them at a developmentally appropriate level. Children should be able to create objects and share them with others. These artifacts can be created in the following ways:

- Only in the virtual world (e.g., virtual bulletin boards)
- In the real world and showcased in the virtual (e.g., digital artwork)

- In the virtual world and produced in the real world (e.g., a newsletter that showcases aspects of the virtual world, including screenshots, that is then printed and mailed to all participants and their families)
- Only in the real world (e.g., activity worksheets)

In today's technological landscape, there is the potential for overuse of technology. Educators and parents should be thoughtful about "defaulting" to technologically based artifacts. Although new technologies provide unprecedented opportunities for new types of artifacts and manipulatives, this does not mean that building blocks, paintbrushes, or other traditional tools for supporting fine-motor skills should be set aside. Instead, virtual worlds—and the associated digital artifacts that could be created in them—should be part of the larger toolbox, along with traditional manipulatives, to support children's development.

Key Questions

- What types of things can children make in the virtual world?
- What are the possibilities for combining traditional manipulatives with virtual manipulatives? How can traditional and virtual manipulatives complement and support children's experiences?

Policies

Policies are the rules and guidelines for the virtual world and/or program that keep it functioning smoothly and ensure that participants are safe. Just as there are rules to define expected behavior for children in real-life environments, rules should exist in virtual worlds as well. For example, when they start school, children are introduced to a new set of formal rules—rules about classroom procedures, rules about how to do classroom work, rules about relationships with others, and rules about the subject matter (Boostrom, 1991). Parents and educators should review policies of the virtual world, which may be included in the "Terms and Conditions" or other documentation to which a participant may have to agree before joining the world.

If a virtual world program is being used within the context of another organization, educators and parents should be familiar with the host organization's rules and policies. This also relates to the attribute of participation—who can participate in the world will partially dictate the policies that need to be in place in the world. In addition, educators and parents should be familiar with common Internet safety guidelines for children; for example, The National Center for Missing & Exploited Children's *Keeping Kids Safer on the Internet* (2009), the statutes of the Children's Online Privacy Protection Act (COPPA), or the Federal Trade Commission's report to Congress entitled *Virtual Worlds and Kids: Mapping the Risks* (2009). Finally, educators and parents should ensure that children understand the policies in place; policies should be written at a level that children can easily understand and the children should be frequently reminded of the policies.

Next, parents and educators need to consider not just *what* the policies are, but *how* they are going to be monitored within the program. Before beginning in a virtual world, parents and educators should understand the protocols for monitoring the safety of the virtual world and how administrators respond to policy breaches; for example:

- If the world is open to children at all times, how is the communication monitored?
- Are there always adults online monitoring the communication?
- Are the communication records reviewed for policy breaches?
- Is there an automatic filter to "catch" certain key words/phrases?
- How are breaches in policies handled?
- Do users receive a warning?
- Are parents or teachers alerted?
- Can users be ejected or blocked from the virtual world, either for a short "cooling-off" period or, as a final step, permanently?

A summary of these steps should be available for both parents/educators and children to view, so that all involved can clearly understand what is expected and how misbehavior will be addressed within the program.

Key Questions

- What are the policies of the virtual world? How are they enforced?
- Are there other Internet safety guidelines that may be applicable to this experience?

Adult Involvement

Issues of safety bring up questions about the roles of adults in virtual worlds. Educators and parents should be aware of the types of support being offered in the virtual world. Adult support in virtual worlds can range from "behind-the-scenes" technical support to true mentoring. As an example of the latter, in a virtual world developed specifically for children experiencing chronic illness and being treated at one hospital, adult mentors in the virtual world worked closely with the doctors, nurses, and child life specialists (trained professionals who specialize in supporting children and families to manage life challenges) to create a bonding community, to develop curriculum in the virtual world that supported the needs of the children (i.e., educating children about medication management), and to support children's development in relation to their particular needs as children with chronic illness.

The extent to which adults are an "official" component of a virtual world is dependent on the purpose of the program. For example, in a stand-alone virtual world, adults may only be in the background, serving a solely technical function. Whereas in a virtual world program designed to teach a particular subject matter, the adult must have the content knowledge to be able to interact and teach the youth. In a virtual world program, adult *mentors* serve a very important function—as the program progresses, they should develop relationships with the youth so that they can provide instruction and support, in the same way that classroom teachers work to develop relationships with students in order to scaffold their learning. More specifically, the influence of adult mentors in virtual worlds programs cuts across all of the previous seven attributes. For example, these mentors are supposed to ensure that the *purpose* of the project is known to participants; to encourage, facilitate, and supervise *communication*; to support and champion youth *participation* in the project; to promote, assist, and engage in *play* alongside the youth; to support and provide aid in the creation of *artifacts*; and to monitor, enforce, and facilitate development of the *policies* of the virtual world. The roles of adults in the virtual worlds must be transparent. To the extent that parents and educators are able, through thorough and critical examination of the world, they should ensure that there are no adults "hiding in the wings" and that children know how to recognize the adult roles in the world.

Key Questions

- How are adults involved in the program?
- What is my comfort level as a teacher or parent with the level of adult involvement in a particular virtual world?

The Relationship Among Attributes in Virtual Worlds

Educators and parents should not consider the attributes in isolation—the entire framework as a whole must be taken into account, as the attributes are closely intertwined with one another. For example, educators and parents must consider not only the mechanisms by which communication occurs (*communication*), but also what content is allowed in user communications (*policies*). The virtual world may include *artifacts* that allow for messages to be left for other users (*communication*) or artifacts that provide an opportunity for users to showcase projects made during the program (*purpose*).

CONCLUDING THOUGHTS:
CAUTIONS ABOUT VIRTUAL WORLDS

I would like to conclude with a few thoughts regarding cautions about virtual worlds. Virtual worlds have the potential to be another wonderful immersive environment that can support young children's development. However, I must acknowledge a very big concern of virtual worlds—the potential for commercialism.

As I have mentioned throughout the chapter, when selecting a virtual world for young children, educators and parents should carefully consider the inclusion of commercial components. The role of advertising within virtual worlds needs to be examined in more depth, for, as KZero Worldswide (2010) stated, "Just as every major toy and TV programme [*sic*] has its own website, we expect them to have their own virtual world" (p. 3). KZero Worldswide also report that almost all of the virtual worlds with more than 10 million regular accounts have licensing and merchandising initiatives, and "tying physical product to virtual products is the key strategy" (Mitham, 2013, p. 17). Furthermore, *The Economist* (2009) reports:

> Online worlds earn most of their money from the sale of virtual goods, such as items to spruce up an avatar or a private room. They are paid for in a private currency, which members earn by participating in various activities, trading items or buying them with real dollars. This sort of stealth tax seems to work. At Gaia Online, users spend more than $1m per month on virtual items, says Craig Sherman, the firm's chief executive. (para. 5–6)

As many child-oriented marketing techniques have shown, youth today have great buying power. However, their increased vulnerability means that consumerism can be both cognitively and physically harmful to them. This concern is not new; Elkind, in his book *The Hurried Child: Growing Up Too Fast Too Soon* (1981), addressed the billions of dollars spent each year on commercials for products that range from violent toys to junk food:

> Children are much less able to recognize commercials than adolescents and adults, and, therefore, are more influenced by them; advertisers hurry children into psychologically and nutritionally unhealthy consumerism. (p. 86)

For example, in some virtual worlds, it is possible to make payments through text messaging on cellphones; one report described the benefits of this payment system to the advertisers:

> Firstly, many younger users are given pre-paid phones, meaning their parents are less likely to monitor their usage. The result here is that these users are more able to purchase virtual currencies/goods. (KZero Worldswide, 2010, p. 3)

A line of academic research regarding online marketing for children examines whether children can recognize the advertisements within virtual worlds (especially in the case of branded games). For example, Calvert (2008) writes about how regulations for online marketing for children should be consistent with marketing regulations currently in place for TV and film:

> Such existing television standards as clear separation of commercial from program content, rules about host selling, consideration of age-based skills in understanding marketer intent, tombstone shots of the unadorned product when the camera shot is still, and limits on the amount of time children can spend seeing marketed content should be considered in the context of newer media. (p. 224)

Although I have only highlighted a small component of the potential negative effects of commercialism in virtual worlds, I want parents and educators to be particularly aware of this issue when they think about children's access to this technology.

In sum, parents and educators need to examine the developmental appropriateness of virtual worlds in the same way that they do for other environments designed for children. The framework presented in this chapter provides one way to do so. Although virtual worlds can be a powerful tool—for community-building, for artifact creation, for supporting communication—their use by young children should be done in a manner that supports children's cognitive, social, and emotional development. In addition, just as there are many new possibilities for scaffolding children's development through the use of virtual worlds, there are just as many new risks. Educators and parents should reflect carefully on the entire constellation of risks and rewards in participating in virtual worlds, in order to determine the best means of implementation for young children.

RESOURCES

General Technology and Children

- Pew Internet and American Life Project: www.pewinternet.org

- National Association for the Education of Young Children (NAEYC): www.naeyc.org
  - ✓ Joint position statement of the National Association for the Education of Young Children and the Fred Rogers Center for Early Learning and Children's Media at Saint Vincent College: www.naeyc.org/files/naeyc/file/positions/PS_technology_ WEB2.pdf
  - ✓ Book, *Spotlight on Young Children and Technology*: www.naeyc. org/store/Spotlight-on-Young-Children-and-Technology
- Common Sense Media, Online Worlds for Young Kids Tips: www. commonsensemedia.org/advice-for-parents/online-worlds-young- kids-tips
  - Children's Online Privacy Protection Act (COPPA): www.ftc.gov/ opa/reporter/privacy/coppa.shtml

Virtual Worlds

- *Journal of Virtual Worlds Research* (free, online, peer-reviewed journal): http://jvwresearch.org/
- American Education Research Association (AERA) Applied Research in Virtual Environments for Learning (ARVEL) Special Interest Group (SIG): http://arvelsig.ning.com/
- Association of Virtual Worlds: www.associationofvirtualworlds.com/
- The Developmental Technologies Research Lab, at the Eliot-Pearson Department of Child Development, Tufts University: http://ase.tufts. edu/DevTech/
- EcoMUVE—Advancing Ecosystems Science Education via Situated Learning in Multi-User Environments at Harvard University: http:// ecomuve.gse.harvard.edu/
- The River City Project—A Multi-User Virtual Environment for Learning Scientific Inquiry and 21st Century Skills at Harvard University: http://rivercity.activeworlds.com/
- The Metauniverse Journal: www.metaversejournal.com/

REFERENCES

Association of Virtual Worlds. (2010). *The blue book: A consumer guide to virtual worlds and social networks* (7th ed.). Available at www.associationofvirtualworlds.com/ publication/the-blue-book/

Barab, S. A., MaKinster, J. G., & Scheckler, R. (2004). Designing system dualities: Characterizing an online professional development community. In S. A. Barab, R. Kling, J. H. Gray, C. Heath, & L. A. Suchman (Eds.), *Designing for virtual communities in the service of learning* (pp. 53–90). Cambridge, UK: Cambridge University Press.

Barab, S. A., Thomas, M., Dodge, T., Carteaux, R., & Tuzun, H. (2005). Making learning fun: Quest Atlantis, a game without guns. *Educational Technology Research and Development, 53*(1), 86–107.

Bartle, R. A. (2004). *Designing virtual worlds.* Indianapolis, IN: New Riders Publishing.

Beals, L. (2011). *A framework for the design and evaluation of virtual world programs for preadolescent youth.* Doctoral dissertation. Tufts University. Retrieved from http://gradworks.umi.com/34/57/3457697.html

Beals, L., & Bers, M. U. (2009). A developmental lens for designing virtual worlds for children and youth. *The International Journal of Learning and Media, 1*(1), 51–65.

Beals, L., & Bers, M. U. (2010). Evaluating participation in an international bilingual virtual world educational intervention for youth. *Journal of Virtual Worlds Research, 2*(5). Available at https:// journals.tdl.org/jvwr/article/view/810/718

Bers, M. U. (2008a). Civic identities, online technologies: From designing civic curriculum to supporting civic experiences. In W. L. Bennett (Ed.), *Civic life online: Learning how digital media can engage youth* (pp. 139–160). Cambridge, MA: The MIT Press.

Bers, M. U. (2008b). Virtual worlds as digital playgrounds. *EDUCAUSE Review, 43*(5), 80–81.

Bers, M. U., Beals, L. M., Chau, C., Satoh, K., & Khan, N. (2010). Virtual worlds for young people in a program context: Lessons from four case studies. In I. Saleh & M. S. Khine (Eds.), *New science of learning: Cognition, computers and collaboration in education* (pp. 357–383) New York, NY: Springer.

Bers, M. U., & Cantrell, K. (2012). Virtual worlds for children with medical conditions: Experiences for promoting positive youth development. In Å. Smedberg (Ed.), *E-Health Communities and Online Self-Help Groups: Applications and Usage* (pp. 1–23). Hershey, PA: Medical Information Science Reference.

Bers, M. U., Gonzalez-Heydrich, G., & DeMaso, D. (2003). Use of a computer-based application in a pediatric hemodialysis unit: A pilot study. *Journal of the American Academy of Child and Adolescent Psychiatry, 42*(4), 493–496.

Boostrom, R. (1991). The nature and functions of classroom rules. *Curriculum Inquiry, 21*(2), 193–216.

Calvert, S. L. (2008). Children as consumers: Advertising and marketing. *The Future of Children, 18*(1), 205–234.

Calvert, S. L., Strouse, G. A., Strong, B. L., Huffaker, D. A., & Lai, S. (2009). Preadolescent girls' and boys' virtual MUD play. *Journal of Applied Developmental Psychology, 30*(3), 250–264.

Cantrell, K., Fischer, A., Bouzaher, A., & Bers, M. U. (2010). The role of e-mentorship in a virtual world for youth transplant recipients. *Journal of Pediatric Oncology Nursing, 27*(6), 344–355. doi:10.1177/1043454210372617

Common Sense Media. (2013, May 10). *Online worlds for young kids tips.* Available at www.commonsensemedia.org/advice-for-parents/online-worlds-young-kids-tips

Damer, B. (2008). Meeting in the ether: A brief history of virtual worlds as a medium for user-created events. *Journal of Virtual Worlds Research, 1*(1). Available from http://journals.tdl.org/jvwr/index.php/jvwr/article/view/285

Dede, C., Ketelhut, D. J., Clarke, J., Nelson, B., & Bowman, C. (2005). *Students' motivation and learning of science in a multi-user virtual environment.* Paper presented at the American Educational Research Association Conference, Montreal, Canada. Available at http://rivercity5.activeworlds.com/rivercityproject/documents/motivation_muves_aera_2005.pdf

The Economist. (2009, July 23). Virtual worlds for children: Online playgrounds. Available at www.economist.com/node/14098380

Elkind, D. (1981). *The hurried child: Growing up too fast too soon.* Reading, MA: Addison-Wesley.

Erikson, E. (1964). *Insight and responsibility.* New York, NY: W. W. Norton & Company.

Federal Trade Commission. (2009). *Virtual worlds and kids: Mapping the risks. A report to Congress.* Available at www.ftc.gov/os/2009/12/oecd-vwrpt.pdf

Glaser, M. (2007). Your guide to virtual worlds. Available from www.pbs.org/mediashift/2007/10/your-guide-to-virtual-worlds283/

Kafai, Y., & Giang, M. T. (2008). New virtual playgrounds: Children's multi-user virtual environments for playing and learning with science. In T. Willoughby & E. Wood (Eds.), *Children's learning in a digital world* (pp. 196–217). Oxford, UK: Blackwell Publishing Inc.

KZero Worldswide. (2013). KZero Universe Q3 2013. Availabile at www.slideshare.net/nicmitham/kzero-universe-q3-2013

KZero Worldswide. (2010). Virtual worlds: 2010 and beyond. www.kzero.co.uk

KZero Worldswide. (n.d.). Virtual World and MMO Universe chart Kids segment for Q3 2013. Available at www.kzero.co.uk/blog/virtual-world-mmo-universe-chart-kids-segment-q3-2012/

Lim, S. S., & Clark, L. S. (2010). *Virtual worlds as a site of convergence for children's play.* Available at journals.tdl.org/jvwr/article/view/1897/1165

Marsh, J. (2010). Young children's play in online virtual worlds. *Journal of Early Childhood Research, 8*(1), 23–39. doi:10.1177/1476718X09345406

Marsh, J. (2011). Young children's literacy practices in a virtual world: Establishing an online interaction order. *Reading Research Quarterly, 46*(2), 101–118. doi:10.1598/RRQ.46.2.1

Mitham, N. (2013, February). *Virtual worlds/MMOs: Key data, metrics and insight.* Presented at the Digital Kids Conference, New York, NY. Available at http://www.kzero.co.uk/blog/virtual-world-mmo-universe-chart-kids-segment-q3-2012/

National Association for the Education of Young Children. (2009). Developmentally appropriate practice in early childhood programs serving children from birth through age 8. Available at www.naeyc.org/files/naeyc/file/positions/position%20statement%20Web.pdf

National Center for Missing & Exploited Children. (2009). *Keeping kids safer on the Internet: Tips for parents and guardians.* Available at www.missingkids.com/en_US/publications/NC168.pdf

Norris, P. (2004). The bridging and bonding role of online communities. In P. N. Howard & S. Jones (Eds.), *Society online: The Internet in context* (pp. 31–42). Thousand Oaks, CA: Sage Publications.

Papert, S. (1980). *Mindstorms: Children, computers, and powerful ideas.* New York, NY: Basic Books.

Preece, J., & Maloney-Krichmar, D. (2003). Online communities: Focusing on sociability and usability. In J. Jacko & A. Sears (Eds.), *Handbook of human-computer interaction* (pp. 596–620). Mahwah, NJ: Lawrence Erlbaum Associates.

Rheingold, H. (1993). *The virtual community: Homesteading on the electronic frontier.* Reading, MA: Addison-Wesley Publishing Company.

Richtel, M., & Stone, B. (2007, June 6). Doll web sites drive girls to stay home and play. *The New York Times.* Available at www.nytimes.com/2007/06/06/technology/06doll.html

Shuler, C. (2007). D is for digital: An analysis of the children's interactive media environment with a focus on mass marketed products that promote learning. Available at www.joanganzcooneycenter.org/upload_kits/disfordigital_reports.pdf

Subrahmanyam, K., & Greenfield, P. (2008). Online communication and adolescent relationships. *The Future of Children, 18*(1), 119–146.

Williamson, D. A. (2009). *Kids and teens: Growing up virtual.* New York, NY: eMarketer.

Conclusion

Environments for Adult Learning

Lisa P. Kuh

In Chapter 1 I asked readers to consider where they do their best work. I wanted readers to ask themselves about the kinds of environmental affordances they "take up" in order to think, learn, interact, or create. Look around the space you are in right now and ask yourself:

- Does it work for you?
- Are you comfortable?
- Could you be in the space for a long time?
- If you are in a class or meeting, how has the leader of this group prepared the environment for your learning?
- How have you structured the experience for yourself and others who are working and learning with you?

It is my hope, and that of all the authors in this book, that readers will take the ideas in our chapters into their hearts and minds and, with some new lenses, think critically about the environments they prepare for young children. However, as a college-level professor who also studies teacher professional development, I know firsthand that the spaces in which future teachers are taught on campuses across the country can be devoid of aesthetic inspiration in terms of furnishings and pedagogical approaches. The contributing authors developed guiding questions within and at the end of each chapter to help readers think about the concepts and ideas presented. However, how to use these questions with students or a staff at a school can be a challenge. Therefore, I offer some guidance on two levels. First, I will briefly review the challenges encountered in spaces for learning in higher education. Second, I have found that implementing particular pedagogical structures with students and teachers can create a space for learning in spite of aesthetically and physically challenging spaces. Using text and observation protocols to dig into readings, promote discussion, and foster new ways of thinking can create an inspiring learning environment.

THE CHALLENGE OF LEARNING SPACES
IN INSTITUTIONS OF HIGHER EDUCATION

At a recent faculty meeting, one of our longtime professors brought up an issue that apparently had been plaguing her for years. She said, "I feel oppressed when I walk into room 109." She went on to say that she craved a space where students could spread out their work and where furniture could easily be arranged so that they could sit in small groups or in a circle to engage in discussions. In addition, I have heard faculty from around the country talk about poor lighting, those ubiquitous chairs with curved "desks" that one must slide into, and rooms with no windows. On college tours with my son, I peeked into classrooms searching for evidence of thoughtfully prepared environments for adults. Although I did find some lovely, well-lit, architecturally beautiful rooms, most classrooms (including the ones in which I teach) were furnished with armchair-style desks arranged in rows, facing a board at the "front" of the classroom. At one institution, I did find some unique small desks that could be easily stacked and arranged in multiple ways—in rows for test-taking, pushed together to create larger surfaces for hands-on work and seminar-style discussions, or stacked and set completely aside for "knee-to-knee" conversations.

A survey of learning space design in higher education showed that although a range of people in higher academia felt that those who use the space should drive its design, the actual control over space was more likely to be in the hands of those who manage, schedule, and maintain the space (Vredevoogd & Grumman, 2008). Those surveyed believed that a primary factor influencing views of design spaces should be the learning style of students, indicating that perhaps traditional spaces are not meeting the needs of diverse learners or multiple pedagogical techniques. In addition, the primary measure of effective learning spaces is the extent to which the environment can support a range of activities, be they presentation by an instructor or the way in which learners participate (Vredevoogd & Grumman, 2008). As discussed in the Introduction and Chapter 1 in this book, designers, those in the field of environmental psychology, and educators have found anecdotally and empirically that a well-designed space that considers factors such as color, light, furnishings, and pedagogical structures can potentially enrich learning experiences, productivity, and well-being (Dudek, 2005).

PROTOCOLS: CREATING "SPACE FOR LEARNING" VIA STRUCTURES FOR TALKING

Realizing that a makeover of our department's classrooms would not be coming anytime soon, I turned to another aspect of my work to look for answers. Part of my research involves observing staff meetings and listening to teacher talk. When teachers meet to talk about their work, they are rarely guided by structures that focus conversations on their own learning, practice, and children (Kuh, 2012). Successful learning communities build time into their work explicitly for the purpose of collaboration—whether it is among teachers in a meeting or students in a college classroom (Cibulka & Nakayama, 2000; Hord, 1997; McLaughlin & Talbert, 2001). It is rare to see an education journal these days that does not talk about collaboration as an important part of a teacher's work. However, there is no particular philosophy or program that explicitly defines what teachers should do, and teachers are often expected to improvise as they go along (Phillips & Bredekamp, 1998). As a result, new teachers are entering environments that do not support inquiry-based conversation, and in-service teachers are subject to isolation in their practice.

Nonetheless, educators do know that successful learning communities adopt tools and structures that help guide the focus on teacher practices (Windschitl, Thompson, & Braaten, 2011). In this book, we champion the development of rich environments for young children within the idea of "teacher practice." Tools such as protocols that guide conversations have been shown to keep teacher talk focused on student learning and teacher practice (Blythe, Allen, & Powell, 2008; Curry, 2008; Dunne, Nave, & Lewis, 2000; Kuh, 2012).

Although we hope that this book will inspire readers to think critically about spaces for young children *and* spaces in which we teach about environments for young children, we also want readers to use the book as a tool for teaching. For this reason, I offer three categories of tools, or protocols, that can shape the way teachers interact with one another. The term *protocols* refers to structured conversations about topics, questions, text, student work, or observations that involve multiple steps and guidelines for participation (Blythe, Allen, & Powell, 2008). In *The Power of Protocols,* the authors go so far as to say that protocols can overcome norms of private practice and create the possibility of new settings for education (McDonald, Mohr, Dichter, & McDonald, 2007). More information about the protocols presented in the following sections can be found on the School Reform Initiative website at www.schoolreforminitiative.org.

Although there are many strategies from which to choose, I cluster my suggestions into three broad categories: (1) examining text; (2) structuring meaningful and close conversation; and (3) looking at environments. The sections that follow describe each protocol cluster and offer one example of protocols that can be used in conjunction with the content and questions raised in this book. Additional protocols for each category can be found at schoolreforminitiative.org.

Examining Text

Protocols for examining text are designed not only to facilitate discussion among participants who have read a particular piece of text, but to help readers get to the essence of the meaning of text and/or understand interpretations of text. A text protocol generally requires the reader to identify passages, a sentence, or even a single word that provoked new thinking, strong reactions and disagreement, or approval. Readers are often asked to share their thinking with others in small groups and to listen actively to others who may or may not share their views. In addition, text protocols can be used with guiding questions, such as those at the end of the chapters. The experience of reading, posing guiding questions, discussing text and listening to colleagues/peers, and identifying new ways of thinking can lead to powerful learning (Breidenstein, Fahey, Glickman, & Hensley, 2012). Depending upon the number of people, the text protocols can be done in whole groups of up to about 18. However, with larger groups, breaking into triads and posing a series of questions that require participants to think more deeply with each subsequent round efficiently allows all voices to be heard. One text protocol, The Final Word, follows, and many others are available on schoolreforminitiative.org.

Structuring Meaningful Conversation: Posing Questions That Inspire

In addition to the text protocols, many of which involve close conversation in small groups, other structures give participants a way to experience conversations in ways that create community and even intimacy. In a Chalk Talk, the protocol on page 188, a question is put in the center of a large piece of paper or whiteboard. Participants respond to the question in silence by writing on the board, using arrows and lines to connect to one another's ideas on the Chalk Talk. After everyone has responded to the question and to one another, participants stand back and reflect on what they notice and what it means to them. The group can go on to discuss implications for teaching and learning. A piece of text could be the inspiration for the Chalk Talk, and participants can read, respond to the Chalk Talk, and then engage in discussion.

Other protocols listed on schoolreforminitiative.org require participants to respond to prompts or questions and engage in listening and speaking with anywhere from one to four other people.

The Final Word Protocol

The Final Word

Adapted from the original by Jennifer Fischer-Mueller and Gene Thompson-Grove.

Purpose
The purpose of this discussion format is to give each person in the group an opportunity to have their ideas, understandings, and perspective enhanced by hearing from others. With this format, the group can explore an article, clarify their thinking, and have their assumptions and beliefs questioned in order to gain a deeper understanding of the issue.

Time
For each round, allow about 8 minutes (circles of 5 participants: presenter 3 minutes, response 1 minute for 4 people, final word for presenter 1 minute). Total time is about a forty minutes for a group of 5 (32 minutes for a group of 4, 48 minutes for a group of 6).

Roles
Facilitator/time-keeper (who also participates); participants.

Facilitation
Have participants identify one "most" significant idea from the text (underlined or highlighted ahead of time), stick to the time limits, avoid dialogue, have equal sized circles so all small groups finish at approximately the same time.

Protocol
1. Sit in a circle and identify a facilitator/time-keeper.

2. Each person needs to have one "most" significant idea from the text underlined or highlighted in the article. It is often helpful to identify a "back up" quote as well.

3. The first person begins by reading what "struck him or her the most" from the article. Have this person refer to where the quote is in the text - <u>one</u> thought or quote only. Then, in <u>less than 3 minutes</u>, this person describes why that quote struck him or her. For example, why does s/he agree/disagree with the quote, what questions does s/he have about that quote, what issues does it raise for him or her, what does s/he now wonder about in relation to that quote?

4. Continuing around the circle each person responds to that quote and what the presenter said, <u>briefly, in less than a minute</u>. The purpose of the response is:
   • to expand on the presenter's thinking about the quote and the issues raised for him or her by the quote,
   • to provide a different look at the quote,
   • to clarify the presenter's thinking about the quote, and/or
   • to question the presenter's assumptions about the quote and the issues raised (although at this time there is no response from the presenter).

5. After going around the circle with each person having responded for less than one minute, the person that began has the "final word." In no more than one minute the presenter responds to what has been said. Now what is s/he thinking? What is his or her reaction to what s/he has heard?

6. The next person in the circle then begins by sharing what struck him or her most from the text. Proceed around the circle, responding to this next presenter's quote in the same way as the first presenter's. This process continues until each person has had a round with his or her quote.

7. End by debriefing the process in your small group.

The Chalk Talk Protocol

Chalk Talk

Developed by Hilton Smith, Foxfire Fund; adapted by Marylyn Wentworth.

Chalk Talk is a silent way to reflect, generate ideas, check on learning, develop projects or solve problems. It can be used productively with any group — students, faculty, workshop participants, committees. Because it is done completely in silence, it gives groups a change of pace and encourages thoughtful contemplation. It can be an unforgettable experience. Middle level students absolutely love it — it's the quietest they'll ever be!

Format
Time: Varies according to need; can be from 5 minutes to an hour.
Materials: Chalk board and chalk or paper roll on the wall and markers.

Process
1. The facilitator explains *very briefly* that chalk talk is a silent activity. No one may talk at all and anyone may add to the chalk talk with words or graphics as they please. You can comment on other people's ideas simply by drawing a connecting line to the comment. It can also be very effective to say nothing at all except to put finger to lips in a gesture of silence and simply begin with #2.

2. The facilitator writes a relevant question in a circle on the board.
   Sample questions:
   • What did you learn today?
   • So what? or Now what?
   • What do you think about social responsibility and schooling?
   • How can we involve the community in the school, and the school in community?
   • How can we keep the noise level down in this room?
   • What do you want to tell the scheduling committee?
   • What do you know about Croatia?
   • How are decimals used in the world?

3. The facilitator either hands a piece of chalk to everyone, or places many pieces of chalk at the board and hands several pieces to people at random.

4. People write as they feel moved. There are likely to be long silences — that is natural, so allow plenty of wait time before deciding it is over.

5. How the facilitator chooses to interact with the Chalk Talk influences its outcome. The facilitator can stand back and let it unfold or expand thinking by:
   • circling other interesting ideas, thereby inviting comments to broaden
   • writing questions about a participant comment
   • adding his/her own reflections or ideas

   Actively interacting invites participants to do the same kinds of expansions. A Chalk Talk can be an uncomplicated silent reflection or a spirited, but silent, exchange of ideas. It has been known to solve vexing problems, surprise everyone with how much is collectively known about something, get an entire project planned, or give a committee everything it needs to know without any verbal sparring.

6. When it's done, it's done.

7. The Chalk Talk can be considered complete at this point or it can become the basis for a further discussion. Questions to raise with the group might include:
   • What do you notice about what we wrote?
   • What do you wonder about now?
   • What was the Chalk Talk like for you?

Protocols are most powerful and effective when used within an ongoing professional learning community and facilitated by a skilled facilitator. To learn more about professional learning communities and seminars for facilitation, please visit the School Reform Initiative website at www.schoolreforminitiative.org

Looking at Environments for Learning: Environment Walks

Because this is a book about environments, I want to include ideas for reflecting upon our own environments or the spaces of others—both in and out of school. The protocol included on the next page, First Classroom Visits, can be used to reflect upon environments in the service of expanding your notions of aesthetics, classroom arrangement, what the spaces tell you about the philosophy of adults who use the space, and what children might be able to do in a given space. The protocols in this category on schoolreforminitiative.org are for both the teacher whose classroom is being observed and for the observer. Sometimes our observations are for the observer to gain more insight into their own practices via reflection on other environments. Other times we observe to give feedback and help another practitioner think more expansively about a question or to simply reflect back to them what we see and make meaning of what we see. With observation protocols, both observers and the observed may need to modify steps and questions to make the observation coherent with the goals for the experience.

Thinking Critically to Reframe Practice

We hope our readers will use the protocols I included in concert with this book, and also the other protocols provided at schoolreforminitiative.org. Observations of spaces are powerful when used in conjunction with text and guiding questions. For example, using an observation protocol, preceded or followed by a chapter in this book, and reflecting on text, observation data, and reflective questions is a way to integrate theory and practice. While protocols alone are not a cure-all for environmental constraints, they open possibilities for learning in spaces where the aesthetics and design are less than desirable.

The need for rethinking and looking critically at environments should be part of a conscious teaching practice, whether working with adults who will teach children or working directly with young children and their families. Notions of bright colors, busy classrooms, catalogue playground equipment, lack of loose parts, and a limited view of children's knowledge and ability limits the possibilities for rich spaces for learning. We hope that readers begin to think of spaces as canvases in which children can participate in the evolution of the environment, with the support of adults who take children's endeavors seriously. This stance and sense of agency on the part of teachers, administrators, those in higher academics, policymakers, and parents might foster the transformation of environments for young children into spaces of creativity, inspiration, intellectual pursuits, choice, and development.

First Classroom Visits

First Classroom Visits

Developed by Paula Evans.

Purpose

The purpose of these first visits to each other's classrooms is to enhance our understanding of our own practice. Before beginning your classroom visits, think hard about a question that you have about teaching and learning. Is there a question that gnaws at you...that keeps you up at 3 AM...that you feel some passion about? It may be that after one or two visits, you may want to change your question. That's OK, too.

Pre Observation

You should let the teacher you are visiting know what you are hoping to learn something about. At the same time, be clear that you are not expecting the teacher to craft his/her lesson around your particular interest. That's not the point. Assume that your question is broad and deep enough that any class will give you a window on some new learning.

During and After Observation

So, you are visiting classes to gain insight into a question that you have framed related to your own teaching. You are not visiting to evaluate or give feedback to the teacher whom you visit. Do have at least a brief conversation with every teacher you visit after the class. What did you learn?

Keep a journal or notebook with your notes and reflections from your visits. If others in the school or grade level or content area team are also taking part, these reflections (though private) will serve us in our collective dialogue, and we will use our learning and these visits to shape our meetings and future peer observations together.

My question is:

Possible questions to guide your reflections in your journal:

- What evidence do I see in this classroom that might address my question [or portions of my question]?
- What particular content or strategies in the classroom are striking to me? Why?
- As I leave this class, what have I learned about myself as a teacher, about our students here at this school, or about teaching? What new questions or insights do I have?

REFERENCES

Blythe, T., Allen, D., & Powell, B. S. (2008). *Looking together at student work.* New York, NY: Teachers College Press.

Breidenstein, A., Fahey, K., Glickman, C., & Hensley, F. (2012). *Leading for powerful learning: A guide for instructional leaders.* New York, NY: Teachers College Press.

Cibulka, J., & Nakayama, M. (2000). *Practitioners guide to learning communities: Creation of high performance schools through organizational and individual learning* (Briefing paper). Washington, DC: National Partnership for Excellence and Accountability in Teaching.

Curry, M. (2008). Critical friends groups: The possibilities and limitations embedded in teacher professional communities aimed at instructional improvement and school reform. *Teachers College Record, 4,* 733–774.

Dudek, M. (2005). *Children's spaces.* Oxford, UK: Architectural Press.

Dunne, F., Nave, B., & Lewis, A. (2000, December). Critical friends groups: Teachers helping teachers to improve student learning. *Phi Delta Kappa Center for Evaluation, Development and research* 28, December. Available at http://www.schoolreforminitiative.org/wp-content/uploads/2014/02/Dunne_et_al_2000.pdf

Hord, S. (1997). *Professional learning communities: Communities of continuous inquiry and improvement.* Austin, TX: Southwest Educational Development Laboratory.

Kuh, L. P. (2012). Promoting communities of practice and parallel process in early childhood settings. *Journal of Early Childhood Teacher Education, (33)*1, 19–37.

McDonald, J. P., Mohr, N., Dichter, A., & McDonald, E. C. (2007). *The power of protocols.* New York, NY: Teachers College Press.

McLaughlin, M. W., & Talbert, J. E. (2001). *Professional communities and the work of high school.* Chicago, IL: University of Chicago Press.

Phillips, C. B., & Bredekamp, S. (1998). Reconsidering early childhood education in the United States: Reflections from our encounters with Reggio Emilia. In C. Edwards, L. Gandini, & G. Forman (Eds.), *The hundred languages of children* (2nd ed., pp. 439–456). Westport, CT: Ablex Publishing.

Vredevoogd, J., & Grumman, P. (2008). *Summary report of a survey of learning space design in higher education.* Conference of the Society for College and University Planning. Montréal, July.

Windschitl, M., Thompson, J., & Braaten, M. (2011). Ambitious pedagogy by novice teachers: Who benefits from tool-supported collaborative inquiry into practice and why? *Teachers College Record, 113,* 1311–1360.

About the Editor and
the Contributors

Lisa P. Kuh is an assistant professor in the Family Studies Department at the University of New Hampshire (UNH). She coordinates the pre-K–3rd-grade Teacher Preparation Program and is the consultant for pedagogy and inquiry at the UNH Child Study and Development Center. She is a coprincipal investigator on the Natural Playground Project, a research endeavor focused on the impact of outdoor environmental design on children's play. She holds a PhD from the University of Washington in curriculum and instruction and teacher education. She also studies how teachers transfer collaborative professional development experiences into daily work in classrooms. Lisa has over 25 years of classroom experience and as a teacher educator at the college and university level. She lives in Cambridge, Massachusetts, with her husband and two sons.

Megina Baker is a doctoral candidate at Boston College and works with the Boston public schools to develop integrated kindergarten curriculum. A graduate of Tufts University and Cornell University, she has spent the past 10 years teaching young children, both in the United States and in Sweden, and mentoring student teachers in the Early Childhood program at Boston University. She is also a member of the Democracy Inquiry Group situated at Wheelock College. In her free time, Megina takes walks in the woods with her 1-year-old daughter, dressed in good clothing, of course.

Laura Beals is a nonprofit evaluator. Her primary areas of expertise are in the design and evaluation of technology to support youth development, nonprofit evaluation, and innovative technology-based research and evaluation methods for use with children. Laura was also a senior member of the Developmental Technologies Research Group at Tufts University and worked at the Tufts Center for Engineering Educational Outreach. Laura completed her PhD and MA at the Eliot-Pearson Department of Child Development at Tufts University, with her doctoral dissertation focused on the design and evaluation of virtual world programs for preadolescent youth.

Leah A. Bricker is an assistant professor of science education at the University of Michigan. She holds a PhD from the University of Washington in the

Learning Sciences. Bricker's research explores STEM-related learning pathways and trajectories. She uses lenses from multiple fields (e.g., science education, learning sciences, science studies), and ethnographic and design-based research methods, to investigate linguistic and interactional elements of STEM-related learning and practice, social disparities related to youth interest and opportunities associated with STEM learning and practice, science communication, "informal" STEM learning, and learning within health-related contexts.

Clement Chau received his PhD at the Eliot-Pearson Department of Child Development at Tufts University with a research focus on new technology and new environments on children and youth development. He is also a co-principal investigator on the Natural Playground Project, a research endeavor focused on the impact of outdoor environmental design on children's play. He works as a learning designer at Leapfrog Enterprises, Inc., with a focus on educational toys and mobile games for young children. He is also the vice president of Ponte and Chau Consulting, Inc., in Belmont, Massachusetts.

Iris Chin Ponte is the director of the Henry Frost Children's Program in Belmont, Massachusetts, which combines the philosophies of Dewey, Montessori, and Reggio Emilia. Her research interests include cross-cultural issues in education and adoption from China, in addition to the impact of natural playscapes on children's behavior. Iris is a coprincipal investigator on the Natural Playground Project, a research endeavor focused on the impact of outdoor environmental design on children's play. She is also the president of Ponte and Chau Consulting, Inc., in Belmont, Massachusetts.

Angela Eckhoff is an assistant professor of Teaching and Learning in the Early Childhood Education program at Old Dominion University. She is also the codirector of the Virginia Early Childhood Policy Center at Old Dominion University. She holds a dual PhD from the University of Colorado–Boulder in Educational Psychology and Cognitive Science. Her areas of specialization include visual arts pedagogy in early childhood education, imagination and creative development during childhood, and informal learning environments for children and families.

Carley Fisher-Maltese is a postdoctoral fellow in the Program for Society and the Environment at the University of Maryland, where she studies the school gardening program in the District of Columbia. Carley completed her PhD in Education at Rutgers, The State University of New Jersey, and her master's in Elementary Education at Teachers College. Her doctoral dissertation focused on a garden-based approach to teaching life science. Previously, Carley was an elementary school teacher and the regional coordinator for Grow Healthy, a USDA-funded program combining gardening, nutrition, physical activity, agriculture, and locally grown foods.

Anna Housley Juster is an early childhood education consultant and free-lance writer. Anna is a PhD candidate in Early Childhood Education at New York University, focusing on maternal-child relationships among 3-year-olds as related to play and roles. She received her pre-K–3rd-grade teacher credential through Tufts University, and was a Head Start teacher before earning a master's degree in Developmental Psychology from Teachers College/Columbia University. With Dr. Herb Ginsburg, she helped develop the early childhood math curriculum Big Math for Little People and was director of content for the preschool television series *Sesame Street.* She regularly consults with a variety of companies developing educational media for young children and designing play spaces in museums and theme parks. After many years in New York City, Anna now lives in Brookline, Massachusetts, with her husband and two daughters.

Tiffany R. Lee is a learning scientist in the School of Education at the University of Colorado Boulder, where she studies research-practice partnerships with a focus on P–12 STEM, equity, and learning across settings. Previously, Lee was a postdoctoral fellow with the Learning in Informal and Formal Environments (LIFE) Center at the University of Washington and the director of Education at Teaching Channel. She has over 10 years of professional experience working with young children in classrooms, homes, and research settings. Lee earned a PhD from the University of Washington in the Learning Sciences.

Morgan Leichter-Saxby is a writer, Playwork trainer, and consultant who has worked on Adventure Playgrounds and on play-ranging teams in the United Kingdom, the United States, and the Gambia. She holds an MA in Anthropology from University College London and researched Adventure Playgrounds. As a playworker and senior playworker with the Play Association Tower Hamlets, she supported children's play in public spaces with high rates of poverty. Morgan later joined Islington Play Association as an access developer, delivering training and providing support to Adventure Playgrounds and mobile play services. She wrote *The Playworker's Guide to Dens and Forts* and researched childhood games among the elderly population and recently arrived immigrants. Her website, www.playeverything.wordpress.com, was the first Playworker blog. As an independent researcher, Morgan has delivered papers and workshops on play at more than a dozen national and international conferences.

Melissa Rivard is currently a researcher at Project Zero at the Harvard Graduate School of Education. From 2002 to 2012, Melissa worked on the Making Learning Visible Project—a long-term collaboration between researchers at Project Zero and educators in Reggio Emilia. She is coauthor of several journal articles and the recently published book on this work, *Visible Learners: Promoting Reggio-Inspired Approaches in All Schools.* She has also produced numerous videos, including *Documentation: Transforming our Perspective* (based on interviews with key educators and scholars in Reggio Emilia), *Kids Are the Experts!*, and *The Color Investigation: Making learning visible in a K0–K1 classroom.*

Judith Ross-Bernstein is an educational consultant based in Ithaca, New York, where she raised three children and currently lives with her husband. A senior lecturer in the Department of Human Development at Cornell University for 25 years, she taught child study classes and supported undergraduate field experiences in local, state, and international early education and care settings. At Cornell, with American and Swedish colleagues, Judith designed and led a curriculum-embedded study abroad experience with Cornell Abroad. Judith was a professional developer with the Danish Institute for Study Abroad in Copenhagen, Denmark. Working alongside Danish and American faculty, she taught comparative courses on Play in Childhood and Children with Special Needs as a senior consultant. Judith is now an adjunct instructor in the Department of Education at Syracuse University and teaches an early childhood integrated curriculum methods course and supervises emerging teachers.

Patricia Tarr is an associate professor in the Faculty of Education at the University of Calgary, Alberta, Canada. She has been inspired by the Reggio philosophy since 1990 when a presentation by Lilian Katz about a Reggio project challenged her to rethink the image of the child she held as an early childhood art educator. She has chaired committees to bring The Hundred Languages of Children exhibit to Calgary in 1997 and 2006. Her research and publications have focused on implications of the Reggio philosophy for North American contexts, particularly classroom environments and pedagogical documentation.

Deborah Valentine is visiting assistant professor of Early Childhood Education in the Teacher Education Department at St. Joseph's University in Philadelphia. In May 2013, she was among the first cohort of doctoral students to graduate from Rutgers–Camden's groundbreaking doctoral program in childhood studies (the first in North America!), where she focused her research on the history of play, playgrounds, and early childhood education in Philadelphia. Prior to attending Rutgers, she spent over 15 years working as a teacher, administrator, and researcher in a variety of early childhood and elementary school programs, primarily in underserved urban communities.

Index